Nicholas Redfern writes on a regular basis for numerous UFO publications, including the bestselling *UFO Magazine*, and has contributed crucial material to Timothy Good's books *Alien Liaison* and *Beyond Top Secret*. He has lectured on his subject at universities in both Britain and the US, and has appeared on a variety of programmes, including BBC TV's *Out of this World*, *The Big Breakfast*, and Channel 5 News. He is the author of *A Covert Agenda* and *The FBI Files*.

Also by Nicholas Redfern

A Covert Agenda: The British Government's
UFO Top Secrets Exposed
The FBI Files: The FBI's UFO Top Secrets Exposed

COSMIC CRASHES:

THE INCREDIBLE STORY OF
THE UFOS THAT FELL TO EARTH

NICHOLAS REDFERN

POCKET
B O O K S

LONDON · SYDNEY · NEW YORK · TOKYO · SINGAPORE · TORONTO

First published in Great Britain by Simon & Schuster UK Ltd, 1999
This edition first published by Pocket Books, 2001
An imprint of Simon & Schuster UK Ltd
A Viacom company

1 3 5 7 9 10 8 6 4 2

Simon & Schuster UK Ltd
Africa House
64–78 Kingsway
London WC2B 6AH

Simon & Schuster Australia
Sydney

A CIP catalogue record for this book is available
from the British Library

ISBN 0-671-03306-9

Typeset by SX Composing DTP, Rayleigh, Essex
Printed and bound in Great Britain by
Omnia Books Ltd, Glasgow

CONTENTS

For Graham Birdsall and Mark Birdsall – true pioneers in the field of UFO research.

INTRODUCTION

WHEN I FIRST BECAME SERIOUSLY INTERESTED IN THE UFO puzzle back in the late 1970s, it became readily apparent to me that, of the many UFO encounters reported by credible sources since the 1940s, a high percentage appeared to relate to sightings of tangible, intelligently controlled vehicles displaying a technology infinitely more advanced than our own.

But no technology, I reasoned, however advanced, could be considered completely flawless. That being the case, I wondered, why was it that those piloting the UFOs did not suffer the occasional mishap? Why did their craft not malfunction in our atmosphere? And, more importantly, why did their ships never seemingly crash to Earth? Then it struck me: perhaps they did. Perhaps it was simply the case that we, the general public, never got to hear of such mind-blowing events.

The idea that a variety of governments throughout the world were purposefully withholding from the public at large actual crash-recovered exhibits of alien technology, and perhaps even alien bodies, was an intriguing one.

Certainly, as far back as July 1947, there had been rumours in circulation that the US military had found a UFO, presumed crashed, in a remote desert area; and as time went on, the stories became more and more elaborate. Witnesses told of seeing dead alien creatures preserved in cryogenic chambers at a top-secret US Air Force base; there were the military sources who quietly revealed their involvement in covert recovery operations of crashed and downed UFOs; there were those few members of the public who, as a result of events beyond their control, had found themselves implicated in UFO crash-retrieval incidents, and who had been sworn to secrecy by Uncle Sam; and there was the mythical 'Hangar 18': a veritable museum housing all manner of recovered alien artefacts and technology. Beyond rumour, however, there was nothing. At least, not until 1980 . . .

It was that year which saw the release of a remarkable book: *The Roswell Incident* by Charles Berlitz and William Moore.[1] As a sixteen-year-old sixth-form student, I read the book eagerly, and was fascinated by its assertions: in the summer of 1947, a UFO had crashed at Roswell, New Mexico, and, along with its crew of dead alien creatures, was retrieved under cover of the utmost secrecy by the US military. For decades, American authorities had been sitting tight on the greatest story of all time; with the release of the Berlitz–Moore book, however, the US Government's 'House of Secrets' was beginning to crumble.

Time and again I read *The Roswell Incident*, and began to dig further into the fairly limited amount of data that existed at the time in support of that particular UFO crash and a number of other, broadly similar, accounts.

From the investigator (and former US Air Force Intelligence operative) Leonard Stringfield I obtained a variety of 'Status Reports' outlining his findings on the crashed UFO issue, and detailing a whole host of such crashes that had occurred throughout the USA. Indeed, Stringfield's research suggested that the US Government was up to its neck in the whole murky business.[2]

For me, the most significant breakthrough came in 1987 with the publication of Tim Good's *Above Top Secret*. A true classic, Good's book exposed to one and all the startling fact that government and military agencies throughout the world were keeping a very close watch on the UFO mystery, and in some cases were classifying their findings on the subject at an extraordinarily high level. More importantly, Good devoted a considerable number of pages to a discussion of the Roswell event and the 'Majestic 12' – a top-secret panel of US scientists, military figures and intelligence personnel whose purpose it was to deal with the whole crashed-UFO controversy.[3]

Shortly after Good's book was published, I wrote to him detailing the experience of my father, who had been implicated in a UFO encounter while serving in the RAF in the early 1950s, and we thereafter became friends and routinely liaised on matters of mutual interest.

In 1991 Tim's second bestseller, *Alien Liaison*, was published. I had supplied Tim with a considerable amount of unique documentation for use in that particular work, and I well recall his words when, over drinks in April 1991, he presented me with a complimentary copy of the newly published book, and asked me, 'Nick, why don't you have a go at writing your own book?'

Admittedly, at the time, this seemed like something of a pipe dream; however, there was no doubting the fact that I had at my disposal a wealth of material that had never seen the light of day. Early in 1990, I had begun the difficult and time-consuming task of trying to make sense out of what exactly British authorities had learned about the UFO subject, and ultimately utilised some of my findings in a chapter for *The UFO Report, 1992*, of which Tim was the editor.[4]

Spurred on by the release of that work, I set about digging further into the British Government's involvement in the UFO mystery, and by late 1995 had completed the initial draft of a manuscript. Tim read it, liked it, and passed a copy on to his literary agent, Andrew Lownie. I was more than pleased that Andrew (who would soon thereafter become my literary agent, too) was enthusiastic about my project: 'As I said on the phone,' said Andrew to Tim, 'I was most impressed with

Nicholas Redfern's script . . . He has uncovered some extraordinary material . . .'

Of that, there was no doubt. I had spent a great deal of time analysing the available RAF and Air Ministry UFO files at the Public Record Office at Kew, and had been able to show that, since at least 1947, there had been numerous occasions when RAF pilots had engaged in potentially hostile encounters with UFOs. Needless to say, I put all of this material to good use in my manuscript, and come mid-1996 Andrew had secured for me a fine two-book deal. The following year *A Covert Agenda* was published; and in 1998 my second book, *The FBI Files*, was released and exposed the involvement in the UFO phenomenon of the United States Federal Bureau of Investigation. What had begun on my part as a dream had turned into a reality. With two books under my belt, however, what next?[5]

Just after the contract had been finalised for the publication of my first two books, Andrew quite naturally wanted to know if I had any ideas for a follow-up. I told him that throughout my research I had come across tantalising rumours that suggested it was not just in the USA that UFO crash-retrieval operations had occurred: I possessed a substantial body of evidence pertaining to several alleged events similar to the Roswell crash of July 1947 that had occurred within the confines of the United Kingdom!

I had devoted a small chapter of *A Covert Agenda* to a discussion of these rumours, but did not really expand on them to any great extent – primarily because much of the evidence was fragmentary at best and required further research. Nevertheless, with my first two books complete, I was now in a position to dig deep into the complexities of each case. Needless to say, the road ahead was not easy . . .

'UFO crashes in Britain? Preposterous!' That was the viewpoint coming from officialdom, and, it has to be said, from the majority of my colleagues involved in UFO research. In addition, another of Andrew's clients was a Ministry of Defence man, Nick Pope, who had himself written a book on his experiences while investigating UFO sightings on behalf of the MOD between 1991 and 1994. 'I've spoken with Nick Pope,' said Andrew shortly after I put my new book proposal to him, 'and I asked him if there had ever been a British equivalent of the Roswell crash. Nick said there hadn't.'

Is that so? I thought to myself, somewhat amused. Nevertheless, I was not one to be easily discouraged, and headed off into what was relatively uncharted territory.

Despite the many official denials I received throughout my journey of discovery, time and again I got to speak with numerous seemingly genuine sources relating utterly remarkable accounts about crashed and retrieved UFOs, dead alien bodies held by a mysterious elite, and high-level British Government conspiracies designed to mask the truth surrounding the whole UFO issue. Most intriguing: the further I delved into the controversy, the stronger the supporting evidence became. A whole host of witnesses, official and unofficial documents, and never-before-heard-of incidents began to surface – sometimes with alarming speed.

There was the employee of ATV who recalled a crashed-UFO incident in Staffordshire in the 1970s and the recovery of 'survivors' from a damaged UFO found in Suffolk in 1980; there was the witness who had caught on film the retrieval by the military of a triangular-shaped UFO from a remote field many years ago; there were the shocking revelations that surfaced when I looked into a reported UFO crash in the UK during World War Two; there were the numerous witnesses to the recovery of a UFO that had impacted on a Welsh hillside in 1974; and there was the woman who had seen a flying-saucer-like device in storage at a sensitive military base in southern England in 1996. But these cases were the mere tip of the iceberg.

As time went on, I found myself digging deep into the heart of Britain's defence and intelligence communities – digging that ultimately left me exposed to a totally bizarre world full of crashed UFOs, dead aliens, top-secret documents on the retrieval of extraterrestrial spacecraft, real film footage of alien autopsies, an off-limits chamber buried deep within an imposing mass of caverns and tunnels beneath the Wiltshire countryside, a strange mind-control operation, the disturbing deaths of a number of sources who had got a little too close to the truth, and a high-ranking group whose purpose it was to ensure that the public remained forever in the dark.

I had the witnesses; I had the documents; I had the information. I began the long and difficult task of assembling everything into a coherent format.

Only time will tell what secrets the publication of *Cosmic Crashes* might ultimately reveal . . .

CHAPTER 1

THE ALIENS, THE ACTRESS
AND THE ASSASSINATION

WHEN I BEGAN CONDUCTING RESEARCH INTO THE CRASH of an alien spacecraft somewhere in the United Kingdom during World War Two, not for one moment did I expect that I would ultimately become embroiled in an investigation that encompassed the deaths of the actress Marilyn Monroe and US President John F. Kennedy. And yet that is precisely what occurred as I dug further and further into the case.

Despite claims that the so-called 'modern era' of unidentified flying objects had its beginnings on 24 June 1947 – the date on which the American pilot Kenneth Arnold viewed nine crescent-shaped UFOs overflying the Cascade Mountains in Washington State – I knew that this was not strictly true.

In the final two years of World War Two, both Allied and Axis pilots had regular encounters with a mysterious aerial phenomenon dubbed the 'Foo Fighters'. According to the reports, the Foo Fighters were relatively small, brightly lit objects, usually spherical or ovoid in shape, which would on occasion bear down on military aircraft as if conducting some form of monitoring operation.

Although it had been suggested by a number of UFO researchers that the Foo Fighters were merely some form of advanced technology developed by the Nazis, I always found this to be a somewhat flimsy explanation. For example, at no time did the Foo Fighters engage in hostile action; nor were sightings restricted to the European theatre: as the war progressed, reports began to surface from other areas of the globe, including the Pacific, where the American military machine was out in force.

In addition, many of the Foo Fighter encounters were reported during the closing stages of World War Two, at a time when the Nazis were, literally, fighting a losing battle. Would they have continued to plough money and resources into financing a relatively obscure project to develop Foo Fighter-type technology, when their empire was teetering on the brink of collapse? I considered the possibility unlikely.

That the Foo Fighters were not a manifestation of offensive Nazi technology was something perfectly demonstrated by the late Michael Bentine – he of 'Goon' fame. As I had learned, during the war Bentine served as an intelligence officer with a Polish bomber wing, and was required to debrief pilots on their completion of routine bombing raids over Germany.

From late 1944 onwards, Bentine began to receive reports from air crews who had encountered Foo Fighter activity – bright lights circling their aircraft as if playing 'tag'; objects closing in and soaring away at speed – and asked the crews for their opinions. When they suggested that the Foo Fighters were possibly Nazi weapons, Bentine, quite reasonably, asked, 'OK, what did the weapon do to you?' When the reply, 'Nothing', was offered, Bentine perceptively noted, 'Well, they're not very effective weapons, are they?'[1]

And this was the problem I had with the Foo Fighters: it seemed to me patently illogical for the Nazis to expend so much money on developing such technology which they then failed to put to practical use. But, if not Nazi in origin, where on Earth (or possibly *off* Earth) were the Foo Fighters coming from and what was their purpose? I recalled the highly perceptive statement of Professor George Valley, who in the late

1940s was attached to the US Air Force's Scientific Advisory Board, and noted, with respect to the UFO mystery:

> If there is an extra-terrestrial civilization which can make such objects as are reported then it is most probable that its development is far in advance of ours. This argument can be supported on probability arguments alone without recourse to astronomical hypotheses.
>
> Such a civilization might observe that on Earth we now have atomic bombs and are fast developing rockets. In view of the past history of mankind, they should be alarmed. We should, therefore, expect at this time above all to behold such visitations.[2]

Considering that the Foo Fighters began to be seen on a regular basis at a time when the US Government was conducting its early atomic research at Los Alamos, New Mexico, I considered Professor Valley's words to be highly significant.

But what bearing did any of this have on the recovery by British authorities of a crashed UFO during the height of hostilities with the Nazis? For years I had been intrigued by a persistent rumour that I had heard time and again from various sources within the UFO research field: that a Foo Fighter had come down somewhere in the UK in the final years of World War Two; however, none had attempted to pursue the case to any great extent. It was time to remedy that situation.

Having recognised that the majority of Foo Fighter reports had surfaced either over mid-Europe or in the Pacific, I first had to determine if there were any reports of UFO activity in the UK during the mid-1940s. After all, if the United Kingdom was free of UFO or Foo Fighter encounters during World War Two, this would tend to negate the rumours of a crash-recovery operation. I spoke to anyone and everyone whom I thought might be able to shed some light on the matter, and succeeded in making a number of very significant breakthroughs. For example, there was Gordon W. Cammell, who served as a bomber captain with the RAF during the war.

In May 1943, Cammell was the captain of a Lancaster bomber aircraft and recalled that, on one occasion while crossing the English Channel after returning from a bombing mission over Germany, all of the crew viewed what appeared to be a 'huge, orange ball' on or near the sea, seven or eight thousand feet below the Lancaster.

The object appeared stationary and was seen by those on board for around ten minutes, during which time there was no change in its brightness. Discussions among the crew determined that the light was not from an aircraft or a ship in distress.

After landing back at the base at RAF East Wretham, Suffolk, the crew reported their sighting to the debriefing officer, who also had no idea of what it was that the crew had seen. The incident remained unresolved.[3]

In addition to the account of Gordon Cammell (whose testimony as a military pilot was absolutely credible) I made a positive advance via Paul Fuller, a respected researcher of the 'crop circle' mystery, and the editor and publisher of *The Crop Watcher* magazine.

I had in the past made available to Paul various pieces of UK Government-generated documentation on the crop circles that I had obtained through the Public Record Office at Kew, and, in return, Paul would pass on to me information relevant to my research.

From Paul, I learned that a retired Royal Air Force pilot had come forward with an account of a UFO incident in the United Kingdom in which he was implicated directly, and which occurred at the very time that the Foo Fighter mystery was at its height.

Paul's source had served in the RAF at the level of flight lieutenant, and in the summer of 1944 had seen a bizarre, wheel-like UFO, around 100 feet in diameter and resplendent with lights, near an RAF station in the Hull area: Home-on-

Spalding Moor. Having ruled out the possibility of some form of secret weapon, Paul's source could only watch in wonder as the strange object traversed the skies of 1940s Britain.

While there was no suggestion from Paul Fuller's informant that the UFO had either crashed or become disabled, this incident did at least serve to show that UFOs were seen within British airspace by credible RAF sources during World War Two. I continued my quest.

Having spoken with a variety of colleagues in the UFO field and having scoured numerous journals and newspaper archives, I was able to state with confidence that the original source for the publicised accounts surrounding the World War Two crash was one Dorothy Kilgallen – a respected American journalist.

On 22 May 1955 (presumably at least a decade after the event occurred) Kilgallen wrote in an International News Service cable:

> I can report today on a story which is positively spooky, not to mention chilling. British scientists and airmen, after examining the wreckage of one mysterious flying ship, are convinced these strange aerial objects are not optical illusions or Soviet inventions, but are flying saucers which originate on another planet.
>
> The source of my information is a British official of Cabinet rank who prefers to remain unidentified. 'We believe, on the basis of our inquiry thus far, that the saucers were staffed by small men – probably under four feet tall. It's frightening, but there's no denying the flying saucers come from another planet.'
>
> This official quoted scientists as saying a flying ship of this type could not have possibly been constructed on Earth. The British Government, I learned, is withholding an official report on the 'flying saucer' examination at this time, possibly because it does not wish to frighten the public.

When my husband and I arrived here from a brief vacation, I had no premonition that I would be catapulting myself into the controversy over whether flying saucers are real or imaginary.[4]

I spoke with Tim Good, who confirmed to me that he had been advised by Gordon Creighton, a former diplomat and intelligence officer, that the crash had occurred at some point during World War Two and that the details had been given to Kilgallen at a cocktail party by an illustrious source in mid-1955. Creighton commented:

As regards the identity of the titled Englishman, I had no doubt at the time as to who he was – a great leader and servant of our country who has represented us well both in one of the highest of our military posts in World War Two and in the political sphere during the early post-war era. Our assumption at the time, and in later years, was that the official in question may very likely have been Lord [Louis] Mountbatten. I wrote to Dorothy Kilgallen at once, seeking further information, but never got a reply from her, and she died a few years later. We may take it as certain that she had been effectively silenced.[5]

If the crash did occur during the 1940s hostilities, where did it take place? This was the question uppermost in my mind and proved to be a matter that I was never able to resolve fully. I was not, however, surprised: the incident had been successfully kept under wraps for more than a decade before Dorothy Kilgallen learned of its reality; and even then the information came out only as a result of a tip-off from a talkative insider.

Moreover, I was able to speak with a long-retired RAF source who had been involved in the recovery of a number of German aircraft which had crashed within the confines of the UK during the war. As he pointed out, given the sheer scale of air-crash incidents that occurred during the time frame

1939–45, it would be an immense task to try to determine if one particular incident involved, say, a German fighter plane or something far more exotic. I agreed, and resolved to try another avenue: if British authorities did indeed have at their disposal a crashed alien vehicle (and possibly its extraterrestrial crew, too), then presumably the craft had to be stored somewhere to allow a detailed examination of both it and its contents to take place. But where? Once again, I made telephone calls, wrote letters, called in favours, and generally pursued just about every source that came to mind. Of the few people who were able to help, they were all saying the same thing: the UFO did not remain in the UK – it was shipped across the Atlantic to the USA.

I determined that my best approach was to contact those former and retired officers in both the US intelligence and military communities who had made positive statements on unidentified flying objects. Again, most knew nothing. But some did.

There was John Lear, for example. Lear, a pilot who had flown covert missions for the Central Intelligence Agency (CIA), and who was the only pilot to hold every airman certificate issued by the US Federal Aviation Administration, told me that while his information was sketchy, he had definitely been advised that the UFO had been 'strapped to a [Boeing] B-17' aircraft and transported to the States.[6]

There was also Leonard Stringfield, the former intelligence officer with the US Air Force. He detailed to me how, in the summer of 1977, he was contacted by a retired US Naval Intelligence officer and was asked to present a lecture on the UFO subject for the Cincinnati, Ohio, Chapter of the World Wings association. Later, after Stringfield had concluded his talk, he was approached by one of the audience, a pilot, who confided in him that he had knowledge of a 1953 UFO crash in Arizona. More startling, he revealed to Stringfield, 'I have seen the bodies', and went on to describe how they were being stored at a secure site at Wright-Patterson Air Force Base,

Ohio.[7] Most important from my point of view, however: the pilot was also aware of the crash of one of the mysterious Foo Fighters on British soil at some point in the 1940s. Was Wright-Patterson the final destination of the mystery space vehicle? I had more secrets to pry open before I could answer that question.

Fortunately, Lear and Stringfield were not the only two to have come across such accounts. I was also able to turn up a copy of a 1958 letter from a Brazilian UFO researcher, Olavo T. Fontes, to the renowned American investigator, Coral Lorenzen, of the Aerial Phenomena Research Organisation (APRO).

In that letter, Fontes revealed how he had been contacted by sources connected to Brazil's Naval Intelligence, and had been quietly informed that the rumours of a UFO having crashed in the UK were true, and furthermore that the recovered craft was practically undamaged! Fontes elaborated and revealed that the British case was not a singular event – there had been other such crashes in North America, the Sahara Desert and Scandinavia. He continued, 'All of these discs were small crafts – 32, 72 or 99 feet in diameter. In all of them were found bodies of members of their crews. They were "little men" and ranged in height from 32 to 46 inches. They were dead in all cases, killed in the disasters. The examination of the bodies showed they were definitely "humanoid" – but obviously not from this planet.'[8]

I studied all of this information very carefully, lest something had been overlooked. It had. Dorothy Kilgallen's alleged informant, Lord Louis Mountbatten, held the title of Admiral of the Fleet; Olavo Fontes's source of information was Brazilian Naval Intelligence; and Leonard Stringfield had secured his data on the Foo Fighter crash after being invited to give a talk by a retired US Naval Intelligence source. All three derived from Naval Intelligence.

As I was keenly aware, Tim Good, in his books *Alien Liaison* and *Alien Contact*, had presented a copious amount of data to show that US Naval Intelligence was deeply involved in covert UFO-related projects and operations.[9] Was there a flow of UFO data between the naval intelligence communities of a variety of nations, including the UK, USA and Brazil? This was a distinct possibility.

Although my enquiries with the Royal Navy to determine the extent to which the UK liaised with the USA on naval intelligence matters received a somewhat frosty reception, the Americans did at least admit to me that on issues of shared interest there would be routine liaison between the two. Moreover, a document forwarded to me by the US Naval Space Command revealed, 'The "space watch" was set up in 1961 when the Naval Space Surveillance Center was created to detect, identify, and track launched space vehicles and satellites.' Launched by whom? I wondered.

The document continued, 'The command operates a surveillance network that can detect objects out to an effective range of 15,000 nautical miles . . . The Naval Space Surveillance Center also maintains a catalog of all Earth-orbiting satellites and supports the US Space Command as part of the nation's Space Detection and Tracking System.'

Quite clearly, the presence of any 'unknowns' in Earth orbit would not have gone unnoticed by the US Navy and its overseas counterparts. And it was not just the naval intelligence communities of Western nations who were aware of the true ramifications of the UFO mystery.[10]

In April 1995 I had filed a Freedom of Information Act request with the Defense Intelligence Agency for access to any and all UFO-related documentation which the DIA had obtained since the time of my previous request in 1993.

In response to my request, the DIA declassified twelve documents which dealt with UFO encounters overseas; and included in the document package was a report which first struck me as being quite amusing. On reflection, however, it did have its serious side, too.

Formerly classified at 'Secret' level, the report was two pages in length, and dealt with information obtained by a US Intelligence agent in Vladivostok. The agent evidently had a number of good contacts in the city, and in 1990 filed a report with the DIA detailing recently gathered intelligence data.

Among the reports (which included the account of a Soviet admiral who was seen slipping into his wife's handbag a pineapple which he had stolen from an official function – pineapples apparently being in short supply in Vladivostok!) was one that related to the activity of a general with Soviet Naval Intelligence who had 'imbibed heavily' at a military reception and let it slip that 'rather than fighting each other [censored] should get together to fight UFOs'! Soviet Naval Intelligence, it appeared, had also been exposed to sensitive UFO data. But back to the case at issue.[11]

I was also intrigued by Dorothy Kilgallen's assertion that the retrieved UFO was examined by 'British scientists and airmen'. As I knew from my researches at the Public Record Office at Kew, in the early 1950s when UFOs began to be seen over the UK with increasing regularity, the Air Ministry's Directorate of Scientific Intelligence (DSI) was one of the divisions that were obliged to examine such reports – many of which were filed by military sources. Dorothy Kilgallen's description of the team who examined the crashed UFO sounded very much like a layperson's description of DSI.

There was also the astonishing fact that when I tried to access a number of DSI files that I knew full well were housed at the Public Record Office, I was met with a stunning response from the PRO: '[B]ecause of the nature of these files many will be under extended closure and so closed for 50, 75 or 100 years.'[12]

Fortunately, this matter was picked up by the late Martin Redmond MP, who in the latter part of 1996 raised the issue of the DSI's withheld files in Parliament. Since that statement from the PRO was made to me in 1990, I was aware that a few

DSI files had been declassified (none of which dealt with UFOs), but was somewhat surprised when, on 28 October 1996, Lord Howe, then Under-Secretary of State for Defence, advised Redmond: 'I can confirm that my Department's Scientific Intelligence Branch holds no records under extended closure for any period in excess of 30 years [and] the PRO has confirmed that the class list giving details of preserved records is available at Kew.'

I was fully aware that the 'class list' of files was available; however, as I also knew, the DSI had most definitely examined a wealth of UFO data in the early 1950s (much of which concerned numerous UFO sightings reported at the height of a military exercise in the North Sea in September 1952) and that material was simply not referenced in the class list at the Public Record Office.

But there was one interesting fact that I was able to ascertain: in 1953, a number of DSI operatives made a special 'visit' to the United States on official business. Was this to examine the UFO retrieved in the UK a decade earlier? The possibility was never far from my mind when addressing the complexities of this particular affair.

In 1995 the case took on far greater significance for me when Milo Speriglio, a court-certified questioned-document expert in the USA, surfaced with a remarkable one-page document (supplied by an unnamed source) which referenced, among other things, crashed UFOs, Dorothy Kilgallen, Marilyn Monroe, the Kennedy administration and a classified government project.

I had come across Speriglio's name more than a decade earlier when I picked up a copy of his book, *The Marilyn Conspiracy*, which sought to determine the facts surrounding the admittedly mysterious death of the actress. This had been preceded by *Marilyn Monroe: Murder Cover-up*, and was followed by *Crypt 33: The Saga of Marilyn Monroe*.

When in 1995 a copy of the document at issue first came to light, Speriglio commented, 'I had [the document] probably about two months before I did anything with it. I looked at it and said, "Marilyn Monroe and aliens, no way!"'

But precisely what did the document say? 'To put it succinctly,' said Vicki Ecker of *UFO* magazine, 'the document suggests that on the day she died, Monroe was going to hold her own press conference, where she was planning to spill the beans about, amongst other things [John F. Kennedy's] secret knowledge of UFOs and dead aliens.'

On acquiring a copy of the document I was most interested to see that it also referenced various 'wiretap' operations which had recorded conversations between Dorothy Kilgallen and an acquaintance of hers named Howard Rothberg; and further conversations between Marilyn Monroe and JFK's brother, Robert Kennedy.

Of course, the questions I wanted answering were: Is this genuine? Does the reference to Dorothy Kilgallen have a bearing on the crash of an alien spacecraft in the United Kingdom half a century ago? And what is Speriglio's opinion?

According to Speriglio, Howard Rothberg was the one-time owner of a New York-based antique shop, and had occasion to meet Marilyn Monroe there. '[Rothberg] also dealt with a lot of photographers who used to film Marilyn,' said Speriglio, adding, 'He got a lot of information about her from them, and he would feed [that information] to Dorothy Kilgallen who was a friend of his.' And of the document itself? Dated 3 August 1962, and purportedly originating with the CIA, the document is now aged and fading, but the discernible sections state:

Rothberg discussed the apparent comeback of [Marilyn Monroe] with Kilgallen and the break up with the Kennedys. Rothberg told Kilgallen that [Monroe] was attending Hollywood parties hosted by Hollywood's elite and was becoming the talk of the town again. Rothberg indicated in so many words, that [Monroe] had secrets to tell, no doubt arising from her trysts with the President and the Attorney General. One such 'secret' mentioned the visit by the President at a secret air base for the purpose of inspecting things from outer space. Kilgallen replied that she knew what might be the source of the visit. In the mid-fifties Kilgallen learned of a secret effort by US and UK governments to identify the origins of crashed spacecraft and dead bodies, from a British Government official. Kilgallen believed the story may have come from the New Mexico area in the late forties. Kilgallen said that if the story is true, it would cause terrible embarrassment for Jack [Kennedy] and his plans to have NASA put men on the moon.

[Monroe] repeatedly called the Attorney General and complained about the way she was being ignored by the President and his brother.

[Monroe] threatened to hold a press conference and would tell all.

[Monroe] made reference to bases in Cuba and knew of the President's plan to kill Castro.

[Monroe] made reference to her 'diary of secrets' and what the newspapers would do with such disclosures.

In essence that was the document. But was it the real thing? Certainly, it seemed impressive, and as Vicki Ecker noted, Speriglio had been able to ascertain that the typeface used in the document did match that commonly in use in the early 1960s. Moreover, an investigative journalist known to Speriglio was acquainted with several ex-CIA agents who had verified the contents, specifically noting that there were certain key words present which implicated the intelligence community as being responsible for the document.[13]

From this side of the Atlantic, I was able to add still further data which tended to suggest that the document was indeed genuine. However, I did encounter some criticism from colleagues. One suggested that it was rank paranoia to believe that the Central Intelligence Agency was in any way interested in the activities of Marilyn Monroe; while another suggested that any link between Marilyn Monroe and a UFO crash on UK soil was sheer fantasy.

'Fair enough,' I replied. 'But how can you say that with conviction?'

'Well, it just can't be true, can it?' came the reply. That was not, I concluded, a well-defined argument.

On a Sunday morning in the summer of 1995, I sat down with a copy of the document and scrutinised it carefully from top to bottom. Most intriguing was a reference at the top of the document to a 'Project Moon Dust'. I had carried out a detailed investigation of Moon Dust several years previously and had succeeded in uncovering around one thousand pages of once-classified documents on the project from a variety of US Government and intelligence agencies.

Although largely a project designed to secure for US intelligence purposes foreign 'space debris' which had fallen to Earth, including satellites, rocket boosters and so on, I was also able to tie Moon Dust in conclusively with the UFO issue. For example, a 1967 Defense Intelligence Agency report I had obtained clearly stated with respect to a UFO encounter over Morocco in January 1967, '[T]his sighting demonstrates a high level of local interest in the subject of UFOs and presages future reporting which could be valuable in pursuit of Project MOON DUST.'

Second, the information pertaining to Dorothy Kilgallen's knowledge of a 'secret effort by US and UK governments to identify crashed spacecraft and dead bodies' did tally with that allegedly divulged to her in 1955 by Lord Mountbatten. In fact the only anomaly with regard to this aspect of the document was Kilgallen's purported belief that the crash had possibly occurred in New Mexico, rather than in the UK, as the former intelligence officers Gordon Creighton and Leonard Stringfield had suggested.

I reasoned that while Mountbatten may well have been talking about a British crash, Kilgallen's reference to New Mexico was possibly an allusion to the so-called 'Roswell Incident' of July 1947. The key point, however, was that this document reinforced the rumours that British authorities had been involved in the secret analysis of UFO debris and alien bodies many years ago, and that the CIA were aware of that fact.

As far as Marilyn Monroe and the Kennedys were concerned, I realised that it would be necessary for me to go off at a tangent into areas unknown.

Having reviewed the document fully, and also having read a number of thorough biographies of Marilyn Monroe, I could not fail to notice that her threat to 'tell all' about what she had learned from her 'trysts' with the Kennedys, and what was contained within her 'diary of secrets', was made only one day before her death on 4 August 1962. Without going overboard, I could not help but consider that which I preferred not to: Marilyn Monroe was murdered for what she had learned about the UFO subject, and this was somehow tied in with a classified Anglo-American investigation of the aforementioned UFO debris and alien bodies.

I had digested enough material on Monroe to know that the circumstances surrounding her death were far from clear, and I took a decision to look into the matter further by filing Freedom of Information Act requests with a variety of US Intelligence and Government agencies. And while I'm doing that, I thought, I might as well have a go at chasing down any documentation existing in US Government files on Dorothy Kilgallen. Most responses were negative; one in particular was not.

While undertaking the research for my second book, *The FBI Files*, I knew that the Bureau (particularly when under the control of the late J. Edgar Hoover) had compiled records on just about anyone and everyone; and sure enough, the reply from the FBI was positive. Within weeks of my requests I had in my possession a mountain of once classified FBI documents on both Kilgallen and Monroe.

On reading the Monroe material, I was amused to see that

the very first entry in the file was a 'Confidential' memorandum from FBI Director Hoover to the Department of State concerning Monroe's activities. More eye-opening: a copy of that same memorandum was circulated to the CIA. So much for the comments of colleagues that the Monroe–CIA link was 'sheer fantasy'!

Furthermore, despite the fact that the document was dated 19 August 1955, the overwhelming majority of it was blacked out in accordance with Freedom of Information Act regulations, which allowed government and military departments to deny the public access to sensitive data if deemed necessary. I could understand that there might well have been personal reasons why aspects of Monroe's file were withheld; however, it was made clear to me that the data was denied release specifically for reasons affecting the 'national defense' of the USA. Surely this related to more than mere Hollywood scandal.

In addition, the FBI's papers also confirmed fully the rumoured affair between Monroe and Robert Kennedy – as was alluded to in the document supplied to Milo Speriglio. A section of one such FBI paper read:

> During the period of time that Robert F. Kennedy was having his sex affair with Marilyn Monroe, on one occasion a sex party was conducted at which several other persons were present. Tap recording was secretly made and is in the possession of a Los Angeles private detective agency.

Again this added weight to Speriglio's document and validated the rumours that Monroe was under surveillance. And I was intrigued to note that the FBI had taken keen notice of an article published in the *New York Mirror* by the columnist Walter Winchell in July 1963 dealing with Monroe's 'suicide', and which was the subject of a detailed Bureau memorandum titled ' "PHOTOPLAY" ARTICLE CONCERNING MARILYN MONROE'S DEATH.' My interest was increasing by the moment.[14]

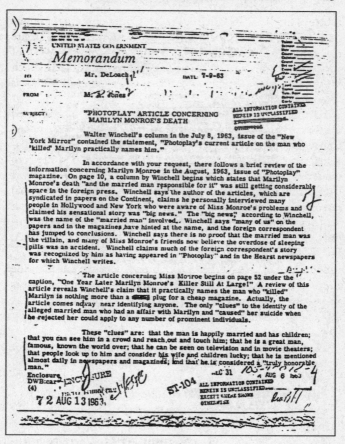

UNITED STATES GOVERNMENT

Memorandum

TO :   Mr. DeLoach   DATE: 7-9-63

FROM :   M. A. Jones

SUBJECT: "PHOTOPLAY" ARTICLE CONCERNING
MARILYN MONROE'S DEATH

ALL INFORMATION CONTAINED
HEREIN IS UNCLASSIFIED

Walter Winchell's column in the July 8, 1963, issue of the "New York Mirror" contained the statement, "Photoplay's current article on the man who 'killed' Marilyn practically names him."

In accordance with your request, there follows a brief review of the information concerning Marilyn Monroe in the August, 1963, issue of "Photoplay" magazine. On page 10, a column by Winchell begins which states that Marilyn Monroe's death "and the married man responsible for it" was still getting considerable space in the foreign press. Winchell says the author of the articles, which are syndicated in papers on the Continent, claims he personally interviewed many people in Hollywood and New York who were aware of Miss Monroe's problems and claimed his sensational story was "big news." The "big news," according to Winchell, was the name of the "married man" involved. Winchell says "many of us" on the papers and in the magazines have hinted at the name, and the foreign correspondent has jumped to conclusions. Winchell says there is no proof that the married man was the villain, and many of Miss Monroe's friends now believe the overdose of sleeping pills was an accident. Winchell claims much of the foreign correspondent's story was recognized by him as having appeared in "Photoplay" and in the Hearst newspapers for which Winchell writes.

The article concerning Miss Monroe begins on page 52 under the caption, "One Year Later Marilyn Monroe's Killer Still At Large!" A review of this article reveals Winchell's claim that it practically names the man who "killed" Marilyn is nothing more than a plug for a cheap magazine. Actually, the article comes nowhere near identifying anyone. The only "clues" to the identity of the alleged married man who had an affair with Marilyn and "caused" her suicide when he rejected her could apply to any number of prominent individuals.

These "clues" are: that the man is happily married and has children; that you can see him in a crowd and reach out and touch him; that he is a great man, famous, known the world over; that he can be seen on television and in movie theaters; that people look up to him and consider his wife and children lucky; that he is mentioned almost daily in newspapers and magazines; and that he is considered a "truly honorable man."

Enclosure
DWB:car ENCLOSURE
(4)

ST-104   ALL INFORMATION CONTAINED
HEREIN IS UNCLASSIFIED
EXCEPT WHERE SHOWN
OTHERWISE

7 2 AUG 13 1963

In 1963 the FBI took a keen interest in the circumstances surrounding the death of Marilyn Monroe

As far as Dorothy Kilgallen was concerned, the Bureau forwarded to me a bulky file consisting of no fewer than 167 pages, several of which dated back to the late 1930s. On reading the file, I realised that Kilgallen was a figure who moved in impressive circles, and had an uncanny ability to uncover sensitive data.

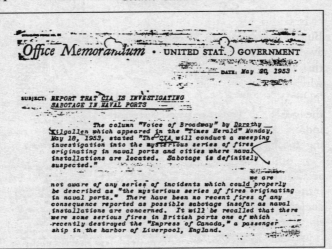

Office Memorandum • UNITED STATES GOVERNMENT

DATE: May 20, 1953

SUBJECT: REPORT THAT CIA IS INVESTIGATING
SABOTAGE IN NAVAL PORTS

The column "Voice of Broadway" by Dorothy
Kilgallen which appeared in the "Times Herald" Monday,
May 18, 1953, stated "The CIA will conduct a sweeping
investigation into the mysterious series of fires
originating in naval ports and cities where naval
installations are located. Sabotage is definitely
suspected."

we are
not aware of any series of incidents which could properly
be described as "the mysterious series of fires originating
in naval ports." There have been no recent fires of any
consequence reported as possible sabotage insofar as naval
installations are concerned. It will be recalled that there
were some serious fires in British ports one of which
recently destroyed the "Empress of Canada," a passenger
ship in the harbor of Liverpool, England.

FBI files concerning Dorothy Kilgallen and the CIA.

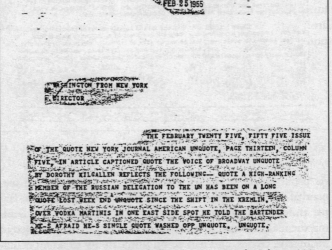

FEDERAL BUREAU OF INVESTIGATION
U. S. DEPARTMENT OF JUSTICE

FEB 25 1955

WASHINGTON FROM NEW YORK
DIRECTOR

THE FEBRUARY TWENTY FIVE, FIFTY FIVE ISSUE
OF THE QUOTE NEW YORK JOURNAL AMERICAN UNQUOTE, PAGE THIRTEEN, COLUMN
FIVE, IN ARTICLE CAPTIONED QUOTE THE VOICE OF BROADWAY UNQUOTE
BY DOROTHY KILGALLEN REFLECTS THE FOLLOWING. QUOTE A HIGH-RANKING
MEMBER OF THE RUSSIAN DELEGATION TO THE UN HAS BEEN ON A LONG
QUOTE LOST WEEK END UNQUOTE SINCE THE SHIFT IN THE KREMLIN.
OVER VODKA MARTINIS IN ONE EAST SIDE SPOT HE TOLD THE BARTENDER
HE-S AFRAID HE-S SINGLE QUOTE WASHED UPP UNQUOTE. UNQUOTE.

*As this FBI record shows, Dorothy Kilgallen was someone to whom the acquisition of
sensitive intelligence data was not unknown.*

In addition to the 'crashed UFO' account, for example, a Bureau document of 27 March 1945 referred to Kilgallen's awareness that 'Marshal Tito, the Yugoslav leader, has agents in this country who beat and terrorize Yugoslavs who disagree with his policies'; while an FBI memo of 18 July 1950 stated, 'New York Office advised that Dorothy Kilgallen's column in the Journal American on May 12th had contained information indicating that an Israeli Intelligence official had been traveling in the United States incognito.'

In other words, Kilgallen was not someone to whom the acquisition of sensitive material was a rare event. And I was intrigued to see that there was a direct link between Kilgallen and Monroe: in 1964 Dorothy Kilgallen was granted permission to conduct an exclusive, private interview with Jack Ruby – the man who shot Lee Harvey Oswald, who was the man who allegedly shot John F. Kennedy, who was reportedly one of those from whom Marilyn Monroe had uncovered some of the information contained within her 'diary of secrets'.

Moreover, Kilgallen also attended Jack Ruby's trial and lunched with his two attorneys, Melvin Belli and Joe Tonahill, and, as the researchers William Jones and Rebecca Minshall noted in 1991,

> On November 8, 1965, fifty-two year old Ms Kilgallen died in her home of acute ethanol and barbiturate intoxication, the circumstances of which were undetermined. A close friend and confidante reportedly died of indeterminate causes two days later. It was reported afterwards that Kilgallen had told a friend she was soon going to New Orleans to break the Kennedy story wide open.

Although the FBI's files did not reflect any evidence of foul play as far as the death of Dorothy Kilgallen was concerned, the Bureau was interested enough to obtain copies of a *Time* magazine article on the JFK assassination, which did indeed make mention of her death and addressed the issue of whether anything sinister lay behind it.[15]

While the information in the FBI's files on Dorothy Kilgallen was certainly provocative, I constantly had to deal with sceptics who maintained it was absurd to imagine that a high-ranking British Government official would simply relate to – of all people – a journalist top-secret data concerning a classified British Government project dealing with crashed UFOs and dead aliens. Indeed, this did seem strange and I had to ask myself: what on Earth would prompt someone used to dealing with sensitive intelligence data to impart such astonishing material? An answer came via a wholly unexpected source: the CIA!

In addition to determining that the FBI was taking more than a passing interest in the activities of Dorothy Kilgallen, I was most interested to discover – officially – that the CIA was doing likewise.

As papers released to me in 1997 by the CIA show, the Agency recognised Kilgallen's ability to obtain sensitive intelligence data (such as that regarding the Yugoslavian Government and Israeli Intelligence) and initiated plans to cultivate Kilgallen 'as a potential source of foreign intelligence information'.

As I read the CIA's previously classified files, I was most intrigued to learn that the Chief of the Security Division had stated in an internal report that Agency approval had been granted allowing Dorothy Kilgallen access to 'information classified up to and including Secret provided discretion is exercised in development as a source'.

In other words, in return for acting as a 'source of foreign intelligence information', Kilgallen was being given snippets of material from CIA files at secret level! Moreover, the decision to allow Kilgallen access to such material was made in 1954 – only twelve months before she was fed the 'crashed UFO' story! In view of this, the idea that Kilgallen would be given details of just such a momentous event did not seem so strange after all.[16]

Returning to the document leaked to the investigator Milo

Speriglio, I could not fail to notice that within a few years of its creation, practically all of those referenced within its text were dead: Dorothy Kilgallen, Marilyn Monroe, John F. Kennedy and Robert Kennedy.

I found it difficult to accept that all of those deaths were in any way directly related to the UFO crash that occurred years before within the UK, and yet credible sources were maintaining that John F. Kennedy's death was at least partly prompted by his decision to reveal to the public the truth surrounding the alien presence on Earth.

The Emmy Award-winning television producer Linda Howe, for example, had uncovered information suggesting that Kennedy was far from happy with the overwhelming secrecy surrounding the UFO issue as a whole; and as the investigative writer Lars Hansson noted in 1991 after having dined with her; 'Ms Howe described her meetings with military intelligence agents a few years before during which the JFK assassination was discussed in some detail. After relating what they imparted to her she was most emphatic about the wisdom of leaving that issue alone.'[17]

From a former CIA pilot, John Lear, too, astounding revelations surfaced surrounding the assassination of John F. Kennedy as it related to the UFO issue.

Referring to the Majestic 12 (or MJ-12) group first publicised by Tim Good in *Above Top Secret*, Lear stated that:

[T]he powers that be had to eliminate President Kennedy because he wanted to release the information on the disks and the aliens in 1963. Since then, we have talked to people who have heard the recording made in the Oval Office when Kennedy pounded his fist and told the representatives of MJ-12: 'You guys better get your stuff together because I'm going to tell the public.'

There were several reasons why [John F. Kennedy] was assassinated. One was the Bay of Pigs fiasco; another was that he had threatened to 'shatter the CIA into a thousand pieces'. A third reason was because he threatened to pull all our Americans from Vietnam by 1965. The fourth was that he intended to expose the alien-disk cover-up.[18]

John Lear's account was certainly fascinating – and not a little disturbing; whether by accident or design, however, the JFK–UFO connection was one I found incredibly difficult to make. The secrecy surrounding this particular aspect of my investigation was, without doubt, all-encompassing.

I uncovered little else of any real significance to the case in question, but felt that I had made some highly constructive progress: there was the investigator Paul Fuller, who was able to affirm that UFO activity in the United Kingdom during World War Two was not unknown; there was the important testimony of the former bomber captain with the Royal Air Force, Gordon W. Cammell; there was Dorothy Kilgallen and her off-the-record encounter with a high-ranking British official who was aware of an ultra-secret British–American investigation of crashed UFO debris and alien bodies; Milo Speriglio had surfaced with an intriguing Central Intelligence Agency document linking well-known figures in both the political and entertainment arenas with that same investigation; there were the accounts of Leonard Stringfield, John Lear and Olavo Fontes; and, finally, there was that mass of Federal Bureau of Investigation papers pertaining to Dorothy Kilgallen and Marilyn Monroe.

Faced with the evidence I had obtained, I recognised that the subject of crashed UFO technology and dead alien bodies in the hands of some mysterious elite was perhaps the most closely guarded secret of all time.

Indeed, as I had learned, it was a subject for which some people would possibly kill to keep concealed. Without doubt, the stakes were high.

But I was ready to gamble.

CHAPTER 2

CRASHES AND CRATERS

ONE OF THE MOST INTRIGUING ACCOUNTS THAT CAUGHT my attention as I sought to determine the full extent to which the British Government was implicated in the crashed-UFO controversy came from retired United States Army Command Sergeant-Major Robert Dean.

According to Dean (who held a cosmic top-secret clearance), between 1961 and 1964, NATO's Supreme Headquarters, Allied Powers in Europe (SHAPE), conducted a classified investigation into the UFO subject which resulted in the publication of an eight-inch-thick document titled 'The Assessment'.

Dean further maintained that SHAPE's studies concluded that a number of extraterrestrial civilisations and species were visiting Earth and were undertaking an in-depth surveillance programme.

Most pertinent to my research, however, was Dean's assertion that in the early 1960s British military forces were implicated in the recovery of a UFO that had crashed on the East-West German border. I decided to look into the facts.

It was 1962, Dean explained, when the incident occurred; and while serving with SHAPE he had access to 'the entire report' relating to both the crash and the retrieval of the UFO.

As he detailed, the UFO fell to Earth near the East-West German frontier on soft soil and, as a result, on inspection was found to be partially intact – albeit half buried. Crucially, the first to arrive on the scene (the location of which was identified as Timmendorfer, near the Baltic Sea) was a corps of British military engineers who succeeded in gaining entry to the machine. And they found no fewer than twelve dead alien creatures – small in stature with large, bald heads, black eyes and grey skin. Dean additionally stated that a series of extensive autopsies of the aliens were undertaken by the British military, who discovered the intriguing fact that all of the bodies were identical: clones or, as Dean put it, 'laboratory products'. 'I saw all the photos taken of the beings and I couldn't believe it,' Dean recalled.

Dean's claim that this event occurred in 1962 was of profound significance to me, mainly because, as I knew from my research at the Public Record Office, in that very year a document had been circulated throughout the British military by the Air Ministry ordering all military-originated UFO reports to be forwarded to a specific department within Air Intelligence.

Were these new guidelines the result of the events at Timmendorfer? Given the remarkable coincidence timewise, this was a distinct possibility. Even more interesting was the fact that 1962 was also the year in which Marilyn Monroe began talking confidentially about her knowledge of British Government involvement in the crashed-UFO controversy. Had she, possibly via her connections with the Kennedys, learned of the incident at Timmendorfer?

Although the information imparted by Robert Dean related to events that occurred nearly four decades ago, data relating to this affair continued to reach me as late as 1998. In April of that year, for example, I spoke with one Stephen Meeson, who, prior to his retirement, had served as an inspector of equipment with the Ministry of Defence. He informed me that he was working with the Royal Electrical and Mechanical

Engineers when Bob Dean surfaced with details of the Timmendorfer UFO crash and attempted to shed some light on what had occurred.

'I tried to look into it,' Meeson told me. 'When Bob Dean's story was first publicised I asked my superior – who was a major in the REME – to make a few enquiries. As I was working for the REME at the time, too, I thought I had a good chance of finding someone who perhaps knew something about it.'

'And did you or the major come across anything?' I asked.

There was a slight and decidedly uneasy laugh: 'Well, the major said he was told: "Leave it well alone." Now this was in England; I wouldn't say where as I don't want things pinning down, but that's what he was told.'[1]

Leave it well alone? This at least suggested to me that there was some substance to the 1962 UFO retrieval near the Baltic Sea; and the fact that the entire matter was still considered a sensitive matter was one that could not be discounted. The British military was truly in possession of some deep and dark secrets, I concluded.

Throughout Nick Pope's term with the Secretariat of the Air Staff, I had regularly questioned him on a variety of issues relating to the UFO phenomenon, and had routinely pressed for greater openness on the part of the Ministry. Nick was always quick to respond to my questions, and I sensed that his involvement in investigating UFO sightings on behalf of the Ministry of Defence was borne out of a real and enthusiastic desire to determine the truth.

My suspicions proved to be correct in 1996 when Nick's book, *Open Skies, Closed Minds*, was released at a time when public interest in the UFO subject was at an all-time high. Sure enough, Nick's book went on to become a bestseller, and he became a key player in the UFO lobby.

Although some research colleagues viewed Nick with suspicion, I never detected any evidence of deception on his part –

my belief was (and still is) that Nick recognised that behind the UFO mystery there lay a very real phenomenon, and he was not afraid to stand up and say so.

To illustrate Nick's helpful attitude towards the UFO research community, in July 1993 he wrote to me advising that January 1994 would see the release of two previously classified files of UFO data held at the Public Record Office.[2]

On making enquiries at the PRO in January 1994, I learned that the files in question covered the period 1961–63 and amounted to no fewer than six hundred pages of never-before-seen material. Needless to say, I wasted no time in securing copies.[3] Although I was keen to see the extent to which the Air Ministry was implicated in the UFO puzzle in the early 1960s, I was also eager to learn if there were any records available referencing an event that briefly attracted major media coverage in the summer of 1963 when it was widely reported that a UFO had slammed into the ground on farmland at Charlton, Wiltshire.

Before examining the Air Ministry's papers, I reviewed my own records on the case at issue in an attempt to ensure I was fully conversant with the facts. I had not studied my files on the 'Charlton crater' for some years, but well recalled that I had been able to put together an impressive body of material on the affair. On a Monday night in February 1994 I sat down and began to sift through the data.

All the evidence suggested that the Charlton crater controversy began in the early hours of 16 July 1963 when several witnesses recalled unusual aerial activity in the Charlton district. There was Leonard Joliffe, who was employed at Manor Farm, Charlton, and reported hearing an unusual explosion in the vicinity; there was a local police officer who recalled seeing an unidentified orange light streak across the sky before disappearing in the Charlton area; however, the most important witness was a farmworker, Reginald Alexander, who discovered a crater-like depression near the aforementioned Manor Farm several hours after Leonard Joliffe heard the explosion.

Concerned at what he had uncovered, Alexander quickly informed his employer, Roy Blanchard, of his remarkable discovery. Arriving at the scene, Blanchard was amazed to see a circular area of flattened ground – eight feet in diameter with outwardly spreading 'spoke' marks – which gave every impression that something tangible had come into contact with the earth . . .

I leafed through the many press reports generated at the time. It transpired that Blanchard, fully appreciating the seriousness of the event, contacted the local police, who quickly arrived on the scene. The police wasted no time in calling in the Army.

Next to arrive was Captain John Rogers, chief of the Army Bomb-Disposal Unit at Horsham; admittedly baffled, he called for backup. By this time, the media had latched on to the case, and launched their own investigations. At that stage in the proceedings, both Roy Blanchard and Captain Rogers were willing to speak out.

'There isn't a trace of the potatoes and barley which were growing where the crater is now,' said Blanchard. 'No stalks. No leaves. No roots. The thing was heavy enough to crush rocks and stone to powder. I believe that we have received a visit from a spaceship from another world.'

Captain Rogers confirmed that he too considered the event extraordinary, to say the least: 'There is no evidence of burn or scorch marks. And I could find no trace of an explosion. My superiors and I are baffled.'

As I continued to scan the various media reports I was intrigued to discover that, whatever the nature of the object that came down at Charlton, it attracted intense interest on the part of the Army. For example, several days after the initial discovery of the crater, the Army's Southern Command revealed that preliminary investigations had led bomb-disposal experts to believe that a large object, probably metallic, was secreted deep within the crater.

Forty-eight hours later, I discovered, the Army brought in a team of impressively equipped individuals. A further, and infinitely more in-depth, study of the crater began. What was the conclusion? I continued to peruse the reports.

One theory which was particularly popular among the bomb-disposal team was that the crater had been formed following the detonation of a long-buried German bomb, presumably dropped by an aircraft during World War Two. The only snag in that theory, I learned, was that further analyses continued to suggest the presence of something tangible within the crater – in other words, if the crater was formed following the explosion of a bomb, what was the nature of the intact object still registering on the Army's detection equipment? It was clear that a deeper investigation was warranted. And then came a breakthrough: the Army announced that it had located something deep within the crater . . .

Scanning a variety of newspaper reports, I was able to ascertain that this particular 'discovery' had sent the media into a frenzy, with numerous rumours circulated to the effect that an alien spacecraft had been recovered from the crater. According to the Army, however, this was not the case. What they had recovered was a weighty lump of rock believed to have been a meteorite.

Since the analysis of meteorite debris was outside the scope of the British Army, on 24 July 1963 the rock was forwarded to specialists at the British Museum for study. On the following day, questions were asked in Parliament:

Mr Mason asked the Secretary of State for Air if he will have an examination made of the crater and other evidence at Charlton, near Shaftesbury, to assess the possibility of its having been made by an unidentified flying object.

Mr H. Fraser: When I know the results of the investigation which the Army are at present making, I shall consider whether further examination would be justified.

Twenty-four hours later, the origin of the mystery lump of rock was resolved, but this only added to the confusion surrounding the entire incident.

According to the British Museum, the suspected meteorite was nothing more than standard ironstone, which was found naturally across the southern portion of the United Kingdom.

I located an official press release issued by the British Museum's Keeper of Mineralogy, Dr G.F. Claringbull: 'It is the sort of thing some people would easily find at the bottom of their garden. Certainly, this specimen is not a meteorite.' So what *was* the cause of the crater? And how did it fit in with the explosion reported by Leonard Joliffe shortly before its discovery?

I continued to review the media's involvement, and discovered that the Army was keen to distance itself from any further investigation, but did reluctantly admit that the matter was still considered unexplained. As a spokesman for Southern Command told the press: 'As far as we are concerned the matter is closed. It is not a bomb so it has nothing to do with us. The cause of the hole and its surrounding "phenomena" is still unexplained, but it is no part of the Army's task to unravel such mysteries.'

Even Joseph Godber, Secretary for War, conceded that the matter had not been satisfactorily resolved; however, I found it curious that no one in officialdom appeared to want to take things further. For example, I was able to determine that the media's reporting of the case led to still further questioning in Parliament:

Mr Wall asked the Secretary of State for Air what were the findings of the two Royal Air Force officials who investigated the crater at Charlton, Wiltshire; and whether investigations by his department are continuing.

Mr H. Fraser: From my inquiries I have no reason to think that anything happened in the area which would justify further investigation by the Air Ministry.

This certainly piqued my curiosity, since there had been very little mention in the press that, in addition to the Army, the Air Ministry was taking an interest in what occurred at Manor Farm. I was certainly intrigued, however, to find that the Air Ministry had taken a sudden interest in the case following the Army's assertion that the event remained unexplained; and despite the Air Ministry's low-key involvement, it appeared that they, too, got no further.

Then came a stunning admission. On 25 August 1963, John Southern, a thirty-seven-year-old television repairman of Wembley, Middlesex, came forward and claimed that he, along with two friends, was responsible for hoaxing the public over the crater. 'I was one of the hoaxers,' he said at the time. 'There were two others in it but I have promised not to tell their names.' He elaborated, and stated that it was the intention of all three to dig a number of craters throughout the country, 'to give the impression that something from outer space had landed'; and to reinforce the hoax, they had decided to leave near one of the craters a car, with its doors wide open and a laced-up shoe inside to make it appear that the driver had been 'abruptly wrenched' from his seat. Southern added that it was the intention to drag the car to the edge of the crater while its brakes were on, thus giving the impression that it had been pulled 'by a powerful magnetic force'. The caper then became more involved: Southern would lie low for a few days, and then, when he had been missed, would turn up with a remarkable account describing his kidnap at the hands of alien beings. 'I was to say I had been to a space station. This would be less complicated than a story about visiting another planet as my observations would be limited and easier to explain.' He expanded further:

> The first crater was dug at a lonely spot near Haddington in Scotland where my friends were staying and the second was then prepared on a farm in Wiltshire.
>
> My friends returned to London and we watched the

papers for the discovery. When the story appeared I remember asking one of my friends why they dug channels coming out of the crater and he said: 'It's the experts who have to do the guessing, not us.'

It all caused quite a stir but not nearly enough. I suppose it was eclipsed by the Profumo affair. However, we decided to look for a site for our third crater. I volunteered to lend a hand at digging this one but my friends developed blisters on their hands digging the first two and if this happened to me it would connect me with the digging when I was later 'found'.

My part of the stunt was getting close now and I was being briefed on the things I should say when I returned to Earth.

But at the last moment I realised I was not cut out for the part. I had been getting steadily more nervous as the scheme went on. I knew I could never have kept up the act after my 'reappearance', apart from the ordeal I put my family through.

My friends were not too disappointed when I let them down because they were not entirely happy about the spot we had chosen. And they had expected more publicity about the first two craters.

They were still keen to go on but neither could take my part in the hoax as their holidays were nearly over. Why am I telling this story now? Because I have been a fool.

As I looked into the considerable media coverage afforded to John Southern's account, I discovered a variety of problems. First, his two 'friends' were rather too conveniently missing; and his version of events could not explain the presence of the metallic object apparently detected deep within the crater by the Army – nor could it explain the reports of strange, aerial activity at Charlton shortly before the crater was discovered.

For its part, the Army seemed willing to accept Southern's version of events. 'We had six men working on this crater for ten days,' said Major H.P. Qualtrough of the Horsham Bomb-Disposal Unit. 'They could have been on much more important work. If it's a hoax I'm prepared to laugh with the next man. We often get hoaxed. Nearly always in Cambridge rag week. We just accept it in good grace. All I can say is that at the time this appeared to be quite genuine.'

I was interested to see that Roy Blanchard, the owner of Manor Farm, was not convinced by John Southern's 'confession': 'I don't believe this story that the whole thing was a hoax. I think anyone who believes it was a hoax is being hoaxed.'

Despite the fact that John Southern's account of how the crater came to be formed attracted a great deal of press interest, it went largely unreported that shortly afterwards he confessed that his version was indeed nothing more than a good-hearted fabrication.

According to Southern, on hearing about the crater, he initially felt that it simply had to be a hoax. By confessing that he was the hoaxer, Southern explained, he felt that this would inevitably force the real hoaxer into the open; he was, after all, reaping the publicity for their efforts. However, silence prevailed and no one else came forward to counter Southern's claim to have made the crater. In an ironic twist, Southern's last word on the matter was that he now considered that a UFO had been the cause of the crater after all![4]

There were other reasons for dismissing the claims of John Southern. In 1992 I had come across the account of one Wallace Binns of Emsworth who recalled visiting the site of the Charlton crater shortly after its discovery. According to Binns, approximately two hundred yards from the crater there was a depression which, in today's terminology, would best be described as a 'crop circle'.

Binns also recalled that the circle was unfortunately trampled by numerous people who wished to examine the crater; however, he was able to speak with an artist who had sketched the circle and recalled that the crops within it had been bent over through ninety degrees and were swirled in an anticlockwise direction. There was also a rather more eminent witness to the circle – the astronomer Patrick Moore.

In a letter to *New Scientist* on 22 August 1963, Moore wrote, 'In the adjoining wheatfields were other features, taking the form of circular or elliptical areas in which the wheat had been flattened. I saw these myself; they had not been much visited, and were certainly peculiar.'

Was the phenomenon responsible for the Charlton crater also responsible for the nearby crop-circle formations? I continued to scan the records in my possession and found yet another correlation. The investigator Paul Fuller told me that in 1992 Graham Brunt of Dorset revealed to him that in the early 1950s he had lived relatively close to the site of the crater, and recalled that a similar crop circle had been found on the farm in either 1951 or 1952. Manor Farm was certainly a most interesting location.[5]

I also turned up several newspaper clippings on an event which may have been tangentially related to the discovery at Manor Farm.

Only six days after the Charlton encounter, an unusual flying object was seen at Parr, Lancashire, by a variety of witnesses. One, Michael Holland, reported:

We saw this thing very high up at first, then it came down very fast. It stopped in the air about 70 feet high. It had a red flashing light on top of it and it flashed like those on top of police cars. It was spinning when it first came down, but then it stopped and the flashing light went out. We were all watching it when something slid back underneath it and what looked like a periscope came out. It swivelled round and pointed at us. Then it went back in and the machine went up very fast into a cloud. We saw it again about five seconds later, then it vanished.

I was able to confirm that details of this account, along with a pencil drawing of a tripod-legged UFO, were forwarded to

Flying Saucer Review magazine, who perceptively noted that an analysis of the drawing showed '[A] central projection at its base which could have caused a hole in the ground had it actually rested on terra firma. The three "legs" might well have made the mysterious radial marks in Mr Roy Blanchard's field.'[6]

My study of the media's treatment of the Charlton crater had ended. But what of the Air Ministry files declassified at the beginning of 1994? Remarkably, they made scant reference to the affair. A dozen or so newspaper clippings aside, the papers consisted of a brief exchange between two Air Ministry divisions (S4 and S6) and centred on the discovery of the lump of ironstone by the Army.

I was, however, able to determine that there was evidence of interest on the Air Ministry's part, beyond that shown by S4 and S6. As I demonstrated in *A Covert Agenda*, the UFO work undertaken by both S4 and S6 in the early 1960s largely revolved around the study of low-grade UFO reports submitted to the Air Ministry by members of the general public; the good-quality reports – specifically those filed by Air Force, Army and Navy sources – were channelled through to Air Intelligence.

A study of the Ministry's reports revealed that in precisely the same week as the crater discovery was made at Charlton, someone within Air Intelligence was greatly interested in obtaining reports of landed UFOs.

On 25 July 1963, for example, a huge, grounded UFO was seen near Salisbury (now Harare), Southern Rhodesia (now Zimbabwe), and a report was filed with Air Intelligence by the Royal Rhodesian Air Force, who had forwarded the details via the British Defence Liaison Staff, Southern Rhodesia.

Curiously, the report sent to Air Intelligence was missing from the documents released to me, but a two-page 'note' forwarded to S6 gave brief details of the landing and convinced me that Air Intelligence had its own reasons for looking into reported UFO 'touchdowns'. I could not discount the possibility that their interest was a direct follow-on from the encounter at Charlton.[7]

Although I located nothing further pertaining to Charlton, I found it significant that in the months that followed further 'impact craters' were discovered dotted around the United Kingdom.

On 25 November 1963 a similar depression to that discovered at Charlton was found on farmland at Home Farm, Belton, near Grantham.

'So far nothing has been found to suggest that there is actually an unexploded bomb in the field,' said Captain J.E. Rogers, Officer Commanding, No. 2 Troop, at Horsham, in answer to questions raised by the Nottingham *Guardian Journal*. 'We have been drilling in the vicinity and inserting metal detectors in an effort to trace any metal which could indicate the presence of a bomb.' Ultimately, nothing was found.

Three months later, on 11 February 1964, another similar crater was located, this time at Slackstead, near Braishfield. The site was once more farmland – the discovery having been made in a newly ploughed field by two forestry workers. Yet again, bomb-disposal experts were rushed to the scene. No bomb was found.

I returned my records to their filing cabinet and considered the implications of the incident at Charlton. John Southern's 'confession' could clearly be discounted, as could the theories that the crater was the result of either a meteorite impact or the explosion of a World War Two bomb. And what of the various crop-circle reports generated in the area? How did they fit into the scheme of things? Decades on, it seemed impossible to say. But there was one thing I was certain of: if the Charlton crater was indeed caused by the crash-landing of a UFO, then in this instance it was obviously a case of 'the one that got away'.

CHAPTER THREE

INCIDENT AT COSFORD

JANUARY 1995 IS A MONTH I WILL LONG REMEMBER. IT marked the beginning of an intense quest on my part to determine exactly what occurred at a relatively anonymous Royal Air Force establishment in the heart of Shropshire on a fateful night in late 1963. As you will soon learn, what began as a straightforward investigation into a long-forgotten UFO sighting soon mutated into a bizarre series of events stretching across the Atlantic and encompassing the landing (and possible retrieval by the military) of a spacecraft from another world; a disturbing 'mind-control' operation to prevent those involved in the case from speaking out; contacts with a shadowy intelligence operative; and my acquisition of a batch of once classified papers relating to the case in question.

Today, the RAF station at Cosford, near Wolverhampton, is perhaps best known for its huge museum, which is home to an impressive collection of vintage military and civilian aircraft. Less well known is the fact that Cosford is also classed as a Technical Training Establishment where Royal Air Force operatives receive expert tuition in a variety of disciplines, including avionics, engineering, electronics and specialist photography.

At around 11.30 p.m. on 10 December 1963, however,

Cosford became briefly famous for an entirely different reason. According to rumours circulating at the time, on the night in question a dome-shaped UFO touched down on the base, bathed the surrounding area in a beam of green light, and was seen at close quarters by two RAF apprentices. At least, that had been the accepted story for four decades . . .

My first exposure to the Cosford event came in 1987 on reading Tim Good's bestselling book, *Above Top Secret*.[1] Perhaps the finest and most objective investigator of the UFO mystery in the United Kingdom, Tim gave a detailed account of the evidence in hand, the bulk of which had been secured in early to mid-1964 by two researchers, Wilfred Daniels and Waveney Girvan, and had not been referenced in UFO investigative circles since that year, when the renowned journal *Flying Saucer Review*, gave the affair pride of place in its pages.[2]

I had good reasons for taking more than a passing interest in what occurred at Cosford: since the late 1970s my father, Frank Redfern, had worked on a voluntary basis at the Cosford Aerospace Museum, and in the early 1980s was almost single-handedly responsible for restoring to its former glory Cosford's Fairey Gyrodyne helicopter – a prototype for the famed Rotodyne – which thereafter became a key exhibit at the museum.

I asked my father to make enquiries on my behalf with personnel at the base, but not surprisingly that led nowhere – a quarter of a century had elapsed and anyone with first-hand knowledge would have long since departed Cosford.

Similar enquiries on my part with staff at the base were equally fruitless: 'Unfortunately we do not keep records that go so far back actually at Cosford,' I was advised by Squadron Leader Carolyn Browning in May 1988, 'but we do write a monthly diary that is eventually retained by our Air Historical Branch; perhaps mention was made of this sighting at the time.'[3]

While conducting the research that led to the publication of *A Covert Agenda*, I had been in touch on a number of occasions with both the Ministry of Defence's Air Historical Branch and its publicly acknowledged division for handling UFO reports – Secretariat Air Staff 2A.

Any documentation relative to the Cosford encounter, I was advised in 1989, would be subject to the 'Thirty Year Ruling', and since Cosford occurred in late 1963 (with the paperwork spilling over into 1964), the likelihood was that nothing of significance would enter into the public domain much before January 1995. For six years I put Cosford to the back of my mind and turned my attentions elsewhere.

In January 1995, as I was putting the final touches to the original manuscript of *A Covert Agenda*, thoughts of the UFO landing at Cosford came flooding back into my mind. Had the Ministry of Defence declassified its files on the case? Was a dusty batch of papers sitting on a shelf at the Public Record Office, just waiting to be scrutinised? A quick phone call to the PRO confirmed my suspicions: the file was available; I could examine it any time I wished. With this information in hand, my investigation began in earnest.

On first examining the file, it became immediately apparent to me that the Air Ministry (the encounter had occurred several months before the formal establishment of the Ministry of Defence in April 1964) had viewed the matter with the utmost seriousness. In total, the paperwork surrounding that one case amounted to an astonishing sixty-one pages! Never before had my research at the Public Record Office uncovered such a large file devoted solely to one UFO event.

In addition to securing the official file, I began liaising with various 'old-timers' in the UFO investigation field, and was fortunate enough to obtain copies of the original research notes and letters of both Wilfred Daniels and Waveney Girvan as they related to Cosford. A remarkable picture began to emerge.

As I began to pore over this 'Aladdin's Cave' of aged and fading documents it became obvious that the UFO landing (or 'crash-landing', as I was later to learn) at Cosford was only one of a number of strange UFO-related occurrences in late 1963. In a letter dated 3 January 1964 to Flight Lieutenant A.R. Stevens at Cosford, Wilfred Daniels, who had previously served with the British Army's Royal Electrical and Mechanical Engineers at the level of captain, wrote: 'On the 12th and 14th of November last, there were UFOs over [the] M6 motorway; at Yarley (my own sighting) and [at] Tittensor (Manchester lorry-driver witness). There were two UFOs between Preston and Southport on Wednesday 12th Nov. 1963, also.'

Daniels also revealed to Flight Lieutenant Stevens (somewhat rashly, in my opinion) that he had uncovered intimate details of the Cosford landing: 'I have learned today, through civilian UFO-investigation channels, that a UFO is reported to have landed recently adjacent to a hangar at RAF Cosford and to have been seen by RAF personnel to sweep the airfield with a green light before taking off and disappearing from view.' In conclusion, Daniels added, 'I do not expect an admission as to the Cosford landing, but I think the foregoing will be of interest to you.'

On investigating further, I was able to determine that Daniels's information had come from J. Leslie Otley of the Tyneside UFO Society, who had published details in the TUFOS journal, *Orbit*. In a letter to *Flying Saucer Review*'s editor, Waveney Girvan, in early January 1964, Otley detailed the event, adding that 'the two young RAF types' watched the UFO for approximately two minutes before seeking out a superior officer. 'The two were interrogated at length by the Camp Commandant and fellow officers. The sighting was reported to the camp over its own "closed circuit" radio.'

At this point in the proceedings, my research showed that something truly remarkable occurred. Before Flight Lieutenant Stevens had a chance to respond to Wilfred Daniels's letter of 3 January, Daniels had a million-to-one chance encounter outside the Albrighton branch of Lloyds Bank. I quote from Daniels's own report, filed shortly afterwards:

On Thursday morning, January 9, 1964, I motored over to Albrighton, close to which is situated the RAF Technical Training Establishment, RAF Cosford on the west side of [the] A41, Wolverhampton to Newport, Salop.

In High Street, Albrighton, at about 11.15 a.m., I came face to face with a young man in clerical garb. When I asked him if he were the Vicar of Albrighton, he replied, 'No, I am the Chaplain at the RAF Station.'

Daniels was quick to capitalise on this astonishing coincidence, and fired off a salvo of questions: 'Do you know the two lads concerned in this business?' 'How did they describe the thing – what shape, what colour?'

According to Daniels, the Chaplain replied, 'Oh! Yes, I've talked about it to them and they really believe they saw it. They said it looked like what you would take for a Flying Saucer. It was down on the ground [and] as they watched it a trap-door in the upper part slowly opened. It was then they ran!' 'They were scared, then?' pressed Daniels. 'Yes. They were scared.' the Chaplain replied.

An in-depth study of both the Air Ministry's file and Wilfred Daniels's own papers showed that Daniels had been careful in correspondence with other researchers not to mention the name of the Chaplain. Nevertheless, as a result of the Albrighton meeting, Daniels had the Chaplain's name on record: the Reverend B.G. Henry, BA, RAF. And Daniels's records also showed that Henry advised that it was 'more than his job was worth' to arrange a meeting with the two witnesses; and that 'he really ought not to be talking about it at all; that security had dropped right down on the whole thing'.

As I continued to scour the files, it became clear to me that what Henry did or did not say to Wilfred Daniels was central to the entire case.

On 22 January 1964 Daniels received a brief, and curiously non-committal, letter from Flight Lieutenant Stevens in response to his letter of 3 January: 'I regret that the reported sighting at Cosford was by very inexperienced observers and after investigation the claim was found to have no substance. We are quite satisfied that in this case the eye was deceived!'

I mused upon Flight Lieutenant Stevens's words. His comment that 'the claim was found to have no substance' I considered a thinly veiled allusion to a hoax; however, his final assertion, '. . . in this case the eye was deceived!', suggests something was indeed viewed, even if that something was not a UFO. This curious blend of double talk was extremely prevalent in the Cosford file. Reading it, I had the impression that the Air Ministry was fearful of committing itself to one particular theory, lest it should shortly thereafter be discredited. And far stranger things were to follow . . .

One week after receiving Flight Lieutenant Stevens's letter, Wilfred Daniels received a proposal from Waveney Girvan, offering an all-expenses-paid trip for the Reverend Henry to meet with a number of influential figures in London society who were both interested in and concerned by the UFO mystery. 'Would the padre be persuaded to come to London as the guest of these people some evening convenient for him during next March, probably at the end of the month? I suppose it would be impossible to bring with him one or other of the two frightened apprentices?'

What was Daniels's response? I sifted through the mound of papers, and discovered a letter dated 2 February from Daniels to Henry:

I have kept faith with you and have divulged your name to no-one . . . I have just received the enclosed letter from Waveney Girvan. Should you decide to respond to the invitation contained in Mr Girvan's letter, the decision would be your own freely made in the knowledge that you have not been previously identified to anyone by me.

Henry's reply was brief and to the point: 'I regret that I am unable to accept the invitation to go to London. Since we met

I understand that you have been in formal communication with the Station, and had a reply. I assure you that there is nothing I can add to that.' This was a far cry from the very frank responses that Henry made to Daniels at Albrighton on 9 January to the effect that a UFO was seen. Had he been silenced at an official level?

While the released papers did not reflect this, they did reveal that Henry's version of his meeting with Wilfred Daniels diverged greatly from that of Daniels himself. In a half-page memo drawn up at the suggestion of the Air Ministry, Henry flatly denied the statements attributed to him:

> Mr Daniels asked me if I could give him any information concerning the incident that occurred at Cosford early in December . . . He then asked me if I could affirm or deny that anything had happened. I told him that I could do neither, since I had no knowledge of the incident, and suggested that he got in touch with the Station Adjutant. When he asked me for the names of the Boy Entrants so that he could interview them I told him that I did not know them, and again suggested that he contacted the Station Adjutant.

Furthermore, as the months progressed, Henry continued to maintain that he had not given Daniels an account of what was purported to have occurred; nor had he commented on any of Daniels's theories as they related to the affair.

Was this a form of damage control, or was Wilfred Daniels in error? A heated debate raged: in addition to the investigations of both Waveney Girvan and Wilfred Daniels, the Wolverhampton *Express & Star* newspaper devoted space to the matter, as did the *Kensington News & West London Times*. Interestingly, I learned that both the Air Ministry and Cosford kept a close watch on what the media in general had to say: 'At the time of the boys' claim some interest was apparently shown by the London press, but nothing was made of the affair.

However, in mid-January of this year, the "Express & Star" of Wolverhampton, in spite of seeking the Station's views, reported the boys' claim.'

As I continued to analyse the data at my disposal, I could not help but notice that as the days passed, and the controversy continued, a variety of frankly absurd and contradictory suggestions were put forward by the Air Ministry as it sought to diffuse interest in the case. This was not lost on Waveney Girvan, who wrote to Cosford on 3 March 1964: 'What puzzles me at the moment is the number of different explanations which are being put out, either by you or by the Air Ministry, as to the truth of the occurrence at your Station last December.'

As Girvan noted, those 'explanations' included: 'nothing at all'; 'two drunk apprentices'; 'a hoax'; and, somewhat amusingly, 'a British Railways steam train'. 'I think you will have to agree,' continued Girvan in his letter, 'that all the above explanations cannot be correct, and I should be obliged, for the sake of the record, to know which version can be regarded as official'.

Before poor, beleaguered Flight Lieutenant Stevens had the opportunity to respond, however, yet another researcher, Mrs M. Harman of London, launched her own investigation. 'Is it true that you have, or had, two RAF apprentices at your Station who saw a Flying Saucer land on your premises?' she enquired of Cosford on 4 March. Echoing Waveney Girvan's comments, Harman added, 'The various reports and explanations that seem to have been handed out are the real cause of my concern.'

Six days later Girvan again wrote to Flight Lieutenant Stevens: 'I have been hoping that I might by now have had a reply to my letter of March 3rd.'

'I have passed your letter to the Air Ministry, from whom you will no doubt receive a full reply in due course,' replied Stevens, two days later. A similar letter was forwarded to Harman. Flight Lieutenant Stevens, I concluded, was keen to absolve himself of further involvement in the controversy.

At this stage in my search for the truth surrounding the Cosford landing, I uncovered a most intriguing entry in the Air Ministry's file. The entire memo was handwritten, and the signature illegible; nevertheless, it was clearly titled: 'Note for action', and discussed the issue of how questions from the general public on Cosford should be handled. As the unknown author of this memo noted, replies to queries should be written 'in the most guarded and general terms consistent with our normal line that we have no evidence to suggest that flying saucers exist'.

Questions flooded my mind. If the entire Cosford story was nothing more than a straightforward hoax, why should any and all replies to the public be written only in 'the most guarded and general terms'? And who was the author of this curious memo? I pressed on.

In addition to informing Waveney Girvan and Mrs Harman that their questions would be answered directly by Whitehall, Flight Lieutenant Stevens prepared a detailed two-page report, titled 'OUTSIDE ENQUIRIES ABOUT AN ALLEGED UNIDENTIFIED FLYING OBJECT AT ROYAL AIR FORCE COSFORD', and circulated it to at least three departments: S4 at Whitehall (the office responsible for handling certain UFO reports received by the Air Ministry in the early 1960s); the office of the Senior Press Officer at Whitehall; and the Air Ministry Information Officer at Corporation Street, Birmingham.

The report was most thorough and detailed the investigations of Girvan, Daniels and Harman; it also addressed the conflicting testimonies of Reverend Henry and Wilfred Daniels; the media's response to the entire controversy; and the various theories put forward to dismiss the case.

Perhaps oddest of all about the report was the fact that it clearly indicated that the initial explanations put out by the Ministry were being quietly withdrawn. 'The boy entrants were not drunk nor hallucinated . . . The remarks about the effects of steam from a locomotive on nearby lights were put forward as a possible explanation only.'

On top of that, in a letter of 17 March to Waveney Girvan, an Air Ministry spokesman, B.E. Robson, also appeared to negate the theory that the event was nothing more than a hoax: 'Hoax is perhaps too strong a word,' Girvan was advised. Despite this curious retraction, the Air Ministry continued to assert that nothing of any real significance had occurred: '[A]s a purely routine measure an officer examined the airfield. He found no evidence of a landing whatsoever.' Strangely, when questioned by *Flying Saucer Review* about the military's examination of the airfield, Flight Lieutenant Stevens made the unusual observation that they had been unable to locate any 'scorch marks' to indicate the presence of a UFO. More than thirty years on, as I shall soon reveal, that statement took on a new significance.

Perhaps most interesting about Robson's letter to Girvan was its denial that Reverend Henry knew any intimate details of the encounter: 'I understand from [Henry]', Robson advised, 'that he did not comment on any of the theories put forward and that he certainly did not give any account of the alleged incident.' None of this was lost on Girvan, who two days later, countered,

> You will forgive me if I say that I am more puzzled after reading your letter than I was before. If the incident was not the result of a hoax, as you hint but do not actually say, then the whole affair is even more mysterious than the Air Ministry has been trying to make it.
>
> My representative added that the padre was emphatic that RAF Security Regulations wholly ruled out any chance of his meeting the boy entrants who had reported the alleged landing. The padre's last remarks were: 'I believe that the two lads believed what they had reported to be the truth, but I do not think you would get any "change" from any of the station officers.

Girvan also revealed that the combined investigations of *Flying Saucer Review*, Wilfred Daniels, Leslie Otley and Mrs

Harman had resulted in the identification of the two witnesses: Ian Jones and, as was later revealed, Ray Wardle. Moreover, Girvan cryptically informed Flight Lieutenant Stevens that he had also secured 'a great deal of evidence from outside the camp'. Quite what this referred to, I never learned, but the implication was that Girvan had accumulated a wealth of pertinent data on the Cosford event.

The next entry in the Air Ministry's file made me stop and think. Despite dismissing both Girvan's and Harman's letters as 'tedious correspondence' (which made me consider how researchers such as myself are viewed by the Ministry of Defence today!) one Ministry man, B.E. Robson, began to wonder if Reverend Henry had indeed made specific comments on the encounter to Wilfred Daniels.

'I know that we have already his formal denials on record,' Robson wrote to the commanding officer at Cosford, 'but I feel bound to ask you to check with him whether he ever made the statements attributed him in Mr Girvan's letter.'

I continued to leaf through the material, and was confronted with a rather irate letter from Wilfred Daniels to the Air Ministry: 'From Mr Girvan I have received a copy of your letter to him dated 17th March 1964 and also a copy of his reply, dated 19th March, to that letter.' It was evident from the letter that Daniels was aggrieved by the Air Ministry's suggestion that he, Daniels, had misrepresented his meeting with Reverend Henry:

> Flt Lieut Henry may have valid reasons for denying that he gave any account of the alleged UFO landing at RAF Cosford in December last but I say that he did, on the 9th January, in the words set down in Mr Girvan's letter to you dated 19th March.
>
> I wish it to be put on record that I resent most strongly the apparent innuendo implicit in the statement that (quote) 'he certainly did not give any account of the alleged incident'.

Daniels then closed his letter with a challenge: 'I say again that Flt Lieut Henry did so make that account to me. Now I shall require you to tell me unequivocally whether or not you mean to imply that my truthfulness in reporting the alleged Cosford UFO incident to Mr Girvan is being questioned?'

Once again, as was so common in this particular encounter, the Air Ministry backed down, and bluffed its way out of a potentially embarrassing situation. B. E. Robson replied:

So far as the Air Force Department is concerned, no one has questioned your truthfulness in reporting the alleged UFO at Cosford to Mr Girvan. Unfortunately Flight Lieutenant Henry's recollection of his conversation with you is different from yours and he does not recollect using the words attributed to him. It is a perfectly common and natural phenomenon for two people to differ in their recollections of a particular incident, and it involves no criticism of anyone. It certainly does not imply any untruthfulness on the part of either party.

Robson was also wise enough to ensure that his own position was carefully covered: 'I was merely passing on Flight Lieutenant Henry's own recollections; I made no categorical statement of any kind on the point.' Quite.

In the meantime Flying Officer R.A. Roberts forwarded a one-page letter to Robson: 'We shall be most grateful to receive copies of all letters you send to Mr Girvan and his friends, although of course, you will not want to let them know this.'

Whatever the true nature of the exchange between Daniels and Henry, as interest in the case refused to die down, Henry made it clear to his superiors that he was 'seriously considering taking legal action against these persons should this correspondence continue'. Daniels was having none of it: '[Henry] did NOT give the impression that he had any idea that the incident was being categorised as a distortion of something mundane or just a silly misapprehension.'

How would the Air Ministry respond to Reverend Henry's desire to take legal action against Girvan and Co.? I was eager to know, and a May 1964 draft letter from B.E. Robson to Cosford told me:

> I have consulted the Directorate of Personnel Services and the Directorate of Legal Services, and they are both agreed that Flt Lt Henry's best course is to do nothing . . . Any rejoinder at this stage is likely only to prolong the contentious series of articles [and] the Directorate of Legal Services is doubtful whether the legal redress which Henry might obtain would be worth the expense involved.

I could find no indication from the file that Henry took the matter any further, and the final, handwritten entry from the Deputy Director of Personnel Services seemed to reflect this: 'I think that [Henry] would be ill-advised to attempt legal redress.'

A photocopy of a letter of 19 June 1964 from the UFO researcher and author Gavin Gibbons to the *Kensington News & West London Times* perhaps best summed up the entire controversy:

> I have been in Shropshire since 1958 and have known Mr Daniels since 1954 . . . He is very reliable and a down to earth scientist, holding a responsible executive position at English Electric in Stafford . . . No crank or unbalanced person could deceive Mr Daniels . . .
>
> But let us not blame poor Flt Lt Henry. Were he to tell the truth he would lose his job. He is in a very difficult position. No. It is the anonymous bureaucrats in the Air Ministry who are to blame. I have not the space to give the countless instances when Flying Saucers have been dismissed as weather balloons, meteorites, hallucinations, hoaxes, clouds, the planet Venus or similar nonsense.

I read Gibbons's final words and realised that, four decades on, very little had changed: 'There is no doubt at all that the Air Ministry, and their opposite numbers in most countries of the world, with a few honourable exceptions, are desperately trying to hide the fact that we are being visited by craft from other worlds and that those in authority are just as in the dark about the mystery as we are.'

I closed the file, and thought deep and hard about those long-gone days of 1963–64. What really happened? Who was telling the truth? Did an alien spacecraft touch down at RAF Cosford, or was the entire matter a ghastly hoax that embarrassed the Air Ministry into silence? I was going to have to dig deeper if I was to unravel the mystery.[4]

Early in 1994, the much-respected Yorkshire-based investigative group Quest International took a spirited gamble and launched its bimonthly journal, *UFO* magazine, on to the news-stands (the gamble paid off, and today the magazine boasts a readership in excess of 100,000 per issue). I had known its editor, Graham Birdsall, and his brother Mark since the mid-1980s and had written the occasional article for the magazine, primarily on intelligence issues as they related to the UFO phenomenon.

Keen to get me on board on a regular basis, Mark asked if I would consider putting together a few articles for the new magazine. I was naturally happy to oblige and began submitting material for publication. When I received the Cosford file, I naturally assumed that this would make an ideal feature for the magazine.

'Put it together, Nick,' said Graham, after I described to him the contents of the file and my proposed article. This I duly did, and the feature appeared in the magazine shortly before Christmas 1995. The article was well received, and as a result of its publication a number of potentially important new sources surfaced, including the Green family of Wolverhampton.

As Barry Green related to me, at the time of the encounter

his family was living about four miles from RAF Cosford in the vicinity of Tettenhall Wood and recalled an event which, time-wise, tied in with the Cosford incident. Barry's own memories were somewhat vague, but other family members could readily remember what had taken place. Barry told me:

> My father and brother were in the kitchen; it was at night [and] their attention was drawn to an object in the clear, dark sky. It had multi-flashing lights; one light which was more visible was a larger, green light [and] it hovered for a while.
>
> My father and brother shouted to the rest of the family in excitement; that's when I came running into the kitchen to find them looking through the window at this object. I noticed the object and remember how nice the colours were.
>
> My father shouted to me to go into the living room; I don't know why, but it was probably because there were so many of my family in there trying to get a look at this object, which was hovering for a while, then all of a sud-den shot off at great speed in the direction of RAF Cosford. [My father] also said that it was no jet; he served in the war and had never seen anything like it. Where my father lives, they're used to seeing jets flying across the sky as it's a main route for air traffic. This object was not very high and was not in line with any main air-traffic lane. It's made us all wonder very much if this object was the one seen on that night at RAF Cosford.[5]

And the Green family were not alone in having witnessed unusual activity in the vicinity of Cosford in December 1963. There was 'Don' from Albrighton, who informed another investigator and author, Jenny Randles, that he was interro-gated at length by two RAF officers after having reported see-ing near the base a 'cigar-shaped' UFO, which was surrounded by an aura 'that caused it to glow with a curious light even in daytime'. Since Don's father was obliged to sign an official 'form' for the officers, Don was cautious about going on record, but did reveal that his sighting had occurred in the same general time frame as the December 1963 encounter.[6]

Then there was Alistair Blake who surfaced with one of those frustrating 'friend-of-a-friend' accounts. According to Blake's information, not only had a UFO touched down at Cosford, but while hovering over a secluded part of the airfield (and I can testify that Cosford is indeed impressive in size) it bizarrely 'split' into three distinct sections – one of which crashed to Earth with an almighty bang! Blake could remember little more, but did recall that his informant for the account, who 'worked for the Air Force in Birmingham', quietly advised him that some form of object or device was removed from the airfield by 'a load of blokes in black overalls'.[7]

Try as I might to resolve this frankly amazing account, Blake could not (or perhaps would not) elaborate further. And yet tantalising corroboration of a sort may have been entrusted to *UFO* magazine. As was reported in the January 1997 edition, '[A] relative of a man based at RAF Cosford, near Wolverhampton [said] that in 1963 it was alleged a UFO landed at the base and the runway bore the burn marks. The press were told that the burn marks came from a nearby barbecue at the bottom of a resident's garden!'[8]

Was there a connection? And if so, was this somehow linked with the comment made to *Flying Saucer Review* all those years ago that a search of the airfield had failed to locate any 'scorch marks'? Considering that it was Cosford, and not *Flying Saucer Review*, who brought up the issue of 'scorch marks', the picture only became more puzzling. But it was not until 18 January 1996 that matters really came to a head.

I had just spent the best part of two hours interviewing a retired RAF officer who informed me that he had engaged in an aerial 'dogfight' with a UFO over Scotland in 1959. I thought the day could not get any stranger. I was wrong.

At around 2.00 p.m. the telephone rang. 'Nick?' said a familiar voice; it was Graham Birdsall.

'Hello, Graham. How are things?'

'Bloody hectic, mate,' Graham replied in his distinctive Yorkshire brogue.

I smiled; I could hear Graham's brother Mark in the background shouting something about deadlines, and a telephone was ringing. It remained unanswered.

'Nick, I've had a call from someone who wants to speak to you about your Cosford article,' said Graham. Who's that? I wondered. 'Ray Wardle,' added Graham.

'Are you sure that's the name? He's one of the two guys who saw the UFO come down at Cosford!'

'That's the guy. He's been living in Las Vegas. Apparently he's back in England and saw the article. I'll give you a contact number.'

Forty-eight hours later, I was speaking with the man who was possibly the key to the entire mystery. Pleasantries exchanged, I asked Ray if I could discuss his recollections of what had occurred at Cosford on that December night back in 1963. Ray was more than willing to talk, and I began by briefing him on the contents of the Air Ministry's recently declassified file. Ray listened carefully and then related to me his remarkable account. It became clear to me very quickly that the released paper told only a fraction of the story. Ray's story went as follows:

Well, me and a friend went out on the evening; we had passes which, I'm sure, covered us until nine p.m. But by the time we got back to Cosford it was nine-fifteen. So I said, 'The best thing we can do is climb the fence.' We went along the side of the fence near these hangars, which were also near to a railroad track.

We didn't see anything at this point; we were still outside the camp site. Then we climbed over a chain-link fence, took a few steps and there was this object. I'm not going to say it was a flying saucer, because it wasn't; it wasn't shaped like one, it didn't look like one.

It was very bright [and] reminded me of a church organ; it appeared to have pipes on it, things like that in the centre of it. But there was no distinct outline to the object at all. And I couldn't tell you if it was on the ground or just above it.

'When you say that there was no distinct outline,' I asked, 'do you mean that the object didn't appear solid?'

Ray was emphatic: 'No, it looked solid, but there was such a glow from it that there were no distinct edges.'

'How big was the UFO?'

We were probably a hundred yards away from it, I would say. This thing was, maybe, twenty feet across by thirty feet high. It was taller than it was wide. I wanted to stay there but the guy I was with didn't. So he ran, and I sort of hovered a bit and then I ran after him and we linked up between two hangars by the side of this thing. He said, 'Let's go back to the billet.' I wanted to report it, but he said, 'You're crazy; they'll know we're late.' Which is true, obviously.

Anyway, I talked him into it, and we did go and report it. Nobody bothered about the fact that we were late back into base; no one said anything. But I can tell you: we were sixteen years old and I can assure you, if we'd have been drunk, we'd have been locked up. That's guaranteed.

But what bothered me was that they refused to come back with us. Nobody would go to the spot that we were telling them about. It was frustrating; it really was. I suppose we were humoured; I really don't know. Nobody said, 'Oh, you're lying.' They just wanted the facts and that was it. It was quite strange, really.'

I pushed on: 'Did anyone go to the site the next day?'

'Not with me they didn't. Not that I recall, no. I'm pretty sure they had a statement. I made a statement, obviously, and signed it. But then another statement of some sort or another from the Wing Commander came out. Something tells me I was pissed [off] about it and I didn't want to sign it. Whether or not I did or not, I don't remember; it's a long time back.'

'You made a statement; a written statement?' I enquired.

'Yes, absolutely,' he replied. 'We wrote down independently more or less what I've just told you.'

'Well, that isn't in the file,' I responded.

Ray continued, 'And we definitely didn't see anything green, or a dome. Or any green lights; that's all bullshit. This object, it was mainly orange, with . . . there was white, yellow. The centre of it was very orange compared to the outer parts of it.'

I then changed tack and brought up the matter of Reverend Henry and the controversy surrounding what he may or may not have said to Wilfred Daniels.

'Yeah, I can remember the padre,' Ray told me, 'well, vaguely. He knew it was true, somehow. I do remember the priest was very concerned, very considerate; whatever you want to call it. He sat and listened. He sympathised with us; he believed us.'

'How about the claim that what you saw was a railway light?'

Ray was adamant: 'The railway light would have been behind us; this was in front of us. In front of a bloody great big hangar!'

At this juncture, the interview took on a far more sinister tone. 'From that day onwards I never remembered it; it never came into my head again,' Ray continued, with a degree of puzzlement in his voice.

'What do you mean?' I asked, the puzzlement spilling over into my voice, too.

'It's odd, isn't it?' said Ray. 'I couldn't tell you who I was with. Now, it had to have been someone I was close to, obviously; otherwise, you don't go out with them. And I've not got a mental picture of the person, or a name or anything.'

'Hang on, Ray,' I butted in, 'are you saying that your memory was deliberately blocked to make sure you forgot about the landing?'

'It was blocked; no two ways about it,' he quietly replied.

I sat back, dumbfounded as Ray related the whole remarkable tale to me. In 1979 he had gone to live in the United States, and opted to settle in Las Vegas. At the beginning of 1988, however, he began to have a number of unusual UFO-related experiences, and on one occasion witnessed two 'Volkswagen-sized' UFOs, 'like two grey bowler hats' operating in close proximity to his home. Ray continued:

Two weeks to the day, my wife called me at work; she'd seen the same things. After that there was a lot of acceleration in things going on. I bought a video camera, because I needed it for my own sanity. I was having people coming into my apartment, but not taking anything; it was like they were playing games.

One day I came in, and sitting on top of my briefcase was my pass from RAF Cosford, the blue pass; and a beige-coloured piece of paper where I'd signed the Official Secrets Act. Then my wife bought me the book, *Above Top Secret*, in about 1989. All of a sudden I remembered it; for twenty-seven years I hadn't remembered it, which is something that you wouldn't do.

I tried to grasp the complexities of the case: 'OK, you recall being stationed at Cosford, but until you began having these odd experiences in the late 1980s, and then read Tim Good's review of Cosford, your memory of the actual sighting had gone?'

'I remembered it the minute I read it. But the years in between it never occurred to me; it never came into my head. Now, the minute I read [*Above Top Secret*], I phoned England

and called my parents, and said, "Did I ever tell you about . . .?" and they said, "Yes." They remembered it.'

As the weeks passed the story began to piece itself together in Ray's memory.

After I left Cosford, I was transferred to RAF Oakington in Cambridge. And here's where I have a problem. Every so often one of us technicians – I was working on transmitters for night flying – would be taken with our senior NCO, if I'm not mistaken, or an officer. We'd drive our vehicle and follow along the Newmarket Road to a place which I'm sure was called 'Eureka'; I don't know why I say that, but I'm sure it was.

It was on the left-hand side about twenty miles north on the Newmarket Road from Oakington. And there would be . . . well, it was an airfield with a bombed-out control tower; it was all in rubble. I had a motorbike at the time and I would have to park it and pull a tarpaulin over it. Now, I can get to going as far as the control tower, and lifting up the trapdoors, but from then it hurts; I can't think of anything else.

This would have been '64, and all I can tell you is it was an underground facility. I could not tell you any more about it because I don't remember it. But it bothers me that I can't; it's a block.

'Did you ever learn the reason why your papers from Cosford turned up in Las Vegas?

I didn't even know they existed. They hadn't been in my mind for twenty-seven, twenty-eight years; then all of a sudden there they are: sitting on top of my briefcase. It goes on and on. I'm sure there's some kind of mind control. Until a couple of years ago, you wouldn't have convinced me that there are ETs, but now I know there are. But I think it's a mixture of two things here.

'Do you think the British Government is somehow orchestrating these events?'

'Well, someone is,' said Ray, forthrightly. 'If I'd heard anybody saying the same story, I wouldn't have believed them, because it sounds too wacko. I can't comprehend it myself.'

We then began to go over old ground, and I sensed that there was little more to be learned. I thanked Ray, and we concluded the interview. It had been a bizarre morning, to say the least.[9]

Two days later, the telephone rang. A solid, cultured voice spoke: 'Nicholas Redfern?'

'That's me,' I replied.

For a moment there was silence. 'You have accessed the Cosford papers at Kew; and you have spoken with Mr Wardle.'

It was a statement rather than a question. 'Er, who's calling?' I asked, quickly flipping the switch on my portable tape recorder. Once again, there was a moment of silence.

'Mr Redfern, please turn off your recording device,' said the mystery voice.

'OK, it's off,' I bluffed.

'No, Mr Redfern,' came the irritated and heard-it-all-before reply. 'Your recorder is not off.'

'Right, it's off now. Who is this?'

'My name is Kent – Francis Kent,' said the caller in true 'Bond – James Bond' style.

As I listened, Mr Kent (if that was indeed his true identity) revealed that the 'numbered landings' at Cosford in 1963 were the subject of several Air Ministry files, and that the papers I had accessed at the Public Record Office in no way told the full story.

'How can I get the full story?' I asked.

Kent laughed softly: 'Air Intelligence would be a good place to start. "Five B" is your speciality, isn't it?' The phone went dead.[10]

Who was the mysterious Mr Kent? And what was his reason

for telephoning? Checks on my part to try to trace the origins of the call led nowhere, and he never contacted me again. It was one of many strange events in my journey to discover the true nature of the British Government's involvement in the UFO mystery.

Kent's reference to 'Five B' in the context of Air Intelligence could only mean Air Intelligence, Technical Branch, 5b. Several years previously I had come across a brief reference to 5b in an Air Ministry memorandum of 14 November 1962, which revealed that the division was exclusively responsible for investigating military-originated UFO reports in the early 1960s.

My attempts to secure the release of 5b's files, however, were spectacularly unsuccessful. Nick Pope, who was at the time working within Secretariat Air Staff 2A at Whitehall, informed me in guarded tones that a discussion of 5b was out of bounds; while the MOD's Air Historical Branch, after having carried out a number of checks on my behalf, ventured that 5b's files had been destroyed some years earlier. As I pointed out in *A Covert Agenda*, however, the papers of another division, S6, which dealt with UFO reports received from the general public in the early 1960s, were openly available for public scrutiny at the Public Record Office. Why destroy high-grade UFO reports received from the military while allowing access to 'lights in the sky' reports from inexperienced observers? I never received an answer, satisfactory or otherwise.

As I reviewed my notes more than two years after my search for the truth began, the Cosford mystery continued to dog me. Waveney Girvan and Wilfred Daniels were both highly respected characters in the UFO research field and conducted their investigation of the Cosford encounter in a professional and straightforward manner – regardless of personal opinions, a perusal of the Air Ministry's papers on Cosford revealed that at all times Daniels and Girvan acted in a wholly creditable fashion.

And what of the Air Ministry's strange reluctance to make an authoritative statement either supporting or decrying the affair? Why the need for double talk and innuendo? As both Daniels and Girvan noted, if the matter was nothing but a hoax, why not say so?

Then there was the issue of Reverend Henry's meeting with Wilfred Daniels outside the Albrighton branch of Lloyds Bank. Again, the Air Ministry stopped short of denying that Daniels's version of events was correct, and even the Air Ministry spokesman, B.E. Robson, was careful not to commit himself: 'It is a perfectly common and natural phenomenon for two people to differ in their recollections of a particular incident, and it involves no criticism of anyone. It certainly does not imply any untruthfulness on the part of either party.'

Of the witnesses, the official file revealed that neither Ian Jones nor Ray Wardle received any form of castigation for reporting their encounter. Considering the many headaches that the case gave the Air Ministry at the time, had a hoax been suspected, both would have been severely reprimanded.

The potentially very important testimonies of those other individuals who recalled the case were not lost on me, either: the Green family of Tettenhall Wood, who saw the UFO on its approach to Cosford; Don from Albrighton who was interrogated by two RAF officers after having viewed a cigar-shaped UFO in the vicinity of the base; Alistair Blake, whose RAF friend guardedly related that a section of the UFO had been recovered from the airfield; and the mysterious Mr Kent.

Of course, the most controversial aspect of the case was Ray Wardle's account of what happened to him after leaving Cosford. In speaking with him, I got the impression that Ray was a level-headed guy, who seemed genuinely mystified by all that had happened to him; and he was certainly disturbed by the 'memory block' he seemed to have undergone at the hands of the military in 1964. And as outlandish as it sounded, Ray's account was not outside the realms of possibility.

Papers released to me under the terms of the Freedom of

Information Act in the United States by the Defense Intelligence Agency, for example, revealed that British authorities had at their disposal some devastating technology for manipulating the human mind. I quote from a DIA report of 31 January 1972, 'CONTROLLED OFFENSIVE BEHAVIOR USSR':

> Psychological torture and physical abuse has been used on Catholic detainees in Northern Ireland. High-frequency sound waves and sensory deprivation research methods that have been outlawed for use on humans by the American Psychological Association were being used to undermine the dignity and destroy the effectiveness of the Catholic minority in Northern Ireland. The case of one 40-year-old released prisoner has been reported. Upon release, the man's mental and physical condition suggested senility – a condition inconsistent with his health at the time of his internment.

A further DIA document in my possession, dating from 1976 and titled 'BIOLOGICAL EFFECTS OF ELECTRO-MAGNETIC RADIATION (RADIOWAVES AND MICROWAVES) EURASIAN COMMUNIST COUNTRIES', revealed that a wealth of research had been carried out for decades to determine the extent to which the human mind could be manipulated via microwave radiation: 'Subjects exposed to microwave radiation exhibited a variety of neurasthenic disorders [including] headache, fatigue, drowsiness, depression, anxiety, forgetfulness, and lack of concentration.'

In light of this, Ray Wardle's experience did not sound so bizarre, after all. In conclusion, only questions remained. Did an alien spacecraft land at RAF Cosford in December 1963? Were parts of the craft removed under cover of the utmost secrecy? Was Ray Wardle silenced for what he inadvertently stumbled upon? And if the answer to all of the above was yes, would my investigations result in a full disclosure of the facts? I resolved to continue my quest.

Even at that stage I had no idea just how bizarre that quest would ultimately turn out to be.

CHAPTER FOUR

UFO DOWN!

MIDWAY THROUGH 1991 A TRUSTED FRIEND AND COL-
LEAGUE in the UFO research field telephoned me with some
startling news. 'Nick, you live near Penkridge, don't you?' she
asked.

'Well, it's not far away,' I replied, 'a few miles.'

'Have you heard anything about a UFO crashing there in
the 1960s?'

That made me sit up and take notice. As I listened it was
revealed to me that the account had just surfaced in the United
States, and furthermore it was not only a UFO that had been
retrieved – alien bodies had been discovered within the
wreckage.

'Do you know where the story originated?' I asked. The
information was sketchy, but the account appeared to have
come from a computer bulletin board in the United States,
having originally appeared in a book.

'I think Leonard Stringfield knows something about it,' my
friend added. That clinched it for me. For years Stringfield, a
former US Air Force Intelligence officer, had devoted his
research activities to chasing down accounts of crashed UFOs
held by US authorities, and regularly issued 'status reports'
summarising his latest findings on the subject. I also knew that

a new status report had just been released in the States and was on its way to me at that very moment.

Despite the fact that Stringfield was often criticised for not releasing the names of some of his sources, his contribution to the UFO investigative community was huge. The author of two first-class books on the subject – *Inside Saucer Post, 3–0 Blue*, which detailed his UFO-related activities with the US Air Defense Command, and *Situation Red: The UFO Siege* – Stringfield was instrumental in locating and interviewing key witnesses to the UFO crash at Roswell, New Mexico, in July 1947, and was among the first to speak with Major Jesse Marcel, whose testimony on Roswell was largely responsible for bringing that decades-old mystery to the attention of the public and media alike.

Three days after I heard about the Penkridge crash, Stringfield's new status report arrived in the mail, and there was indeed a mention of the event in question. The information was scant, to be sure, but there was enough data to work with. I contacted Stringfield some time later and he kindly allowed me to make use of his source's testimony. Once again, I was to become enmeshed in a deep and dark mystery involving a key witness; the Ministry of Defence police; long-forgotten UFO encounters with the military; an official (or perhaps *un*official; I never really knew) telephone monitoring operation; and the recovery of a strange object from a Staffordshire field more than thirty years ago.

My first step was systematically to evaluate the information given in the first instance to Leonard Stringfield. Timewise, all Stringfield knew for certain was that the crash had occurred 'some time in 1964' (I was later able to pin the date down to either February or March of that year), that information having been supplied by Stringfield's key source, 'S.M. Brannigan', a former third class petty officer with the US Navy.

At the time of the crash, Brannigan was stationed aboard a 'specially rigged LST, a flagship (AKA, "spy ship")' attached to a naval amphibious force at an unspecified point in either the

Caribbean or the Atlantic. Brannigan's speciality was the translation of intercepted Soviet military transmissions, and he well recalled one particular instance when an amazing coded message was received at the ship's 'crypto-machine room'.

The message was given to Brannigan and he set to work on translating its contents. Almost immediately, he realised that this was no ordinary interception: it told of a UFO overflying Europe which, for reasons unknown, malfunctioned and plummeted to earth. Whether by accident or design, as the UFO descended, it broke into two parts – the chief section of which crashed at Penkridge, Staffordshire, while 'the remains' hurtled on until they smashed into the ground somewhere in West Germany.

As Brannigan continued his work, more information came to the fore: US Air Force Intelligence was implicated in the recovery – and not just of the UFO. Three dead personnel had also been found. As the enormity of the event became apparent, other US forces became involved, as did various elements of NATO.

Interestingly, despite the crash having occurred in the mid-1960s, Brannigan was still fearful about revealing too much information, as Stringfield noted:

Brannigan admitted there was more to the incident, involving coded information, that he preferred to keep confidential. The Brannigan disclosure, while sketchy, may spotlight only the tip of the iceberg as to the scope of military crash/retrieval operations in foreign lands.

Researchers know that reports of crashes are worldwide, from pole to pole, on every continent, and in many countries even in remote Madagascar. If such incidents are to be secreted, it is my suspicion that US special retrieval teams have been, and still are, prepared to 'go into action' into any crash location within its sphere of military or economic influence such as was exercised with NATO in the 'artifact' retrievals in England and West Germany.[1]

But how to evaluate Brannigan's information? First, the Penkridge reference was interesting. I knew the town and was also aware that both it and the surrounding area – the sprawling mass of forest which was Cannock Chase – had had more than its fair share of UFO sightings over the years.

I had spoken with witnesses who had seen huge triangular-shaped UFOs manoeuvring over the forest in the early hours of a winter's morning in 1988; I had met with a woman who had come into contact with one of the dreaded 'Men in Black' – dark-suited figures who terrorise UFO witnesses – after having seen a UFO in the area; and I had spoken with a family who described to me a nightmarish encounter with a group of diminutive, troll-like creatures who surrounded their broken-down car shortly after midnight in 1975 at the nearby Slittingmill. There was also Andrew Hill, who had shown me a fascinating piece of camcorder footage of an unusual black object overflying the racetrack at Hednesford – another nearby town. In other words, the entire area was a beacon for strange activity.

Since most of these accounts were given to me in confidence, Brannigan's reference to Penkridge as being the crash site was certainly provocative. More importantly, there was the fact that Brannigan was a US citizen. At the risk of offending its inhabitants, I would describe Penkridge as a modest-sized town in Staffordshire. I doubt that the majority of British citizens are acquainted with the town, let alone someone thousands of miles away on the other side of the Atlantic!

There was also Brannigan's intriguing reference to 'coded information' with respect to NATO which he preferred not to discuss. Again, this rang true and suggested that he had some intimate knowledge of intelligence protocols.

For many years there has existed in Britain what was until relatively recently known as the 'D Notice System'. As the Ministry of Defence noted in 1993, the 'D Notice System', now known as the 'Defence Advisory Notice System', '. . . is a means of providing advice and guidance to the media about defence and counter-terrorist information the publication of which would be damaging to national security. The system is voluntary, it has no legal authority and the final responsibility for deciding whether or not to publish rests solely with the editor or publisher concerned.'

It is interesting to note that both the old 'D Notice System' and the revised 'DA Notice System' make reference to precisely the type of information on which Brannigan declined to comment: 'It is requested that no details be published, without prior consultation, of HM Government's highly classified codes and ciphers, related data protection measures and communication facilities, or those of NATO or other allies.'

I was convinced that Brannigan was a valid source of information. But what of the three bodies recovered from the Penkridge site? Leonard Stringfield, I knew, had uncovered an enormous amount of information relating to the physical nature of at least one species of alien visiting the Earth, much of which came directly from trusted sources in the intelligence and medical communities.

From several such sources, Stringfield learned that the typical alien was three and a half to four feet tall; its weight was approximately forty pounds; the eyes were 'large, almond-shaped'; the nose and ears vague; the torso 'small and thin'; and the arms long. To get an idea of the overall make-up of the alien, Stringfield was told, 'Take a look at a five-month human foetus.'[2] I tried to imagine the scene of carnage and the inevitable shock that would have overcome those unsuspecting individuals tasked with securing the crash site when confronted with such creatures.

Before commencing my investigations as a whole into the Penkridge recovery, I reviewed my research notes for *A Covert Agenda*, and discovered something I had previously forgotten.

It was inevitable that, purely for reasons of space, I would be unable to use in *A Covert Agenda* all of the various accounts of UFO activity in the UK that I had come across; some would have to be omitted. Browsing through that material one afternoon, I noticed something of extreme significance: I had in my possession a file full of UFO reports dating from February and March 1964, precisely the time frame in which the crash at Penkridge occurred! Was there a connection?

As I scanned the material, it became clear to me that not all of the accounts in my files could relate to the Penkridge retrieval, but they did serve to illustrate that the UK was swarming with UFOs in both February and March 1964.

At shortly after 10 p.m. on 3 February 1964, a Mr Jardine of Cleveleys, Lancashire, had seen a 'large, round object with three round lights underneath' which approached from the sea at a high speed, veered off to the north, and disappeared in the briefest of moments.

On the same day, the *Southern Evening Echo* newspaper reported that an 'unusual silent object' had been seen flying erratically above Winchester before exiting the area, also in a northerly direction.

Two and a half weeks later, a spectacular encounter took place at the Proof and Experimental Establishment at Shoeburyness, Southend-on-Sea.

The witness was Police Constable 392 W. Crook, who was attached to the War Department Constabulary. At 9.55 a.m. on 20 February he was standing at the 'Northern Corner' of the base, when his attention was drawn to three unidentified objects in the sky travelling due south. 'They were evenly spaced and in line and appeared to be about the size of a normal saucer,' said PC Crook. 'The colour was "Off White" or "Pearl Grey" with no glistening effect, and the shape appeared to be oval. They were above cloud height and were travelling at great speed; no sound was discernible at all.'

I learned that a copy of PC Crook's report reached the Air Ministry's Air Intelligence Division, who responded that the constable had merely seen a formation of RAF Lightning jets. Did these jets have the ability to take on a circular shape and fly in complete silence?[3]

Only days after that event, UFOs were out in force over

both Staffordshire and Shropshire: a huge red object was seen by a Mr Harris of Wolverhampton; and Mr Fred Burton of Madeley, Shropshire, telephoned the *Express and Star* newspaper to report his sighting of a 'round object, whitish-orange, with four red lights' which passed directly overhead.

As I continued to review my records, I came across a report that I confess I had not given much thought to at the time I received it. In light of S.M. Brannigan's account of a UFO tumbling to earth on British soil, however, the report took on a new significance.

The date was 19 March 1964, the time, the early hours of the morning, and the witnesses were Captain E.D. Morrison, pilot of a London-bound Boeing Clipper jet en route from New York, and Captain R.A. Botthos, a DC-8 pilot who at the time of the encounter was two hundred miles west of Land's End. Both pilots watched awestruck: 'something' had entered the Earth's atmosphere and was bearing down on the UK . . .

'I have seen hundreds of meteors and things of that nature,' said Captain Morrison, 'but I have never seen anything like this before. It woke up the sky in a great white flash.'

Captain Botthos elaborated: 'I saw the object, which was travelling on a north to south trajectory, explode in a big flash and trailing columns of smoke on re-entering the atmosphere. I was flying at 29,000 feet. It was a spectacular sight. I don't know what it could have been.'

Was this the same object that Brannigan was talking about? Had Captains Morrison and Botthos inadvertently caught sight of the stricken UFO on its final flight? I made a mental note, and dug further. The next report almost hit me square in the face.

Only two days after the encounter of the two pilots, there was a curious UFO 'landing' at Penrith, Cumbria. Scouring both government and private archives for material on UFO activity in the UK in the early 1960s, I had come across an unusual report filed with the Air Ministry by the Reverend T.E.T. Burbury of Clifton Rectory, Penrith, on 23 March

1964. Reverend Burbury wrote to the National Physical Laboratory at Teddington, who in turn forwarded his letter to the Air Ministry via the Meteorological Office at Bracknell.

> Does an apparent column of blue light about eight feet in diameter and about fifteen feet high which disappears and leaves a mark of very slightly disturbed earth, the same diameter, mean anything to you?
>
> I examined the ground which is about one hundred yards from the nearest building and there are no pylons near. There was no sign of burning, either by sight or smell; the grass growing between the exposed ground appeared quite normal. There were no signs of bird tracks or droppings: the ground simply appeared to have been lightly raked over in an almost perfect circle.

Shortly after obtaining a copy of this report I mailed the details to Paul Fuller, a recognised authority on the crop-circle mystery, as the reference to the ground being raked over 'in an almost perfect circle' was highly reminiscent of a modern-day description of a crop circle. Paul was intrigued and began looking further into the case. With the help of another researcher, Maria Ceresa, he was able to locate the original witness who filed the report with Reverend Burbury: Robert Ellis.

As Robert recalled, on the night of 21 March 1964 at around 9.30 the family's working dog, which slept in an outbuilding, began to howl. Thinking that some stock might have broken loose, Robert went to check and noticed that the tops of two nearby apple trees were lit up by a blue light. He told Paul Fuller:

> Approximately one hundred yards from where I stood was a vivid 'electric blue' light. It's shape was elliptical . . . It stayed in a horizontal position, remaining motionless and making no audible sound. I could see no detail within the light; in fact I had to shade my eyes with my hand, the light was so intense. I was quite frightened –

being alone – and quickly went indoors. By that time I had calmed down and opened the curtains and shutters of the front window to look out again in that direction; all was in darkness.

According to Robert an inspection of the area on the following morning revealed a circular depression as described by Burbury, and Robert added, 'In some places the disturbance was two inches deep as if the area had been vigorously raked. The roots of the grass were damaged and the circle remained visible well into May of that year.'[4]

As these reports (along with a dozen or so other minor accounts) told me, the Penkridge UFO crash was only one of many UFO incidents that occurred both above and on mainland UK in early 1964.

Indeed, as time progressed I began to see a pattern emerging: practically every reported UFO crash in the UK I had come across had been preceded by a wave of other weird events. The World War Two crash, for example, had followed quickly on the heels of both the Foo Fighter reports and that of Gordon Cammell of the RAF. Similarly, the Cosford event followed a wave of encounters that had been chronicled in letter form by Wilfred Daniels. And this was a trend that was to continue throughout my investigations.

I considered it reasonable that regular, intense studies of our society by otherworldly beings might result in one or more accidents on their part. Perhaps the loss of the occasional craft was deemed acceptable. But I needed facts – not speculation. In 1996 those facts emerged.

During the summer I was asked to deliver a lecture at Aston University on behalf of the Birmingham UFO Society. At the close of the lecture (which centred on the Ministry of Defence's involvement in the UFO subject) a woman whose face I recognised came up to me to say hello. It was Irene Bott, President of the Staffordshire UFO Group (SUFOG). I had first met Irene earlier in the year when I was introduced to her by the investigator and former civil servant Matthew Williams at Quest International's annual UFO conference at Solihull.

'Would you like to give a talk at our anniversary conference in September?' asked Irene. I said I would be happy to, and from then on we became firm friends and worked closely on a number of UFO investigations.

Irene's conference at the White House on Cannock Chase was a resounding success, and all the speakers (including myself, Nick Pope, Busty Taylor and Matthew Williams) were well received.

At the close of the conference we retired to the bar for drinks, and I weaved my way to Irene's table for a chat. As we got talking the subject of crashed UFOs surfaced. 'You know, I heard this story a couple of years ago,' I said, 'about a UFO crashing at Penkridge in the mid-sixties. Have you ever come across it?' Irene hadn't, but as Penkridge was only a stone's throw from her house, she resolved to look into it.

Several weeks later I met with Irene for lunch and it transpired that she had made a breakthrough. Keen to promote her group throughout the Staffordshire area, Irene had given an interview to the *Burntwood Post* newspaper and made a brief reference to the Penkridge crash, without giving away any pertinent details. Several days later, she received a letter.

'Take a look at this, Nick,' she said. It was from one Harold South, whom I noted lived close to my home. According to Harold, not only did he know the location of the crash site, he had witnessed the recovery of the object by the military, and, as a result of this, was both interrogated and warned to stay silent by the civilian police! Needless to say, we took steps to speak with Harold South at the first opportunity.

Because of commitments on both our parts, Irene and I were unable to speak with him before 11 December. We were greeted by a man who I estimated to be in his mid- to late sixties. We exchanged greetings, retired to Harold's flat and began chatting. It transpired that Harold was a bachelor, retired, and a rail enthusiast with a specific interest in the restoration and preservation of trains; looking round his living room I also noticed an impressive collection of vintage model cars and lorries which adorned a wide windowsill.

Both Irene and I found Harold to be a credible character, with a wide range of interests, and not at all obsessed by the strange situation he had found himself in more than thirty years previously. For all that, however, something seemed to be concerning him. He leaned forward in his chair and spoke quietly: 'I've just had a phone call from the Ministry of Defence police.'

Irene and I exchanged glances, unsure what to make of this stunning revelation. Barely an hour previously we had rung to confirm our arrangements to meet with Harold, and here he was telling us that within minutes of our call the Ministry of Defence had contacted him. I could see that this was becoming horribly complicated, and I asked Harold to start at the beginning.

Well, it was about quarter to ten on a morning; a weekday. Either February or March 1964. At the time I was working for Bendix washing machines. My area was north of Cannock and I'd been over there to drop off a part before starting my calls.

At the time I was living in Pelsall; the reason they put you on an area not too near your home was so you wouldn't make too many friends with the customers. [He laughed.]

Well, I was driving my works van towards Penkridge from Cannock. About two miles after Cannock, I came to a roadblock.

'Can you describe it?' I asked.

It was manned by Army, police and RAF personnel. The police were shepherding the traffic, but the military were standing by. I didn't see any arms, but they had batons, you know? The truncheons.

Anyway, I looked over to the right and there was a 'Queen Mary', one of the RAF's aircraft transporters, in a field; they used to call them Queen Marys – usually a Bedford unit and trailer. I thought, Oh, it's an aircraft they're transporting. But it was funny it being in a field.

Well, being a railway enthusiast, I always used to carry a camera in the van and at any opportunity I got to see anything of railway interest, I could immediately go and snap it. I thought, I'll get a shot of this. But before I had a chance – we were stuck in the roadblock – the police came over and said, 'You'll have to make a diversion.' I said, 'What the hell's happening?' I wasn't in a very good mood; I'd already been held up through dropping that part off.'

At that juncture, Irene, who was well acquainted with the area in question, asked Harold if he could recall the location of the crash site. He could indeed: an open expanse of fields near the New Penkridge Road. Irene made notes.

As Irene and I listened, Harold revealed that he obeyed the orders of the police: he turned his van around in the middle of the road and headed back towards Cannock.

'Me being a nosy person,' said Harold and smiled, 'I stopped the van about half a mile up the road and sneaked back across a couple of fields.'

As he approached, Harold developed the impression that all was not as it should have been. Keeping his distance for a while, he could not fail to see that the field was by then swarming with people – some in RAF uniforms, others in Army fatigues.

Most interesting of all, there was a group of people 'who looked like scientists' closely examining specific areas of the field. 'There were about four or five that were digging a hole; I should imagine there were about twenty or thirty in the field altogether.'

Spurring himself on, Harold edged closer, careful at all times not to give away his position. It was then that he was able to obtain a clear view of the RAF transporter vehicle: the 'Queen Mary'. Next to it was a mobile crane adorned with Army insignia. But that was nothing compared with what was stretched out on the transporter's trailer . . .

Straining for a better look, Harold noticed that a large object had been lifted on to the trailer and had been partially covered by a tarpaulin. Harold explained to us, however, 'I noticed something very unusual about the load.' Now able to obtain a distinct view of the object's outline, Harold realised that far from resembling a normal aircraft's fuselage, it appeared to be a triangular- or, as Harold preferred, 'delta'-shaped device. Fortunately for Harold, the rear of the object had not been sufficiently covered and he had a clear view of its overhanging edges. 'Instead of being a normal shape, it seemed to spread over the trailer wider,' he elaborated. 'When they transport aircraft they take the wings off and rope them to the sides of the aircraft. But where this was bulging wasn't where any wings should be. It was sticking out over the sides of the trailer at the back by about three or four feet. Of course, a million thoughts went through my mind.'

Anxious to obtain some form of record, Harold had wisely remembered to take his camera with him from the van and duly managed to secure 'a couple of snaps'.

Unfortunately for Harold, his decision to photograph the mystery vehicle had caught the attention of the police contingent coordinating the roadblock. Concerned by this unwelcome attention, Harold hastily headed for his van and exited the area with the utmost haste. He continued:

Anyway, I carried on with my rounds, then went home. I got back, put the van in the garage, and my mother said, 'You've got to report to Bloxwich police.' 'Now what the bloody hell's up?' I asked. She said, 'You've been reported for cutting up a motorcyclist.' I thought, Well, that's bloody strange. Being a motorcyclist myself, that's the last person I'd cut up.

Well, I thought I'd better not go to the police station in the van; although we used to use the vans for pleasure, we were not supposed to. So, I got on my motorbike and went to the police station and I was ushered upstairs. In this room there was a police inspector by the name of Reid; a PC by the name of Robert Bull – what struck me about Bull was that he was the smallest copper I'd ever seen; and a female plain-clothes person taking notes.

'What's all this about me cutting up a biker?' I asked. Well, they started questioning me, asking me what I was doing around [Penkridge] at the time. They said I was observed taking pictures. I said, 'If I want to take pictures, I'll take pictures.' Of course, Reid said, 'Don't come the old acid with me!'

He said I'd been observed taking photos of an incident at Penkridge and they wanted the film. The motoring offence was just a ploy to get me to the police station; they forgot all about that, then.

Meanwhile, while I was being held, they'd got a search warrant out to search my home; and the officers that went there told my mother they were looking for a stolen camera. My mother, being a bit naive, said, 'Oh, he's got a camera, but he hasn't stolen it; it's in the van. He always keeps it in the van.' She gave the camera to them, and they gave her a receipt. Now, my mother always wanted to know the ins and outs of everything and said, 'Who's given you the search warrant?' They said, 'It's a magistrate by the name of Handley at Cannock.'

'What time were you released from the police station?' I asked.

Be about midnight, I should imagine. I was there five or six hours. The police didn't even mention the object; they just wanted to know what I was doing out there and why I had a camera with me. Then shortly afterwards, about three weeks, the camera was returned to me by post; it was in a parcel postmarked Melksham, Wiltshire. There were a few RAF bases around there.

I pursued this issue further: 'Did you get the pictures back, too, or just the camera?'

'No, only the camera; and I was very, very annoyed because I'd got railway pictures on the film. But they had put a new film in.'

Shortly after his camera was returned to him, Harold set off on his motorbike to visit the crash site for a second look: the entire area had been swept clean; not a trace of debris or evidence of damage to the ground remained. He continued with the story:

Well, me being a bit nosy, I started asking people in the area if they knew what had happened. First, I heard that there had been some UFO activity in the area; on the motorbike club night at Hednesford, I was asking one or two of the people. I didn't mention anything about what had happened to me, but they said that there had been some UFO scares. I was also told that there was a rumour going round that a UFO had crashed and had been retrieved by the military. The RAF people, from down by Melksham, were apparently put up in a pub – the Red, White and Blue at Featherstone.

Irene and I both tackled Harold on various points of his extraordinary account, and every time he related the same account: never speculating; never wavering. Thinking back to Leonard Stringfield's information, I asked Harold if he had seen any evidence that the 'crew' had been recovered, too. Harold had seen no bodies, but stressed that there was a heavy military presence, and the recovery operation was well under way by the time he had come across it. We then turned to the most bizarre aspect of the entire business.

'When we arrived,' I said, 'you mentioned that you'd just received a call from the Ministry of Defence. What was all that about?'

Harold looked somewhat concerned, but nevertheless was keen to obtain our opinions. 'This was about a quarter of an hour after you phoned,' he explained, looking at Irene. 'The phone rang; I picked it up and said, "Who is it?" "The MOD police," they said.'

The call had flustered him, and he was unsure of everything said to him; however, he was certain on two points: 'They said something about a complaint and gave me a number I was to phone them back on. But I didn't.'

'That's the number, is it?' asked Irene, pointing to a sheet of paper on Harold's desk.

'Yes,' replied Harold, his voice dropping ever so slightly.[5]

'Can I dial 1471?' enquired Irene. 'We'll see if we can find out who they were.'

Sure enough, a number was available; curiously, however, it was a different one to that which Harold was asked to call. With Harold and me looking on, Irene dialled the number that we had obtained via 1471. It was a Midlands-based operator service controlled by the military.

Sustained questioning on Irene's part revealed that the military operator was responsible for channelling calls both to and from military establishments in the Midlands area; in other words, the call to Harold could have come from any one of a number of locations in the general vicinity including Birmingham, Sutton Coldfield, Shrewsbury and Lichfield. Since any such calls would come through the operator's office, however, dialling 1471 would reveal only the operator's number and not the original source of the call. Fortunately, we had the number that Harold had been given to call. Once again, Irene dialled . . .

'Guardroom,' said an unidentified male voice.

'Hello,' said Irene. 'Could you tell me what this number belongs to, please?'

'This is the Guardroom.'

'The guardroom?'

'Yeah.'

'I'm a little confused here,' said Irene. 'I'm dialling a number that was given to a gentleman at this address to ring.'

'Can I have your name, please?' said the unidentified voice.

Irene wavered: 'Well, I'd like to know why he would be getting a call.'

'I wouldn't know, flower,' came the good-natured reply. 'I really wouldn't know. Nobody's called from here in the last twenty minutes; I've been here. Where are you?'

'Well . . . I'm in Brownhills. You're where?'

'Lichfield,' came the quick reply. 'This is the Army base at Lichfield.'

'So you're at Whittington?' asked Irene.

'Yes, that's right.'

'What's your name?' she continued.

'My name's Mr Law from the MGS.'

'MGS. What does that stand for?'

'Ministry of Defence Guards Service.'

'Ministry of Defence Guards Service,' repeated Irene, her voice echoing incredulity. 'Oh, gosh. It gets worse.'

Mr Law laughed, but was keen to stress, 'The call hasn't come from here.'

'OK,' said Irene. 'The line of work I'm in, I can't tell you too much, but it's very weird nevertheless. If we need to get back to you we will do.' The conversation was terminated.[6]

For ten minutes the three of us sat musing on the implications of the morning's events: at 9 a.m. Irene telephoned Harold to advise him that we were on our way to interview him about his recollections of a strange craft retrieved from a Staffordshire field in 1964, and, within fifteen minutes of our call, the Ministry of Defence police were on the phone to him.

The possibility that this was mere coincidence seemed remote in the extreme. And why else would the Ministry of Defence police be telephoning Harold, a retired washing-machine repairer living in a small Brownhills flat? We all agreed on one thing: there had to be a connection with the events of early 1964. But two questions remained. First, was the call to Harold from the MOD evidence that our activities were being monitored? And second, what was so important about that decades-old incident that warranted continued MOD involvement more than thirty years on?

At approximately midday Irene and I said our goodbyes to Harold, promising to keep him informed of any further developments. We made our way to a local pub for lunch and tried to make some sense out of the affair.

As incredible as it seemed, it did appear that someone, somewhere, knew we had made arrangements to meet with Harold. Since the only contact with Harold had been via telephone, this was disturbing and suggested the presence of some form of eavesdropping operation. There was another important point: although Irene's 9 a.m. call to Harold had been made from my home, she had used her own mobile telephone. As Britain's Royal Family found out to its cost several years ago when the 'Squidgygate' scandal broke, mobile telephones are far from secure . . .

In the course of my work I had come across a number of people implicated in the UFO subject who appeared to have been monitored at an official level. There was Omar Fowler, a well-known investigator of the 'Flying Triangle' mystery, who was quietly informed by a British Telecom source that his telephoned was tapped.

In *A Covert Agenda* I reported on the fact that, in 1977 at least, Graham Birdsall's telephone was surveyed by the National Security Agency station at Menwith Hill, Yorkshire.

In 1989 I had begun to conduct tentative research (with a view to writing a paper) on claims that elements of the British intelligence community routinely monitored certain people involved in the promotion of animal-rights organisations. While I was able to put together a convincing body of evidence, I was soon taken up with other matters, and shelved the project; however, during the course of my research I hooked up with an official source with tangential ties to the Ministry of Agriculture, Fisheries and Food, who was able to provide me with some useful leads.

Over drinks in October 1992, he asked what I was up to, and during the discussion I mentioned that I was liaising with one Mary Seal, a researcher of conspiracy theories who hit the headlines in early 1993 when she hired Wembley Indoor Arena to try to expose the 'machinations' of what she termed a 'global elite' who had been responsible for manipulating the human race for centuries.

My acquaintance asked a few questions, I gave a few answers, and we soon got on to another topic. Shortly afterwards, I received a package in the mail, postmarked Guildford, the home town of my source. Inside was a transcript of a telephone conversation between Mary and a well-known UFO researcher. The conversation centred on Mary's decision to feature the American conspiracy researcher Bill Cooper at her Wembley conference.

As this information had been given to me anonymously (but almost certainly via my Ministry of Agriculture source) I thought long and hard about what to do, but eventually, when invited to Mary's home not long after, I gave her the details of the phone conversation between herself and the researcher without, of course, revealing the name of my source. Faced with this piece of evidence (which I was convinced was utterly genuine) Mary looked at me dumbfounded. 'I knew it,' she seethed. 'The bastards have got me monitored, haven't they?'

In other words, Harold's experience was not isolated; it seemed that practically everyone in the UFO community had a story to tell about covert monitoring operations.

Shortly after the interview with Harold, I met with a friend in the field of private surveillance and relayed to him the basics of the matter, without going into too many specifics. As he explained, virtually anyone can purchase a scanning device to listen in on supposedly private, mobile-phone conversations; however, the user of the scanner usually has no control over which conversation he or she listens to – that is a random matter, largely dictated by factors such as the range of the scanner and the location of the caller. 'Based on the information you've given me,' he concluded, 'you have almost certainly attracted official interest.'

Perusing the Interception of Communications Act of 1985, I learned that domestic telephones can normally be monitored only with the permission of the Home Secretary; however, 'in an urgent case' a warrant can be issued by a senior civil servant.[7] Interestingly, while there were 843 official warrants issued for the interception of communications in 1992, in the following year the *Daily Express* learned that no fewer than 35,000 calls were tapped by the Government Communications Headquarters at Cheltenham during the period 1 January to 31 December 1992 . . .

The 1964 UFO at Penkridge aside, there were other reasons why both Irene and I might have been under surveillance in late 1996. Early in October of that year, there had been a major UFO encounter over East Anglia, into which Irene had conducted an intense investigation. Her enquiries had taken her to the Ministry of Defence; the RAF station at Neatishead, Norfolk; the Civil Aviation Authority; RAF Kinloss, Scotland; the civilian police at Norwich; the coastguard at Yarmouth; and the *Conocoast* oil tanker, whose crew had reported seeing mysterious lights over the North Sea.

Anyone in officialdom with an interest in what was being said about the East Anglian encounters would certainly have benefited from acquainting themselves with Irene's research activities.[8]

For my part, late 1996 was an equally hectic time. I had just delivered the final manuscripts of *A Covert Agenda* and *The FBI Files* to my editor Martin Fletcher at Simon and Schuster; in addition I was busy both giving and attending lectures at locations as diverse as Bristol, Blackpool, Birmingham and London. But that was not all.

In September 1995 I had lunched with Tim Good, to whom I had promised to show a copy of the original manuscript of *A Covert Agenda*. Tim was impressed and asked if he could use a few snippets of information in his forthcoming book, *Beyond Top Secret*. I certainly had no problem with this; I knew that Tim's book would attract a massive amount of attention and welcomed the exposure that his work would give my forth-coming book.

As Tim revealed in *Beyond Top Secret*, while snooping around the files at the Public Record Office, I had discovered that in the mid-1960s three previously unheard-of divisions of the Ministry of Defence were regularly receiving data on UFOs: DI10, DI61E and DI65B. I had also discovered that certain records of the old Air Ministry's Directorate of Scientific Intelligence (which was implicated in UFO research as early as 1952) were being withheld from public disclosure for 100 years.

In October 1996 both the above issues were brought up in Parliament by the late Labour MP Martin Redmond:

> To ask the Secretary of State for Defence . . . what is the current function of DI65B, DI61E [and] DI10. What was [their] function (a) five years ago and (b) ten years ago; and if he will make a statement.

> To ask the Secretary of State for Defence if he will list the titles of the records of the Ministry of Defence's scientific intelligence branch in respect of correspondence sent to Mr Nicholas Redfern by the Public Record Office, Kew on 21 September 1990.

While the replies from the then junior minister for defence, Nicholas Soames (forwarded to me by Nick Pope), did not reveal a great deal, they at least confirmed that my name was being bandied around the defence intelligence community.

Here, then, was ample proof that both Irene and I were in a position that could have led to an official monitoring of our UFO-related activities in late 1996, if not before.

As 1996 drew to a close Irene and I considered the experience with Harold South and his strange call from the MOD police. To both of us, it almost seemed as if a game was being played: when speaking with Harold, the Ministry of Defence made no attempt to block their telephone number (we had their number via the 1471 facility in seconds); they even gave Harold an internal number at Whittington Army Barracks to phone back!

I came to only one conclusion: somebody in the intelligence or Defence community wanted to let us know that, by probing into the complexities of the Penkridge crash, we had opened up a sensitive can of worms. If the intent was simply to keep everything under wraps, why not employ someone to pay Harold a visit and request his silence? Had this occurred, and Harold had merely told us he had changed his mind about talking, neither Irene nor I would have been any the wiser.

By letting us know that Harold's decision to talk had sparked renewed interest on the part of an anonymous agency, however, was the intent to scare us off? Or was it possibly a subtle attempt to spur us on? After all, both of us were by then convinced of the overwhelming validity of the case.

Other questions began to surface: if the call to Harold was indeed an attempt to convince us that the case was valid, was the call officially sanctioned or did we have a sympathetic informer in our midst who was trying to break the case open without compromising his or her identity?

Try as we might, we never found out conclusively one way or another. We were merely left with a mountain of un-answered questions. Who was Harold's mystery caller? Were Irene's and my activities matters of official interest? Why was Harold treated in such an odd manner at Bloxwich Police Station? And, most important of all, what was that mysterious craft recovered from a Penkridge field by the military all those years ago?

Clearly, it was not standard practice to hold a member of the public in a police station (with no charges being brought against them) simply because they happened to photograph an aircraft. In addition, while air-accident investigation teams do on occasion solicit the use of both still and moving picture images of aircraft crashing to earth, this is largely to assist in any follow-up investigation. In Harold South's case, however, the object had crashed some hours before he came across it. The implication was obvious: Harold's film was confiscated not because it was felt his shots would aid the investigation team in determining how the vehicle crashed, but because he had photographed something that the military wanted kept under wraps.

In view of this, could the object have been some form of experimental aircraft? Taking into consideration the unique shape of the craft, the testimony of S.M. Brannigan as related by Air Force Intelligence officer Leonard Stringfield, the ongoing interest in the case on the part of the Ministry of Defence more than thirty-two years later, and the large number of UFO encounters reported throughout the United Kingdom in precisely the same time frame, I found this possibility most unlikely.

My search for the truth surrounding the British Government's involvement in 'crashed UFO' incidents had taken a major step forward. The next step was to make a full assault on those Ministry of Defence files concerning unidentified flying objects that had been released into the public domain and were housed at the Public Record Office at Kew.

Only time would tell if I would uncover the elusive 'smoking gun'; however, if buried deep within the Public Record Office there were indeed government and military files pertaining to crashed and retrieved UFOs, then I would not stop until I had that crucial evidence in hand.

Researching *A Covert Agenda* had shown me that if one

knew the right place to look, one could find a wealth of RAF and Air Ministry files on UFOs which, having been declassified under the terms of the thirty-year ruling, were just crying out for inspection.

CHAPTER FIVE

ACCESSING THE ARCHIVES

WHILE BROWSING THROUGH A VARIETY OF AIR MINISTRY and Army files at the Public Record Office to try to uncover data pertaining to the UFO crash at Penkridge, Staffordshire, in the early part of 1964, I came across a solitary newspaper clipping relating to an incident that occurred at Walthamstow only weeks later.

The inclusion of this clipping in the file was itself curious, since there was no evidence that the department with whom the file originated (S4) conducted any form of investigation into the encounter. However, there was enough information contained within the article to convince me that the event was worth looking into.

According to the newspaper clipping (which was in a somewhat dishevelled state) at 8.43 p.m. on the evening of 13 April 1964, a Walthamstow-based bus driver, Bob Fall, was driving alongside the River Lea in Walthamstow when his attention was drawn to a fast-moving aerial object, which barely missed his bus, and plunged into the river. At the time, Bob recalled:

I just glanced into the sky and saw something coming towards me very, very fast. It flew straight across the road and, had I been a few yards further forward, it would have hit the top deck of the bus.

At first I thought the back windows of the bus had come in and, as I turned around, I saw all the passengers looking out towards the river. There was a big splash in the water. I stopped as soon as I could to report it.

As I continued reading the article I was amused to see that a police spokesman ventured the possibility that the object was merely 'four ducks' flying in formation!

Bob Fall quickly discounted this possibility: 'The thing was at least nine feet long, cigar-shaped and silver. If it had been a bird or birds I [would] have seen the wings. Besides, it was going too fast.'

That was all I needed to persuade me to look into the case further. There was of course a possibility that the object, given its small size, was part of an aircraft, or, worse still, a stray missile dropped inadvertently from a passing fighter plane. It should be noted, however, that the press clipping was contained within a file devoted solely to the investigation of UFO encounters.

I scanned other files at the Public Record Office for any papers relating to an incident involving a downed aircraft, but had no luck. I was not discouraged, however – I had come up against cases more difficult than this in the past, and approached my investigation with relish. Then came a welcome advance.

Digging into the event, I learned that the investigator Ronald Caswell of Harlow, Essex, had looked into the crash and had uncovered a phenomenal amount of data that had been almost completely forgotten by the UK's present-day UFO researchers.

Caswell was undoubtedly on to something, and he made an intriguing move. Reviewing a letter that he had written to the Air Ministry two weeks after the mystery object plunged into the River Lea, I noted that he had elected to inform the Air Ministry of the details of his investigation.

Two years previously I had spoken with a budding writer who was conducting research for a proposed manuscript (which, alas, never came to fruition) on the crash of an atomic-bomb-laden aircraft on British soil in the 1960s. He, too, made the move of informing officialdom that he was looking into the case and this led to a curious series of events: every time he located someone with intimate knowledge of the near-disastrous affair, it transpired that the person in question had then recently received a 'visit' from an authority figure and had been warned that if they spoke out publicly, they would be in violation of the Official Secrets Act. Thanks to one letter to the military, the entire book project collapsed.

While Ronald Caswell's very open stance with the Air Ministry might have led to a similar clampdown, his work did at least show me that the matter was indeed of significant interest.

Anxious to ensure that no stone was left unturned, Caswell mounted his own investigation of the Walthamstow crash and made a personal visit to the reported crash site.

He informed the Air Ministry: 'From newspaper reports it appears that an object approx. 9 feet in length, shaped from the side like a cigar, silvery in colour, fell from the sky, skimmed past the front of a 123 bus, struck the bank and crashed into the River Lea, just missing the Ferry Lane Bridge. He continued that he went to Ferry Lane to make enquiries and learned that the object had ploughed into a set of telephone wires. He informed the Ministry:

> I have a piece of one of the telephone wires broken by the object. A newspaper shows great coils of it on the tow-path. The police spokesman's suggestion that a duck, or even four ducks, could have broken those wires is ridiculous. Neither could a swan. The length of the wire across the river would have moved away at the pressure of a plummeting bird, and the bird would certainly have been badly injured, if not killed.

Caswell further added that while walking the length of the river, he had come across a 'river policeman' working near to the lock-keeper's house. It transpired that the very talkative policeman had himself been present at 11 p.m. on 13 April 1964 and he assisted officers from Greenleaf Police Station in dragging the river.

Curiously, however, when Caswell indicated the area of river that he had been examining (the towpath on the main river stretch), the river policeman revealed that he was looking in the wrong place. 'He took me across a private foot-bridge and around a grassy "island" to a spot overlooking a silted-up channel forking off from the main river. This was certainly no more than 4–6 feet deep. The policeman said that this was where they had dragged, and nothing unusual had been found.'

Caswell then revealed his hand: 'This differs from information I had earlier received to the effect that when it was late enough for the general public to have cleared off, heavy lifting equipment was brought in and a find was made in the early hours of the morning.'

Caswell also offered the intriguing possibility that the river policeman knew far more than he was telling, and 'was himself misled, or he tried to mislead me, as to the area of the fall'. He continued: 'The driver, as he later confirmed, was on the larger of the two bridges when he slowed down to hear the bubbling and hissing, just where he saw the object dive in. And at this point, as the river policeman – who ought to know – kindly informed me, the river could be 30–40 feet deep.'

Caswell then fired off a barrage of questions: 'Why did the police talk of ducks breaking wires, and of water from 4–6 feet deep? How could all these points check with the driver's statement? Why the hissing and bubbling? Why did the police confine their search to a narrow, silted-up area of water, at least during the hours before midnight? Did they receive instructions from higher up?'

Caswell then closed his letter somewhat cryptically: 'Why did a wing commander from the Air Ministry take all the trouble of driving to Walthamstow to interrogate the bus-driver on the 25th April, almost two weeks after the incident?'

Commenting on the alleged 'duck vandalism', Caswell signed off: 'Was [the wing commander] perhaps, in private life, also an honorary member of the RSPCA?'

A further examination of the evidence showed me that on 14 May Caswell received a reply from Mr R.A. Langton of S4, who confirmed that he had no further reports on the Walthamstow incident. 'I hesitate to suggest any possible identification for the Walthamstow object,' he added.

Interestingly, Langton seemed far more intrigued by Caswell's assertion that Bob Fall had received a visit from an unidentified wing commander: 'If a wing commander from the Air Ministry took the trouble of driving to Walthamstow to interrogate the bus-driver on 25 April, I should be most grateful for any further information you may have that would enable me to identify him.'

I saw no further indication that Ronald Caswell had any additional dealings with the Ministry with respect to the Walthamstow crash, but R.A. Langton's letter of 14 May certainly caught my attention.

I knew from my previous research for *A Covert Agenda* that Langton's division, S4, was only one of at least five in the Ministry that received UFO reports in the 1960s; and I also uncovered several documents that showed that, in certain instances, UFO reports filed with the Air Ministry had bypassed S4 and gone directly to Air Intelligence (soon thereafter combined with the intelligence divisions of the Army and the Navy to create the Defence Intelligence Staff).

Was Langton aware that he was not getting to see all the data that the Air Ministry had acquired on UFOs? I could not rule it out.

A few other newspaper clippings aside, my search for additional information on the Walthamstow crash uncovered little else. Whatever the nature of the object retrieved under cover of darkness from the River Lea in the early hours of 14 April 1964, it had long since vanished.[1]

In the latter part of February 1997, my efforts to ascertain the truth behind the various crashed-UFO incidents in the UK received a major boost. In checking the latest releases of data at the Public Record Office in December 1996, I had noted that the following month was due to see the declassification of two files of Ministry of Defence papers covering the period 1964–66. This was a development I could not afford to ignore, and, come February, I had in my possession almost one thousand pages of crucial data. The contents of the files, never before seen by anyone outside of officialdom, were eye-opening.

Scanning the files, I was most intrigued to note that the very first entry in the documentation was an eleven-page batch of material concerning an unidentified object that was seen to come down in the vicinity of March, Cambridgeshire, on 5 January 1965. Of those who witnessed the phenomenon, one, Max Beran, quickly wrote to the Meteorological Office Unit (MOU) at Huntingdon Road, Cambridge.

Whilst in the sunlight it remained visible, giving the appearance of a curved object. Perhaps a parachute, but I would have thought too fast for that. Before falling too low to be visible in the low sun it appeared to be falling to a point perhaps a mile or two south east of the town centre from where I was watching. What could the falling object have been?

What indeed? I flipped through the files and saw that the Senior Meteorological Officer at Cambridge rapidly apprised his headquarters at Braknell, Berkshire, of Beran's letter. Recognising that this was a matter for the Ministry of Defence, Braknell prepared a one-page memorandum for the MOD outlining the facts. Immediately, the Ministry swung into action. When I began to look carefully at the MOD's response to

Max Beran's report, what interested me the most was the fact that the file could in no way be considered complete. For example, a one-page handwritten note from the MOD noted that the police at March had been directed to look into the matter. '[The police] sent a car out to look for the object in the vicinity of the "Sixteen Root Drain" but without success,' stated the MOD. Had the impact site of the object been identified? If so, the available files failed to reveal how such an identification had been arrived at. Moreover, the files of the March police were curiously absent . . .

There was also the significant fact that the MOD had put numerous questions to a host of other departments as it sought to locate and identify the UFO, including the Royal Navy, the Ministry of Aviation, and various civil aviation bodies. Whatever the origin of the object, a piece of military hardware was conclusively ruled out.

'Things which may on occasion fall from aircraft include external fuel tanks, drag-chutes, cockpit canopies, access panels or doors, and sometimes accumulations of ice,' the MOD informed Max Beran. 'We have looked carefully into all these possibilities so far as our own aircraft are concerned, but have drawn a blank.'

Despite this seemingly authoritative letter, however, it was abundantly clear that the Ministry of Defence was keeping its opinions on the case close to home. 'If we have nothing to say, the sooner we say it the better!' recorded one MOD official in an internal report on the case. If the Ministry had learned anything further, I speculated, then those answers were still held tightly under wraps at Whitehall.

Several hundred pages further into the file, I located a piece of data which, in view of everything I had learned thus far, was potentially of great importance.

Robert S. Suter, an American UFO investigator of Savage, Maryland, had written to the Ministry of Defence on 27 April 1966 seeking to obtain 'verification of a persistent rumour here in the USA'.

The rumour referred to nothing less than an unidentified flying object that had been 'shot down' over the United Kingdom 'several years ago' and which contained 'the remains of a once living organism'!

Predictably, Suter received a reply from the Ministry of Defence denying any knowledge of such an occurrence; however, the timing of Suter's letter was important. Only months before I obtained copies of this three-decades-old material, Irene Bott and I had spent a great deal of time evaluating the evidence surrounding the UFO crash at Penkridge in early 1964.

The letter referred to a UFO retrieval within the UK 'several years ago'. Was this, perhaps, the first reference to the Penkridge crash to turn up in officially released MOD files? Certainly, the information passed on to the former US Air Force Intelligence officer Leonard Stringfield confirmed the recovery of alien bodies at the Penkridge site. Was there a connection between those same alien bodies and the 'once living organism' described by Robert S. Suter? Search as I might, the Ministry of Defence was not going to give up its secrets that easily. I made a mental note of this thirty-year-old exchange and continued to plough through the documentation.

Despite the fact that Suter's letter to the MOD was dated 1966, it was evident to me that, at some point, the Ministry's filing system had gone awry: the next two reports of relevance to my quest dated from 1965!

Interestingly, both reports originated from Wales, and both attracted the attention of the MOD's Defence Intelligence Staff (DIS).

With a large official stamp stating WARNING. NO UNCLASSIFIED REPLY PERMITTED. CONFIDENTIAL, the first report, dated 3 April 1965, read thus:

SIGHTING OF UNUSUAL PHENOMENA.

LOCATION: CAPEL CURIG, WALES.

MR GWYN WILLIAMS THROUGH VALLEY CONTROLLER
VIA POLICE AT CAERNARVON SAW BRIGHT LIGHT
DESCENDING FROM SNOWDON ENDING IN A VERY
BRIGHT FLASH. DIALLED 999 REPORTED TO LLAN-
DUDNO POLICE THEN TO CAERNARVON POLICE THEN
TO CONTROLLER RAF VALLEY.

The second report, this time stamped PRIORITY, told a
similar story:

17 DEC 1965. SIGHTING OF UNUSUAL PHENOMENA
BETWEEN RUTHIN AND MOLD ON A494 MAP
REFERENCE 172584, MR KENNETH WILLIAM REECE
[WITNESS'S ADDRESS] SAW A WHITE LIGHT DESCEND-
ING INTO VALLEY WHERE IT EXPLODED AND DIS-
INTEGRATED ON THE GROUND AT POSITION MAP
REFERENCE 196526 LLANDEGLA.

In both cases, I was interested to see, no fewer than five
copies of each report had been circulated to the MOD's highly
secretive DIS for analysis. Did, perhaps, the DIS send operatives out to inspect the two impact points? And if so, was anything of substance recovered?

In 1994 Graham Stanley of the PRO's Government Services
Department advised me:

The registered files of the Defence Intelligence Staff
which have been selected for permanent preservation
have been assigned to a Public Record Office class
(reference DEFE31). All of them are retained by the
Ministry of Defence. These records are retained because
they contain information relating to the security and
intelligence agencies and are obviously highly sensitive.

Despite not being given carte-blanche access to the 1960s
files of the DIS, I did come across one report in the file (which

had possibly been overlooked by the MOD's censors) concerning the DIS's on-site investigation of a UFO encounter reported by Police Constable Colin Perks at Wilmslow, Cheshire, in January 1966. In other words, the possible presence of DIS personnel at the Welsh sites could not be discounted. While the 1964–66 files told me nothing more, I was not finished.[2]

Of those crash-retrieval incidents where I was able to determine that documentation had been generated at an official level, certainly the most remarkable occurred on 8 September 1970. The case was made all the more remarkable by the fact that what was retrieved was not a UFO, but a military aircraft that crashed into the North Sea subsequent to its encounter with an unidentified aerial vehicle!

'This is a story you almost certainly won't believe. It is a story we have no means of verifying. The people we have asked officially have denied all knowledge of it. Those we have asked unofficially have said quite simply, they don't know.' Thus wrote Pat Otter, editor of the Grimsby *Evening Telegraph* – the newspaper that first brought the controversy to light in October 1992. And what a controversy it was . . .

The established facts were relatively straightforward. On the evening of 8 September 1970, Captain William Schaffner of the United States Air Force lost his life after his RAF Lightning aircraft 'ditched' into the harsh waters of the North Sea. The Ministry of Defence had stated that this was simply the result of a tragic accident that occurred in the midst of a military exercise. Or was it? Information published by the *Evening Telegraph* suggested that, at the time of the 'accident', Captain Schaffner had been pursuing a UFO – a pursuit that led, either directly or indirectly, to his death.

By Pat Otter's own admission, most of the *Telegraph*'s information on the affair had come from a source who declined to go public; however, the information imparted to the newspaper was, without doubt, fascinating. According to the *Telegraph*'s source, on the night of 8 September unusual aerial targets were tracked overflying the North Sea by radar operatives at RAF Saxa Ford. Aircraft from RAF Leuchars were scrambled to intercept, as was USAF Captain William Schaffner, who was on an exchange visit with the Royal Air Force, and stationed at RAF Binbrook, near Grimsby. In addition to these basic facts of the case, Pat Otter had received a word-for-word transcript of the exchange between Captain Schaffner and radar staff at RAF Staxton Wold:

Schaffner: I have visual contact, repeat visual contact. Over.

Staxton Wold: Can you identify aircraft type?

Schaffner: Negative, nothing recognisable, no clear outlines. There is . . . bluish light. Hell, that's bright . . . very bright . . . It's a conical shape. Jeez, that's bright, it hurts my eyes to look at it for more than a few seconds . . . Hey, wait . . . there's something else. It's like a large soccer ball . . . it's like it's made of glass . . . coming straight for me . . . am taking evasive action . . . a few . . . I can hardl . . .

At that moment, radio contact was lost. But more was to follow. A radar operator who had been monitoring the movements of both Schaffner's aircraft and the mystery object was astonished to see both targets merge into one, decelerating in speed until they finally came to a halt six thousand feet above the North Sea! Shortly afterwards, the single blip separated into two, and radio contact was re-established. By that time, it was clear that Captain Schaffner was severely disorientated and in deep trouble:

Staxton Wold: . . . . What is your condition? Over.

Schaffner: Not too good. I can't think what has happened . . . I feel kinda dizzy . . . I can see shooting stars.

Although he apparently had plenty of fuel remaining, on the orders of Strike Command Headquarters, Captain

Schaffner was instructed to ditch his aircraft in the North Sea. Schaffner followed his orders to the letter. It was an action that was to cost him his life.

It was some weeks before the aircraft was recovered from the North Sea, but Captain Schaffner's body was never found. With the aircraft in hand, however, it was immediately transferred to RAF Binbrook and placed in a secure hangar, where it awaited study by air-crash experts from RAF Farnborough.

On investigating the aircraft, however, the Farnborough experts found that several pieces of crucial cockpit instrumentation – including the compass and voltmeter – had been removed. On whose orders? While this was never fully determined, throughout the investigation, the Farnborough team was monitored closely by five mysterious individuals – all of whom were civilians, and at least two of whom were American. On completion of their examination (which was inconclusive as to what had caused the crash), the Farnborough team was called into the main office and advised that under no circumstances were they ever to discuss their analysis of the recovered Lightning. How much of the above could be readily verified? According to Pat Otter in 1992:

> I first came across the story six years ago when an outline was related to me by Barry Halpenny, an aviation enthusiast and author . . . There was more to the story than met the eye, he told me. I had anticipated difficulties in investigating a 16-year-old ditching incident in the North Sea, but not on the scale I was to encounter over the next few weeks.
>
> Normally helpful press contacts in the Ministry of Defence responded initially by promising to help, but then became very reticent . . .[3]

It has to be said that, were it not for the diligent research of Pat Otter and, later, Tony Dodd, a retired police sergeant, my interest in the case would have been minimal. Both men made a good case for something truly extraordinary having occurred, and further information and additional witnesses subsequently surfaced. In an attempt to be objective, however, I deemed it necessary to obtain the opinion of the Ministry of Defence.

If the incident did occur as described, I reasoned that the MOD would be most unwilling to discuss the matter with outsiders. In *A Covert Agenda*, I had detailed the extraordinary series of UFO encounters that occurred near RAF West Freugh, Scotland, in 1957, and revealed that at the time the Air Ministry was most concerned by the fact that the press had uncovered pertinent details of the encounters. I was surprised, therefore, to learn that the Ministry had no qualms about entering into debate on the Lightning crash of 1970.

When I first met with Nick Pope of MOD division Sec(AS)2A in 1994, I seized upon the opportunity to ask him about the many rumours surrounding the crash and retrieval of the Lightning. Did he know what had taken place?

A smile came across Nick's face:

Oh, yes, I know about that case. What I can tell you is I was approached a couple of years ago by a number of UFO researchers – including Tony Dodd, who had in turn got the story from Pat Otter – who had all suddenly got hold of this story that an RAF Lightning had crashed in the North Sea subsequent to its encounter with an unidentified flying object that it had been vectored on to by Fighter Control.

I thought that that was quite an extraordinary story, and did my best to find out the facts. I got in touch with the Flight Safety people, and actually called for the full Board of Inquiry file, which is about four inches thick. That file was classified, as all Board of Inquiry files are. I spent a long, long time going through that file with a fine-tooth comb. I also checked the enclosure numbers to make sure there had been no funny business with anything being removed or crossed out. I felt duty-bound to check, because I knew the allegations would almost certainly surface that there had been some sort of cover-up, and I wasn't getting the full story.

The basic story was that the Lightning was part of an exercise – a tactical evaluation exercise. It was being vectored on to a Shackleton aircraft, and the aircraft was practising the night-shadowing and shepherding of low-speed targets. That's connected with the sort of job that the Lightning might have to do in an operational situation. So, it was basically on a military exercise. The Lightning pilot reported seeing the lights of the Shackleton, and I think sounded disorientated, and subsequently the aircraft crashed into the sea.

What I can tell you is, from the file, there's absolutely no reference to anything UFO-related at all; the word 'UFO' did not appear once in the file. The phrase 'uncorrelated target' did not appear. Absolutely no indication at all. So, I honestly can't tell you where the story started from.'

'Is it likely that that Board of Inquiry file will one day be declassified?' I asked Nick.

Nick mused for a moment:

I don't know. I don't see why not. You'd probably have to ask the Public Record Office about declassification of Board of Inquiry files. But I can tell you, I've seen that file; I've been through it. I have found nothing UFO-related at all. It's simply as one would imagine the story of an aircraft crash is: a very tragic story of a combination of factors leading to the aircraft crashing into the sea.

Well, when I got about half a dozen letters from different researchers, I thought the time had come to pull them out of the standard correspondence file and open up a file on this one incident, simply so that everything was in one place. But all the pressure was coming from UFO

researchers. There were no original documents to suggest
that anything unusual had happened.[4]

I truly did not know what to make of this case. Nick Pope,
I was certain, was speaking truthfully. However, as I was able
to show in *A Covert Agenda*, the office in which Nick worked
in no way saw all of the UFO data that entered the Ministry of
Defence. Had the 1970 incident over the North Sea been
genuinely of a UFO nature, would Nick have been able to
access the Board of Inquiry file with such apparent ease? I felt
confident in saying no. Uncertainties remained.

Tony Dodd (who had an exemplary career with Yorkshire
Police) learned from an informant that 'some authorities have
been prepared to go to great lengths to keep hidden the official
reports'; and Dodd's source also informed him that one contact who knew the full story of the Lightning crash died in
unusual circumstances in Germany several years ago.[5] And
there were three other significant factors, too.

There was Mr S. Bentley of Leeds, who had revealed to the
investigator Arthur Shuttlewood that in January of 1972, he
had requested 'confirmation of a date relating to a certain
North Sea incident'.

'The result', Bentley informed Shuttlewood, 'was a visit by
two CID chaps, who asked where I had obtained some
information.'[6]

Second, in 1992 the Ministry of Defence revealed to me
that in 1970 (the year in which the Lightning crash occurred)
the MOD received no fewer than 181 UFO reports. In other
words, UFO encounters were common throughout the
country in the immediate post-1960s era.

Finally, there was the fascinating account of one Rita Hill
which paralleled very closely the crash of the RAF Lightning
jet in 1970. Rita also had first-hand knowledge of a series of
almost identical incidents that had occurred more than twenty
years prior to the events of 1970!

In the late 1940s Rita entered the Royal Air Force as a nurse (having done her training at RAF Halton), ultimately rose to the rank of sergeant, and received a posting to RAF Boscombe Down – from where the RAF conducted (and to this day continues to conduct) tests on radical and new experimental aircraft. Rita told me:

> There were always crashes with experimental aircraft. These weren't little biplanes; we're talking about jets and so on. At times we would have a crash a week. I was in charge of a crash crew and had two lads with me. When we went to a crash site, everything had to be found – buttons off the tunics, scraps and so on. Sometimes it would take us weeks to find everything; and from there the wreckage of the planes would be taken to Farnborough for reconstruction.
>
> Well, with UFOs, I'll tell you what I can – but it was all top secret at the time. When the test pilots had finished their tests, they would have briefings, which we would sometimes attend – these were all very hush-hush. Sometimes, the pilots would report seeing strange lights and objects in the sky – they weren't called UFOs at that time. But they would say that when they saw these strange lights, the instruments on the aircraft would go haywire and sometimes the altimeter would just stop! Which is a disaster in itself!
>
> 'What the hell was that? What the hell was that light?'" Those are the sort of things we'd hear them say. In these cases, the reports went to Whitehall and we were all sworn to secrecy. It's only now that I've said anything about what I saw.[7]

Although, by her own admission, Rita had only partial access to the evidence (largely due to the fact that official secrecy stamped on the encounters in an instant), her account fascinated me and suggested that face-to-face encounters between military pilots and UFOs in British airspace had proliferated for decades; and, as will later be revealed, Boscombe Down's involvement in the UFO puzzle is ongoing to this day.

I felt that my study of a variety of crash-retrieval cases that were supported by a degree of official documentation had taught me a valuable lesson: buried deep within the Public Record Office there was indeed a wealth of credible data on crashed and recovered UFOs. It was simply a matter of knowing where to look.

Slowly but surely I was getting there. But I was not prepared for what came next. From time to time I had come across those witnesses to UFO sightings and encounters whose testimonies proved to be invaluable in my search for the truth; however, from a source with long-standing media connections in both the United Kingdom and the United States, I learned of a series of UFO incidents that shook the military and governmental establishments to their cores.

CHAPTER SIX

OFFICIAL CENSORSHIP

EARLY IN JUNE 1996 I WAS CONTACTED BY ADELENE ALANI, A producer with the BBC, who was then working on a documentary series – *Out of this World* – dealing with various facets of the paranormal. My agent, Andrew Lownie, had sent Addy a copy of the synopsis for *A Covert Agenda*, and, having read it, she was keen to feature me in one of the programmes.

Since *A Covert Agenda* largely dealt with the Ministry of Defence's involvement in the UFO problem, both Addy and I thought it would be a good idea to film me at the Public Record Office, where I could discuss the various UFO files that had then been recently declassified under the terms of the thirty-year ruling.

This was my first exposure to television work and I was keen to get some experience in that area. As it happened, things went very well: I was able to demonstrate that the British Government had long been implicated in the investigation of UFO sightings; and Addy and her team were granted permission to film me in the vaults of the Public Record Office – an area largely out of bounds to the general public. Standing in those vaults, surrounded by myriad shelves packed with box after box of classified files, it made all of us appreciate that, in the UK, official secrecy was a fact of life.

Midway through July 1996 the programme in which I was featured aired, and my interview was included in a segment that dealt solely with the British Government's interest in the subject: Nick Pope was featured speaking about his three-year term with Secretariat Air Staff 2A; Matthew Williams discussed the involvement of RAF Rudloe Manor; and a host of other sources were cited, all of whom added to the credibility of the piece. It was a job well done.

As a result of the broadcast, a dozen or so people surfaced with important new information. There was the retired RAF man who recalled a top secret Ministry of Defence project – 'Poison Chalice' – designed to monitor and intercept UFOs operating in British airspace in the early 1970s; there was the ex-Royal Marine who was confronted with a landed UFO on the Yorkshire Moors in 1979; there was the Norwich housewife blessed with a visit from two representatives of the Ministry of Defence after seeing a UFO near RAF Coltishall in the early hours of an October 1983 morning; and then there was Roger Chambers . . .

Roger initially introduced himself to me by letter in early August 1996: 'Watching you on "Out of this World" re cover-ups about UFOs brings back many memories when I worked for ATV in Bridge Street, Birmingham.'

Roger revealed that he had been directly involved in two UFO incidents while working with ATV (which became Central Television) in the early 1970s that had attracted the interest of the British Government. More importantly, one of those incidents concerned the crash-landing of a UFO at Cannock Chase, Staffordshire – only a few miles from where another UFO had crashed in early 1964.

'If you would like to meet and talk about these things, please phone me,' wrote Roger in closing.[1]

On receiving Roger's letter I telephoned him, expressing a keen interest in what he had to say. Even in that brief, four-minute telephone conversation, I realised that his case was perhaps one of the most important to have caught my attention. A personal meeting was vital.

I knew that any meaningful dialogue with Roger would probably entail several days' work on my part, and with numerous obligations, I was forced to wait until December before I was able to speak with him in person. In the early morning I set off for Skegness, where Roger, a Midlander through and through, had settled to run his own business.

The train journey from Birmingham was largely uneventful and I settled down with a Robert Ludlum novel. Three and a half hours later we arrived at Boston, and I smiled to myself at the sight of the 'Boston Stump' – a large church tower over-looking the town. Only weeks before there had been a series of unexplained radar returns picked up at a number of RAF stations in the area, and the 'Stump' had been squarely blamed as the culprit. 'Freak weather patterns,' the RAF had said . . .

The next stop was Skegness.

I stepped off the train and walked in to the practically deserted station. I could see no sign of Roger and headed for the waiting room. Ten minutes or so later, a man entered and looked around cautiously. Fifty-something with thick, greying hair, he approached me. I stood up.

'Nick?'

'You must be Roger.'

We shook hands, exchanged small talk, and headed off to the nearby car park. Roger and his partner, Jennie, lived only a short distance from the station, and we were there in minutes. I was delighted to be greeted with a splendid chicken casserole cooked by Jennie.

Over lunch, rather than discuss the UFO encounters in which Roger was implicated, I opted to obtain some background information. Roger was fifty-one and had begun working for ATV in 1970 on a freelance basis as a driver and mechanic. From late 1972 until 1977 he worked for the company on a full-time basis, and then returned to freelance work. He finally left ATV for good in 1979.

But it was not just television work on which Roger was

involved: his talents were put to use on a number of well-known films, including *Raise the Titanic*, *McVicar*, and *Too Late the Hero*. And in later years Roger moved to the United States, where he worked on documentary programmes and met a number of well-known personalities, including the actors Glen Ford and Doris Day.

He regaled me with his memories of Oliver Reed, Lord Lew Grade and Diana Dors, among others. 'The things I could tell you about ATV,' he said with a smile.

After lunch, I brought up the subject of UFOs, explaining my interest in determining what the British Government had learned about the subject.

'As I said,' Roger began, 'I started as a driver/mechanic; that was my original job. And then, John Rose, who was our transport manager, said I was for better things, and he put me on to OBs – outside broadcasts. Then we had this thing on Cannock Chase.'

As Roger recalled, it was a harsh winter's evening in January 1974.

> I was working on the news team at the time. There was me; Dennis Shaw was the producer; Keith Lindsay was the cameraman; Barry Bakewell, sound recordist; and Robert Ball, second cameraman.
>
> We got a call off John Rose; he said there'd been a UFO sighting over the Chase, and this was news. They sent me to pick up Keith Lindsay.
>
> This was about eleven o'clock at night. By the time we got back to the studio, most of the crew were there and it was snowing; real thick snow. Snowing like hell.

'Can you recall the exact site?' I asked.
'Cannock Chase, in the Hednesford area,' Roger replied.
I listened carefully as Roger continued his remarkable narrative. He was unsure from where John Rose had obtained details of the incident, but it was clear that somebody at ATV

had uncovered the precise location and the team was dispatched. Having driven through Hednesford, they headed for the Chase. On arriving at a clearing in the forest at around 1.30 a.m., Roger and the crew could not fail to see that something remarkable was taking place in a nearby field.

'When we got there,' said Roger, 'everybody was there: the Army; police minibuses; a lot of police. Never seen anything like it; it was unbelievable. Troops, lorries, the lot.'

'How many are you talking about?' I asked.

Oh God, blimey! Thinking about it, military vehicles, we must have passed ten. At least ten lorries. But the troops, I couldn't count the number of them. It was a madhouse. There could have been up to a hundred, maybe. There were loads; it was swarming.

We pulled up by the field, just after a road cordon. We had to pass the cordon, first. We had 'ATV' on the side of the minibus. They stopped us, and we said, 'We're ATV News,' and they allowed us to pass.

We got to the edge of the field – they wouldn't let us go any further – and there was an old A60 car there. There were two guys in the car. One had the door open; that was the driver. It was a freezing-cold night and the guy was sitting with his legs sticking out of the car. He was sweating like a pig. All he had on was shirtsleeves; it was untrue.'

'So you drove through the forest, were confronted by a military cordon, were allowed to go as far as the edge of the field, and saw the two guys parked in the car near to the field?'

'That's about right.'

'Did the Army people allow you to speak to the driver of the car?'

'Well, they wouldn't really let us speak to him; they weren't happy about it, that was clear. But we did a vox pop on him; we forced ourselves on him.'

'What did he have to say?'

'Him and the other chap had been driving along, and they'd seen what looked like a fireball coming down. He thought it was a plane crashing in the field; so as they got closer they pulled into a slope by the gate, and he couldn't back up because it was thick snow.'

I continued to dig for answers: 'Did John Rose say anything about a plane crash?'

No, John just said it was a UFO sighting; the only person to mention that he thought it was a plane crashing was the driver. Now, when we started to do the vox pop, the driver, whose name was Brummel, said that he jumped out of his car and had gone into the field. He'd seen this thing; he'd actually seen it. And it wasn't an aircraft. His friend was frightened and wouldn't go with him.

But the driver, he walked up to this thing; real close to it. Right up to it. And he said it was a flying saucer.

'He was talking about a circular-shaped device?' I wanted clarification.

'That's what he said: a flying saucer.'

'Did he mention anything about the colour or texture of the UFO?'

He said it was very bright, but he was a bit disorientated. Now, what's interesting is he didn't see the thing leave the field. He went back to his car, but couldn't get it out. So him and his mate, they just sat there. He wasn't at all well when we spoke to him. Like I said, he was sweating like a pig. Well, an ambulance came along, an ordinary ambulance. He didn't want to go in the ambulance; he went under a lot of duress.

Since the driver had been unable to extricate his car from the ever-deepening snow, it struck me that it was most unlikely that he was the one who notified the Army that the object had crashed. Roger agreed.

'Obviously it was well documented before he saw it, I think. It was very secretive. The Army had the entire road completely closed off.'

'So you think the military knew that the object had crashed, or was likely to crash?'

Roger answered forthrightly: 'Oh, yes. Definitely.'

'What happened next?' I asked, anxious to keep Roger talking.

'Well, once the Army got [the driver] into the ambulance, they said we had to go. They kicked us off, but we just backed up, further up the road. We sat there for two, maybe three, hours.

'Now, Keith Lindsay, him being a bit of a sleuth, he disappeared . . .'

'He was away all this time?'

Yes. It was over two hours. We don't know how he found his way in, but he went through a few hedgerows and got into the field. He'd disappeared; he'd just gone! Now, the Army, they didn't know that the full crew wasn't in the minibus. When we backed up, Lindsay was out the back doors and off with his camera; he was a hand-held cameraman.

As I said, two hours or so later, he was back. The rear doors of the van burst open and he jumped in. 'You won't believe what I've just filmed,' said Lindsay. Those were his exact words. I thought he'd filmed the UFO, but he hadn't. What he did film was a massive, circular burn mark in the field.

'If other people had been driving by, would they have seen the burn mark from the road?'

'No, you couldn't see it. Not from the road. Now, Lindsay, he filmed this burned circle, but he couldn't get any perspective, you know, like a man? He shot some hedgerows, but that didn't really show the real size of it.'

'It was big then?'

'I always remember his words. He said, "You could put the Rotunda in it three times." '

The Rotunda, a famous landmark in the centre of Birmingham, is an impressive building with a large circumference. If the object that came down on the Chase was three times the size of the Rotunda, then it was gargantuan, to say the least.

'Was this a burn or just a depression?'

'It was a burn. It must have been hot because there was no snow on it, but the snow was pouring down. And Lindsay walked right the way round it. Lindsay's a good cameraman; not just average, he's good.'

I wanted to know what happened next. 'From the time that you arrived at Cannock Chase, at the crash site, to when Keith Lindsay finished filming, what sort of time span was that?'

'We were there about three hours. We got back to the studios about half past five in the morning. Bill Carr, he edited the film, and we put it on "Preview" and had a look at it, to see what Lindsay had shot. Now, the film lasted for about two and a half minutes; that's what he managed to get. It was in colour and you couldn't believe it.' The emotion in Roger's voice as he recalled the event was plain to hear.

A serious expression came over his face: 'Then the next morning, the government came in.'

'How did that come about?' I asked. 'Were you taken into a room or something?'

'It happened in preview. In the theatre,' Roger explained.

'So you preview a piece of film before it's broadcast?'

'Oh yeah. The government people were always coming in. They vetted the film. Decided it was "blacked" and took it with them. Anything they don't want you to see is blacked – end of story. But Lindsay had made a copy,' he said quietly, a sly smile forming on his face.

'Can I get a copy of his copy?'

'I'll see what I can do,' Roger replied, knowingly.

Regrettably, Roger was ultimately unable to secure a copy of the film; however, he had more to impart. I asked him if he knew which department the government officials represented.

There was no doubt in Roger's mind. 'It was the Home Office.'

'What had happened to the man who had seen the UFO come down: Brummel?'

Well, the next day, I'd been doing filming for *Up the Workers*. John Rose knew the guy's name and he'd been phoning round all the hospitals. He eventually found out they'd taken him to Cotteridge General Hospital, the other side of Wolverhampton. After filming, John came up to me and said, 'You know that guy you filmed last night? He died of radiation burns this morning in Cotteridge General.' John had passed himself off as a relative, or something. But we could never understand why they took him all the way to Cotteridge.

Roger recalled that all of the team were concerned at that point that their health had been put in jeopardy. Fortunately, this did not prove to be the case. Roger's voice then took on a somewhat sad tone as he discussed the strange feeling that came over him when he realised that a man with whom he had been speaking only hours before had died.

I backtracked, anxious to ensure that nothing had been forgotten. 'You mentioned that the guy in the car had seen the UFO crash. He described it as a fireball, like an aircraft crashing?'

'That's right,' confirmed Roger.

'But he didn't see the UFO take off again?'

'No, he didn't.'

'What about the Army? Was there any evidence that they removed the craft from the site?'

'Well, we didn't know. We didn't see them do that, but it was maybe two hours after getting the call that something had come down before we got there. And you don't have a hundred troops and ten lorries there for nothing, do you? I tell you what, Nick,' Roger added, 'it looked like a military operation.'

I had to agree.

Having discussed the various facets of the Cannock Chase crash, I asked Roger to detail for me the other UFO incident he recalled while working with ATV. Although this appeared not to involve a disabled or retrieved UFO, it was important since it led me to conclude that the British Government was fully aware of the many complex issues presented by the UFO mystery.

We were in Oxford doing some filming. This was 1974, too. It was 'Hot Cross Bun Day'. We were at the Randolph Hotel and we were going to film the 'bun-throwing' ceremony at Abingdon, where they throw the buns off the clock tower.

Well, John Rose called again, and said that a farmer had had all his cows poisoned in a field.

'Where about was this exactly?' I asked.

Between Woodstock and Abingdon. So we drove towards Woodstock and took all the back roads. We were told the field was by a petrol station. We passed it probably a couple of times, and the third time we found it. We went into the field and there were a lot of police there. This was in the daytime, but it had happened the night before.

As I said, we went into the field; Keith Lindsay was the cameraman again. There were all these cows lying down dead – a full herd. Loads. And there was a farmer ranting and raving that a rival farmer had poisoned them all. That's what he said. But three of his herd were missing.

Now, Robert Ball said to Lindsay, 'Film the trees.'

They were all burned; all the trees at the back of the field. All the leaves were burned; serious burns. And the farmer couldn't understand why three of his herd were missing.

'Did you get the burned trees on film?'

Oh yes. We got all that on film, and the cows. Now, we found out later that autopsies had been carried out on the cows, and it was like they'd been cooked in a microwave. The film went back to the studio; the 'outriders', kids on motorbikes, they'd taken the films back. Now, when the film got back, someone at ATV made a phone call. Somebody came in to vet the film, and that one disappeared, too.

'Did you get any indication as to where all this film footage was being taken?' I had visions of some vast archive filled with all manner of evidence relating to alien activity.

Roger shook his head. 'Off the face of the Earth?'

This case was of more than passing interest to me: in 1989 I had managed to obtain from the FBI a pile of once classified papers relating to 'cattle mutilation' events in the United States. And, significantly, a high proportion of such reports surfaced in the direct vicinity of where UFOs and strange aerial lights had been seen. I supplied Tim Good with copies of the aforementioned papers (who subsequently cited several in his bestselling 1991 book *Alien Liaison*) and later incorporated the documents into my second book, *The FBI Files*.

As Roger's evidence showed, cattle mutilations were not exclusive to the USA. And what of the burned trees? Had some form of aerial vehicle landed in the field? What was the cause of the horrific microwave-like burns suffered by the animals? And what had become of the three missing cattle?

Were alien beings harvesting Earth-based life forms? The evidence presented in the FBI documents certainly suggested that some type of advanced technology was at work. And that same technology had now broadened its horizons. Was a cosmic 'Jack the Ripper' on the loose? The speed with which the film was confiscated from ATV suggested that someone within the bowels of government knew far more than they were publicly willing to admit.

Roger was not involved directly in any further UFO incidents during his time with ATV, but he did hear, 'on the grapevine', that other regional television studios throughout the country had had film confiscated by the same group of people who acquired the ATV footage. More importantly, some of that footage related to other 'crashed UFO' incidents involving British authorities. I asked Roger to elaborate.

'Well, we heard these accounts, but we were never in the right place at the right time. There was one off the Isle of Wight in 1978. This didn't make the news, either. The rumour through the studio was that this thing, this UFO, had come in over the north side of the Isle of Wight and was shot down. That was the rumour.'

Roger thought for a moment: 'It may have been Thames [Television] who covered that. I know there had been a few UFO sightings in the area at the time. But I definitely heard that divers were out there and warships. It did sound very suspicious. Why should they send warships out? If they send navy divers out, they aren't doing it for nothing, are they?'

At that point in the interview it became obvious to me that there was something else Roger wished to discuss, but he was clearly unsure whether he should. He leaned forward in his chair.

'I shouldn't talk about this; I was told not to talk about this.'

I wondered what could be so important. Suddenly it all became clear. As remarkable as it seemed, Roger was aware that a freelance news team had captured on film the crash-landing of a UFO at Rendlesham Forest, Suffolk, in December 1980!

I had devoted a full chapter of *A Covert Agenda* to a discussion of the Rendlesham events, and it was clear that something of extreme importance had taken place on land near to

the joint RAF/USAF military complex at Bentwaters/
Woodbridge at the time.

There was the testimony of a wealth of military figures who
asserted that a UFO was seen to manoeuvre in and out of the
forest; Colonel Charles Halt, Deputy Base Commander at
Woodbridge, had prepared an official report that confirmed
that he, too, had witnessed unidentified aerial phenomena;
and there was the complicity of the British military, the civilian
police and the Ministry of Defence. There were even claims
that diminutive alien beings had been seen by some of the airmen. But never before had I heard that the event had been
captured on film. This was a first.

'Don't put my address down; I don't want a bullet in my
head,' said Roger.

I persuaded him to open up. It transpired that shortly after
the initial UFO sighting by the military in Rendlesham Forest
early on 26 December 1980, a still-unidentified airman on the
base tipped off a nearby freelance television crew that a UFO
event had taken place.

Wasting no time, the crew quickly headed for the forest.
Sure enough, from their position on the road the entire team
could see an array of unusual lights deep within the forest:
reds, yellows, purples, all manner of colours.

For reasons of personal safety, the crew opted to film the
object at a distance of about half a mile. The UFO, however,
could still be seen clearly. Roger continued quietly:

> What was seen was definitely not from this planet. And
> I'll tell you, as well as the Americans, there were a lot of
> British there. I think I heard they were from Brize
> Norton.
>
> I know there were all sorts of rumours going round the
> base. The team were definitely told by two American air-
> men at Woodbridge that there had been some sort of air
> crash. But the saucer, whatever it was, wasn't captured.
> Not the saucer . . . but whatever was in it.

'Are you saying the military captured the crew of the UFO that came down in Rendlesham Forest?'

Roger looked at me for a moment.

I asked again: 'Is that what you are saying, the crew were found, or captured, and taken away by the military?'

Roger stayed silent, but nodded to confirm that I was on the right track.

'Well, what happened to the film footage?' I asked.

Silence.

'OK. Do you want to name anyone on the shoot?'

'Well, one of them was Robert Ball; he was the cameraman. When ATV became Central, he left and became freelance. But that was a good exclusive.'

I asked again about the film.

'What happened to the film, I never really knew. I, er, I know it went back to Edgbaston, but from there, I don't know.'

'Is there anything else you can recall hearing about the crew of the UFO being captured?'

'About the only other thing we heard was that the crew had been taken to a laboratory in Kent. These were survivors; they weren't dead.'[2]

There was nothing more that Roger could add and we duly concluded the interview. The entire experience had been astounding. I stayed with Roger and Jennie for another day, and then headed off home.

Sitting on the train as I made my way back to Birmingham, I put on my headphones and played the interview tapes. Listening to Roger's voice, I sensed no attempt on his part to deceive me; when he did not have an answer to a question he simply said, 'I don't know.' In addition, I tackled him on each point several times over the course of the two days I was with him (and on three occasions by telephone), and his account was the same. I had no doubt that Roger was relating a series of remarkable, and utterly genuine, experiences.

And Roger's account of a UFO crash-landing at Cannock

Chase in January 1974 was all the more provocative since, in terms of time, it tied in with yet another reported UFO crash near Bala, Wales. In that case, a new witness had just surfaced – a retired military source who claimed to have knowledge of alien bodies recovered at the crash site! I had to press on.

CHAPTER SEVEN

THE MOUNTAIN OF MYSTERY

IN *A COVERT AGENDA*, I MENTIONED AN UNUSUAL EVENT that occurred on the evening of 23 January 1974, when an unidentified aerial object impacted on a remote peak in the Berwyn Mountains, North Wales.

This incident was made all the more remarkable by the fact that numerous witnesses in the vicinity recalled what had occurred, and, as a result of their testimonies, I was able to paint a clear picture of the events as they unfolded.

Annie Williams of Llandrillo said, 'I saw this bright light hanging in the sky. It had a long fiery tail which seemed to be motionless for several minutes, going dim and then very brilliant, like a dormant fire which keeps coming to life. It would have been like an electric light bulb in shape, except that it seemed to have rough edges. Then [it] fell somewhere behind my bungalow, and the earth shook.'

Similar testimony came from David Hughes of the village post office at Ysbyty Ifan. 'The whole house shook violently and suddenly. It began quite suddenly, lasted for a few seconds, then stopped just as suddenly.'

And then there was Police Constable Gwilym Owen. 'There was a great roar and a bang . . . The sky lit up over the mountains. The colour was yellowish but other people in the valley described seeing blue lights.'

As I was researching *A Covert Agenda*, I also came across a nurse who, at the time of the crash on the Berwyns, had rushed to the scene with her two daughters (they initially believed that an aircraft had come down) and witnessed a huge egg-shaped device sitting high on one of the peaks.

In the days that followed, numerous rumours flew about Llandrillo and the surrounding towns and villages: Bala, Llandderfel, Corwen and Crogen. There was talk of the military coming across a large, disabled, unidentified object on the mountains; there were whispers of a carefully coordinated operation to remove the mysterious device; and claims of a high-level cover-up abounded. But that was not all.

In precisely the same time frame, other matters of a bizarre nature were afoot throughout the country. In the Midlands, there was a huge wave of sightings of strange lights and unidentified helicopters.

One day before the crash at the Berwyns, for example, numerous reports of the mysterious helicopters surfaced from Darley Moor in Derbyshire, Bramhall, Prestbury and Scholar Green in Cheshire, and in the vicinity of Aston Cantlow near Stratford-upon-Avon.

Police at Cheshire were baffled as to what was going on and to whom the helicopters belonged and they were keen to solve the riddle. In the days that followed, Special Branch and the Royal Air Force were queried. No answers were forthcoming. Who were flying the helicopters and why remained mysteries.

However, considering that the helicopters were seen in precisely the same time frame as a mystery craft impacted on the Berwyn Mountains, perhaps the most pertinent comment came from the investigator Tommy Blann, who had a contact – a lieutenant colonel – in the US military. Blann said, 'The colonel stated that underground installations, as well as isolated areas of military reservations, have squadrons of unmarked helicopters, which have sophisticated instrumentation on board, that are dispatched to areas of UFO activity to monitor these craft or airlift them out of the area if one has malfunctioned.'

Were the helicopters seen over Cheshire, Staffordshire and Derbyshire attached to a covert UFO crash-retrieval team? This seemed a strong possibility – particularly when rumours surfaced in *The Times* that in mid-January 1974, there had been a sudden influx to the UK of CIA agents from the United States! The whole country, I concluded, was awash with strange goings-on.[1]

At the time I wrote *A Covert Agenda*, those were the facts. However, in late 1996, the case suddenly took on a whole new significance, with the startling account of a retired military source who claimed involvement in an operation to recover alien bodies from the crash site on the Berwyns. Most controversial about this revelation was the fact that it contradicted sharply the official line.

The military had no qualms about admitting that, as a result of the mysterious blast on the Berwyns, an investigative team was dispatched to examine the immediate vicinity; however, according to those in authority, nothing was found.

The *Guardian* of 25 January 1974 was quick to state, 'An RAF mountain rescue team from Anglesey, a posse of Gwynedd police and schoolchildren couldn't find the object.'

The *Wrexham Leader* newspaper, meanwhile, reported on a fantastically original theory that the strange lights seen in the area were merely torches used by men out hare hunting! And the mysterious tremors? 'Coincidence,' reported police and the Royal Air Force.

Reviewing a wealth of newspaper clippings on the case at Birmingham Library, what amazed me the most about the controversy was the speed with which it was killed off: with the assertions of the military in hand, practically all comment in the media ground to a halt in a matter of hours.

It was time, I concluded, to seek out those in the UFO research field who had first-hand knowledge of the incident on the Berwyns. I began with the one woman who, more than anyone, had looked into the many and varied complexities of the crash: the Llangernyw-based investigator Margaret Fry.

I explained the situation to Margaret: I was looking into a variety of crashed-UFO incidents that had occurred within the UK and considered the Bala event to be of prime importance. I was also aware that Margaret had conducted some sterling research into the case and was interested to know her thoughts and feelings on the controversy.

Margaret was more than happy to help, and was instrumental in convincing me that the case was of profound consequence. We began with the nurse.

'You want the correct version?' asked Margaret.

'Indeed, I do,' I replied.

This is what happened. She and her daughters were alone in the house on the night of 23 January 1974. They were alone because her husband worked as a long-distance lorry driver and was away at the time.

I think they felt the earth shake first, and it was very severe. Well, this frightened them enough, but then they heard a very loud explosion. Straight away, she thought there'd been an aeroplane crash on the Berwyns. Being a nurse, she'd been called out two years previously when a military plane had crashed at almost the same spot.'

She promptly picked up the telephone, rang the Colwyn Bay Police and said, 'I've heard this terrific explosion; I think a plane's crashed. Shall I go?' The police replied, 'Yes, please do. We'll inform the appropriate authorities.'

So, she then got in the car with her daughters. They were fourteen and fifteen years of age. They wanted to go with her. They rushed up this little zigzagging hillside; it's not a road: it's virtually a track leading from the village where they live up on to the main road, which is the B4391. And that takes fifteen minutes from their village up on to the road.

They then drove on to the Berwyns, and across the Berwyn Mountains. Up they went, right to the top. There, they had to stop. It's on the highest part of the Berwyns, and below there's a sweep; not a sheer drop but a sweep right down to a gorge. On the other side of the gorge there's a pine forest. Here, the Berwyns are very bare, very bleak and frightening-looking.

Well, just above this area, above the pine trees, there was sitting a great big, roughly egg-shaped object which she said was very clearly defined. It was letting out diffused light. They stood there in amazement, because they weren't expecting anything like that, and they just stood and watched it. As the crow flies, they were about a quarter of a mile away.

Now, after they'd been there about ten, fifteen minutes, they saw little white lights zigzagging up from the pine forests area, up towards the object. The girls started to feel a bit uneasy at that point and said, 'Come on, Mum. Let's go. There's nothing we can do; it's not a plane crash.'

As far as the nurse was concerned, that was just about it. But there were others.

There was another witness, a Miss Wynne. She didn't know anything about the nurse, and, in fact, when she told me about her involvement, I didn't at first connect the two. But she used to tell me about it very often.

Along with her brother and father, she'd gone out to visit relations on the day at a nearby town. They were driving back that night and were approaching Corwen when they felt the earth shake, and they, too, heard an explosion. They looked up towards the Berwyns and could see a big glow in the sky; just like you would get if something had exploded.

They were a bit curious and said, 'Come on. Let's go and see what's happened.' They went along the Forestry Commission road, which is right at the bottom of the

Berwyns. It's a very narrow road; no cars can turn around there. Well, there were police and military all along this road at the base of the mountain. And they could actually see this object sitting just beyond the forested area on the mountains.

'How did Miss Wynne's description of the object compare with that of the nurse and her family?' I wondered.

It was exactly the same. Her description was exactly the same. They said to the police, 'What's it all about?' The police replied, 'It's nothing to do with you. Turn around.' Of course, the road being narrow, and because there were a lot of other drivers who'd followed them to have a look, too, it meant that they got the chance to have a very good look at this thing. So, there were dozens and dozens of people who saw it.

'Who are still to come forward, presumably?' I asked.

Oh, lots of them have come forward. That's the point. I've had people tell me how it came down; who actually saw it coming down on the mountain.

On another occasion I happened to be in Wrexham visiting Miss Wynne, and I had to stop off at a photo-copying shop. When I was in there, the girl behind the counter said, 'I can't help but notice that what you're photocopying is all to do with UFOs.'

'Yes,' I said. 'I'm giving a talk on television tonight, and I'm getting some material together.' Well, she was very interested and said, 'You know, my mother would be very interested in this.'

She told me exactly the same as Miss Wynne. She said that her mother had been near the Berwyns on 20 January and saw a whole pile of cars on the road, which the police were trying to turn around. And they were all able to see this huge thing sitting on the mountainside. I said to her, 'What shape was it?' She replied, 'Mother said it was somewhat egg-shaped.'

'Were any of the witnesses able to gauge the size of the UFO?' I asked Margaret.

'It was absolutely enormous,' she said. 'Maybe several hundred feet in height.'

'In height?' I exclaimed.

In height, yes. And not quite as wide. But I think that more than one UFO was around that night. Some of the people I've spoken with said that they'd seen a huge, orange object in the skies at about eleven the same night, which is very puzzling. And there were a number of villagers who had seen something in the air at around nine-thirty: a big orange ball which headed over their village towards Welshpool.

There were several UFOs in the locality of North Wales that night. I've had reports – nothing to do with the ones on the Berwyns – of people seeing UFOs a few nights before and several nights afterwards.'[2]

There was no doubt in my mind that something of great significance had occurred on the Berwyns. But what? The all-encompassing presence of the military suggested that they were looking for something of supreme importance. And what of the absolutely gigantic, egg-shaped object seen high on the mountains? Was it possible that a disabled alien spacecraft had come down on the Berwyns?

It was clear from what Margaret Fry had to say that the object seen by the nurse, her daughters, Miss Wynne and a host of other witnesses was tangible in nature: it was not a ball of gas or something insubstantial – such as a rare atmospheric phenomenon, as had been suggested in some quarters.

Second, the revelations that the retrieval of the craft was

under way practically by the time that Miss Wynne arrived on the scene helped explain why, later on the following day, an examination of the area failed to locate the object: it had been removed from the crash site by sources unknown either late on the night of 23 January or during the very early hours of 24 January.

But who was responsible for coordinating the retrieval operation, and exactly what was found? At this point I was obliged to examine certainly the most controversial aspect of the mystery: the claim that the bodies of alien creatures had been found at the crash site.

It was late 1996 when this new slant on the case first caught my attention. The original source of the account was the investigator Tony Dodd – who had expended a great deal of time looking into the RAF Lightning crash in the North Sea in 1970.

Tony's source was a retired military figure given the pseudonym of James Prescott. According to Prescott, in January 1974 he was stationed at an Army barracks in the south of England. 'I cannot name my unit or barracks as they are still operational,' Prescott stressed to Tony as he detailed how on 18 January his unit was put on 'stand-by to move north at short notice'. Twenty-four hours later, the unit was directed to make its way towards Birmingham . . .

'We then received orders to proceed with speed towards North Wales,' Prescott elaborated. 'We were halted in Chester in readiness for a military exercise we believed was about to take place. On 20 January, the communication to us was "hot". At approximately 20.13 hours we received orders to proceed to Llangollen in North Wales and to wait at that point.'

On arrival at Llangollen, recalled Prescott, the unit noticed a great deal of 'ground and aircraft activity' in the area. Extraordinary events were unfolding. But it was shortly after 11.30 p.m. when things really began to take shape.

'We, that is myself and four others, were ordered to go to

Llandderfel and were under strict orders not to stop for any civilians,' said Prescott.

The team soon reached Llandderfel, whereupon they were ordered to load two large oblong boxes into their vehicle.

'We were at this time warned not to open the boxes, but to proceed to [the Chemical and Biological Defence Establishment at] Porton Down and deliver the boxes.'

A number of hours later, they reached Porton Down and the mysterious cargo was quickly taken inside the facility.

'Once inside,' explained Prescott, 'the boxes were opened by staff at the facility in our presence. We were shocked to see two creatures which had been placed inside decontamination suits.'

The staff at Porton began the careful task of opening the suits.

'When the suits were fully opened it was obvious the creatures were clearly not of this world and, when examined, were found to be dead. What I saw in the boxes that day', Prescott detailed to Tony, 'made me change my whole concept of life.

'The bodies were about five to six foot tall, humanoid in shape, but so thin they looked almost skeletal with a covering skin. Although I did not see a craft at the scene of the recovery, I was informed that a large craft had crashed and was recovered by other military units.'

Most remarkable was what Prescott had to say next: 'Sometime later we joined up with the other elements of our unit, who informed us that they had also transported bodies of "alien beings" to Porton Down, but said that their cargo was still alive.'

In conclusion, Prescott added that this was 'the only time I was ever involved in anything of this nature. This event took place many years ago and I am now retired from the Armed Forces.'[3]

Live aliens loose on the Berwyns? The case was becoming more extraordinary by the minute. Frankly, were it not for the fact that I knew Tony Dodd to be a wholly trustworthy source of information, I would have been highly cautious about accepting such incredible revelations at face value. Tony's background could not be denied, however: for twenty-five years he had served with the North Yorkshire Police and had risen to the rank of sergeant. His pedigree was exemplary.

Moreover, Tony had the opportunity to see first-hand evidence pertaining to James Prescott's military background. I saw no reason to doubt that Tony had spoken with Prescott and that the man was indeed just what he claimed to be. But it was not just Tony who was acquainted with Prescott and his extraordinary account . . .

Both Margaret Fry and Matthew Williams had also spent time looking into the claims that alien bodies had been found in the Berwyn Mountains. It was time to secure their views on the controversy. Matthew told me:

I spoke to Tony Dodd at the Cardiff UFO Conference just after this story came out, and I also spoke with him on the phone. Tony won't reveal the real name of James Prescott because he thinks that the guy will be traced back to the Army camp or the operational unit he worked for. So if Tony does reveal his name, he'll end up being given a very hard time by the government.

But as I said to Tony, 'There aren't going to be many people who (a) were at a UFO crash-retrieval in North Wales with a specific set of circumstances; and (b) who are now talking about it. I'm pretty sure that the government are going to find out who he is, anyway, aren't they?'

The obvious problem was that if the Army or the government got to Prescott before he had the chance to speak with anyone else, he would be in a lot more trouble than if his name was out in the open. That way, if the Army did anything against him, they'd be seen doing it.

If Prescott does exist – and I think he probably does exist – he'd be far better off talking to people. But Tony said that the guy was on an Army pension and was concerned that he'd end up losing it.

Tony says that he has checked the credentials of James Prescott. How far that goes and what it means, I don't know. But he's happy with them. Tony was happy that after all the research he'd done, Prescott was who he said he was.

From his conversations with Tony and Margaret Fry, Matthew was also able to fill in the blanks with respect to what occurred between the time that Prescott and his unit departed from the crash site with the bodies and their arrival at Porton Down. 'The crates were loaded on to the back of the Army vehicle. They eventually got on to the main roads and headed on to the motorway. At one point, they decided to pull off the motorway and stop at one of the services – just for a cup of tea. They weren't particularly worried, because at this point they hadn't been told what was contained in the crates.'

Alien bodies on the car park of the Little Chef? I asked Matthew to continue.

'They stopped at the services; however, as they went to get out of the cab, they realised that they'd been followed by another vehicle. The people in that vehicle came up to the cab and said, "No. Get back in your cab and get straight back on the road. Don't stop. Just get straight down to Porton Down." And apparently they were shadowed all the way to Porton.'[4]

The Chemical and Biological Defence Establishment at Porton Down was, I knew, a massive and incredibly secretive complex. With an annual budget of no less than £65 million and a staff of nearly one thousand, Porton Down was at the cutting edge of research into advanced chemical and biological technologies – the majority of which was undertaken on behalf of the military. If the British Government did indeed have at its disposal both dead and still-living alien creatures, then Porton Down was the logical location to contain such unique specimens.

Margaret Fry had strong opinions on these extraordinary developments.

'I think Tony Dodd definitely interviewed James Prescott,' said Margaret, forthrightly. 'The military were definitely there that night between nine and eleven. That's definite. But the bodies? I don't know. Who would ever know? James Prescott isn't going to say anything [on the record]; he'd be killed if he did.'

'You've spoken with Tony about this, haven't you, Margaret?' I asked.

'Oh, yes,' she replied. 'Tony told me that James Prescott said that his unit was parked on the B4391 road, and they were given the bodies. I don't know how. Either Tony hasn't been told, or he hasn't told me. But there were, apparently, some soldiers already on the mountain and it was they who brought the bodies down to the little road. James Prescott was handed the bodies on the road; he didn't go on to the mountainside at all.'

'Are you saying, then, that the military who were scouring the Berwyns for the UFO literally stumbled across the bodies?'

'Presumably. But Tony did tell me that there was talk in the barracks afterwards, and that pieces of something or other were taken away.'

'From the crash site?'

'Yes. Some people . . . some lorries took away pieces, debris. Others took away bodies. And, according to this man, at least one was still alive. This is just evidence of one man, but all I can say is that everything I've collected since all points to the fact that this was correct.'

'When you spoke with Tony, did he seem impressed by James Prescott?'

Margaret was quick to answer: 'Tony says that he thinks that Prescott is perfectly genuine. But he's very afraid. He's had all sorts of individuals from the Ministry of Defence coming to him. The MOD don't know for certain that it's [Prescott] who is talking, but they're hinting darkly of the things that can happen if he says anything.'

'This has happened since the case broke in late 1996, has it?'

'Yes,' replied Margaret. 'And now, Prescott has said to Tony that he wants to let it lie. He's sorry; he doesn't want to say anything further for the moment, because he's too afraid.'

'And he's definitely received some form of visit from the Ministry of Defence?'

'Yes. As I say, they don't know for certain that it's him. But his house, it's a military house; he got it by "grace and favour" when he retired. Now they're telling him that if it is him who told Tony, he could end up losing his home. He wasn't just your common-or-garden private; he was very high up in the military. He's got a hell of a lot to lose.'[5]

But how had the military been able to access the crash site with such apparent speed? Matthew had some ideas:

Margaret invited me up to North Wales and I went through some of the witness statements. Where the event was supposed to have taken place – the Berwyn Mountains – we actually went there. We drove up there, stopped the car and had a look across the range to where the crash supposedly happened. It's quite a long walk, so I first looked at it from a distance through binoculars for ten to fifteen minutes. We looked at the topography to see whether or not it was possible to get somebody up there in such a short time, and Margaret's impression was that it would have to have been done on foot. It would have taken a long time to walk up there: possibly up to an hour or more.

The fact that the military were already there to recover the bodies and maybe the UFO suggests they must have had advance notice that the crash was going to happen. We know that James Prescott said that they had a couple of days notice. So the things we found out at the crash site did tend to support his account.[6]

The recollections of Tony Dodd, Margaret Fry and Matthew Williams were invaluable. But I wanted to obtain further expert opinion.

Jenny Randles had proved to be a vital source of information when it came to determining what the British Government knew about UFOs, and I was naturally interested to know what she thought of James Prescott and his account of retrieved aliens – both deceased and living. If his account could be validated conclusively, I explained to Jenny, then we were perhaps on the verge of making a significant breakthrough. Jenny's views, related to me in 1997, were most enlightening and elevated the case to a new level . . .

I was aware of the Llandrillo case at the time it occurred because there had been various media stories published, and I'd just become really interested in UFOs about a year earlier. But the stories had never really connected it with anything significant. The event had simply been written off as a meteorite.

Well, at about the same time as the Llandrillo crash occurred, I was involved in setting up an organisation known as the Northern UFO Network, or NUFON. The original concept of NUFON was to be a kind of liaison scheme to bring local groups together.

I think it was more than coincidence that, as all this was happening, a mysterious organisation turned up on the scene known as APEN – the Aerial Phenomena Enquiry Network. The first thing I ever got through the mail from them was a cassette tape, which was very bizarre because it began with what was later identified as a Nazi war march. The tape was filled with lots of voices shouting and screaming, and heavily accented people – some Welsh, mostly Americans, and some guy calling himself James T. Anderson, Supreme Commander.

Over the next few months, it gradually dawned on me that several other people in NUFON had been sent similar tapes. Then towards the end of 1974, letters started to arrive on APEN stationery. There were all sorts of different names given, and strange James Bond-style coding. But these letters had been posted from all across the country; we could never track them down.

Was there a link between the mysterious APEN and the Llandrillo incident?

It was towards the end of 1974 that a letter arrived from APEN which suggested that there had been a UFO landing in North Wales, and that APEN were considering whether or not to send me the full report on the case. It was going through all the chains of command, they said.

APEN claimed that this UFO had landed rather than crashed; it was an alien craft, and was similar to one which had supposedly impacted on the Rossendale Valley in the summer of 1972. There was also supposed to be a former military officer who lived in a remote cottage on the mountain who was allegedly involved. This was all quite bizarre.

That was one of the last things I got from APEN. But about a year later, around February 1976, I moved house. Literally nobody knew the new address, but when we arrived at the new house, sitting on the doorstep was a card saying, 'Welcome to your new home.' And inside was a sticker with the APEN sign on it, saying, 'Never call anyone bigger than yourself stupid.'

The last indirect contact I had with APEN came in the mid-1980s. I had been contacted by a local UFO group in Crewe which went by the name of FUFOR – the Federation for UFO Research. They, too, were a NUFON-affiliated group, and told me that APEN had approached them and had informed them that the Rendlesham Forest UFO crash of 1980 actually involved something else. I think the innuendo of it was that the case was somehow connected with an incident involving a nuclear missile.

Jenny told me that among her colleagues in UFO research there was a great deal of debate as to who APEN were. There were those who favoured the theory that the group comprised characters on the fringes on ufology; others asserted that the organisation had ties with various right-wing political groups; while others favoured the intriguing theory that APEN was a British Government-sponsored group designed to disrupt civilian UFO research within the UK. Jenny continued:

> Whoever they were, APEN weren't just crackpots; they had employed some fairly nasty tactics. For example, there was one group in Leicester who got into deep trouble. APEN had telephoned the local police, passed themselves off as the Leicester UFO group and sent the police on a wild-goose chase after a nonexistent UFO sighting.
>
> Well, the group were hauled in for wasting police time. But shortly afterwards, this same group received a letter from APEN saying, 'This is just to tell you that we're around and you should watch out for us.'
>
> There was also a claim that APEN had broken into a building in Nottingham, had stolen some UFO files which were held there, and had ransacked the place.

I listened carefully as Jenny told me that APEN employed other devious tactics as it sought to fracture the attempts of a number of UFO investigators to forge links between various UFO organisations within the UK.

Although Jenny was reluctant to ascribe APEN's activities firmly to some hidden governmental body, she did advise me:

> You do have to wonder if some of the sinister things they did would really have been perpetrated just for the sake of it. And I think the most serious aspect was that APEN did attempt to destabilise NUFON. I have no doubt whatsoever that that was the case.

Similarly, at the same time, the British UFO Research Association [Bufora] was attempting to bring together the various British groups in a liaison system. Well, then those groups, too, began to receive letters from APEN telling them not to associate with Bufora.

In the late 1970s, Bufora, through its then chairman, Roger Stanway, attempted a direct liaison with *Flying Saucer Review* magazine and exactly the same thing happened.

I was intrigued to see that APEN's destabilising tactics had begun shortly after the incident on the Berwyn Mountains in January 1974. By attempting to drive a wedge between the various British UFO groups, and by releasing its own 'version' of what occurred on the Berwyns, was APEN's role specifically designed to mask the truth behind that incident? Jenny had had similar thoughts.

That's one of the things about the APEN story which really makes me wonder about them. Because they did see the significance of Llandrillo years before anybody else did. And, of course, they also recognised that the Rendlesham Forest case was more than it appeared to be on the surface, before, I think, many other people did. To me, that suggests an element of sophistication; so, I have to admit that that's one of the things about APEN that does make me still take an interest in them.'

Jenny's involvement in APEN aside, there were other reasons why she had taken a keen interest in the incident on the Berwyns.

Two years ago, in 1995, I was lecturing in London at the *Fortean Times* Unconvention Conference; I gave a talk on crashed-UFO incidents and mentioned the Llandrillo case.

It was at the end of my lecture that a man came up to me. He was attached to the science editorial team of the *Sunday Express*. He said that he was fascinated by what I had to say because of something which' had happened around 1993.

The *Sunday Express* had been approached by a doctor living in the area around Bala. This doctor had told the *Express* that he had been building up a dossier over the previous twenty years, to indicate that there was definitely some cause of higher levels of childhood cancers in the area; and his thesis was that this was connected with a nuclear power station in the area. He'd reported it to the *Sunday Express* in that context.

The science journalist who was at the Unconvention had gone to North Wales to investigate it, and spent a couple of days trying to find whether there could have been a scenario that might have caused this. He said that he couldn't find any substance to these allegations, and so the *Express* just simply wrote off the story. But as he said, 'Of course, if you are now introducing another potential source of radiation in the area twenty years ago that might have provoked things which the doctor had never even known about. It might make the story more interesting.'

Indeed it might. And what of the account given to retired police sergeant Tony Dodd: that alien bodies had been recovered on the Berwyns? Jenny had views on this, too:

The whole scenario of this is curious. About six weeks prior to the 'alien bodies' story breaking, I had written a big article on the Llandrillo case for *Sightings* magazine. In that article I mentioned the possibility that the UFO story could be a cover for a nuclear accident – as I'd always done when referring to the incident.

Then, shortly afterwards, the story appeared in which this soldier had come forward to Tony Dodd, and who told Tony how he had ferried the bodies from the area. But the very day on which that story appeared in the newspapers, there was a *World in Action* programme on TV which dealt with a nuclear accident at Greenham Common in the late 1950s in which radiation leaked from a nuclear weapon. Local doctors had since noted that this was apparently related to a rise in childhood leukaemia in the area, and they had been trying very hard to establish a link through government documentation.

World in Action stated that they had been pressurising the Ministry of Defence for the last few weeks to admit things, and they were getting the runaround. So it did occur to me that in the period between July and September 1996, you had the Llandrillo case brought into the open in a big way through *Sightings* magazine – which sells about thirty to forty thousand copies per issue – and linking it with a nuclear accident at the same time.

By coincidence, Granada Television – the makers of *World in Action* – were pressurising the Ministry of Defence on another incident which might have been very similar in nature. It's conceivable that someone in the Ministry of Defence might well have got tetchy about this, and was fearful that if Granada Television made a case for the incident at Greenham Common in the 1950s, someone might start to dig into other possibilities.

It might have been the ideal opportunity that the Ministry of Defence needed to try to emphasise the alien-contact aspect of the Llandrillo case by bringing out a story which reaffirmed that.

Now, that is pure supposition on my part because I have no idea who this anonymous soldier is. I don't know if he believes what he's saying. But the timing was certainly interesting.[7]

I thanked Jenny for her thoughts on APEN and the Bala

event. It was now time to try to make some form of assessment of what had actually taken place on the Berwyn Mountains back in 1974. In trying to do this, there was one point on which I was certain: there had to be a link with the equally astonishing encounter at Cannock Chase, Staffordshire, in the same month, as reported by Roger Chambers of ATV.

In both instances, unidentified flying objects were seen to fall to earth in fairly secluded areas; both impact sites were secured quickly by the military – who appeared to have prior knowledge that the crashes were going to occur; both UFOs were reportedly of impressive dimensions and of a similar configuration; and, most interesting, there was evidence to show that at both crash locations a significant amount of deadly radiation had been deposited by the craft. In the Staffordshire case there was the unfortunate witness to the crash who died soon after coming into contact with the UFO itself; and in the Berwyn incident there was the rather alarming increase in childhood cancers in the immediate vicinity.

Considering the remarkable parallels between the two cases, I gave a great deal of thought to the possibility that both events involved the same stricken UFO.

Initially, I had suspected that the heavy Army presence at the Staffordshire site was an indication that the UFO had been retrieved there and then. After all, the prime witness to the encounter had told Roger Chambers and the ATV crew that he had seen the UFO crash. But what if the UFO had only been disabled? What if it succeeded in exiting the area before the military appeared on the scene, and was able to continue its flight before finally coming down on the Berwyn Mountains?

I thought back to what Tony Dodd had been told by James Prescott: 'We, that is my unit, were put on stand-by to move north at short notice. On the night of 19 January 1974, we had moved up towards Birmingham . . .'

Considering Birmingham's close proximity to Cannock Chase, there was a distinct possibility that Prescott's unit was the very same one that Roger Chambers recalled swarming over the Chase.

But what of the deeper, and far more sensational, allegations concerning the alien bodies recovered on the Berwyns? As a retired police sergeant with a quarter of a century of experience in the force, Tony Dodd was without doubt a more-than-credible mouthpiece for the account of James Prescott; and more importantly, Tony had had occasion to view evidence pertaining to Prescott's background in the military. I did not doubt that James Prescott was exactly whom he claimed to be.

As Jenny Randles pointed out, however, Prescott had surfaced at precisely the time that high-level questions were being asked about nuclear accidents within the United Kingdom. Was Prescott's account a subtle ploy by the intelligence community to mask the fact that an atomic weapon of some sort had been dropped inadvertently on the Berwyns?

This was an ingenious theory, but it suffered from one major flaw: it could in no way account for the wealth of additional anomalous phenomena that was in evidence during precisely the same time frame: the many UFOs seen throughout Wales only days before and after the crash; the strange lights and unidentified helicopters reported throughout the Midlands; and the experience of Roger Chambers.

As soundly argued as Jenny's theory was, I leaned towards accepting the extraterrestrial hypothesis. Admittedly, however, there was an abundance of questions still outstanding. From where did the mysterious APEN surface? What was their real role in the case? What happened to the alien bodies recovered on the Berwyns? Were they still at Porton Down? And, most importantly: what of the still-living alien creatures recovered at the site?

Perhaps one day those questions would be answered conclusively. The country-wide UFO encounters of January 1974 were, I concluded, truly earth-shaking.

CHAPTER EIGHT

STUMPED!

ON COMPLETION OF MY ENQUIRIES INTO THE BALA incident of 1974, I sought to determine the full extent to which British authorities were implicated in crashed UFO events that postdated that encounter. In no time at all it became clear to me that, following the Welsh crash, a near impenetrable wall had been constructed to prevent those involved in any successive crash-retrievals from speaking out.

If this had occurred only once or twice, I would have considered it mere coincidence; however, time and again, whenever I tracked down anyone with intimate knowledge of such matters, I was met with silence, obfuscation and, most interestingly of all, an overwhelming degree of fear.

To illustrate, in 1995 I had been given the name of a former soldier who was involved in a second UFO-retrieval operation in Wales – this time in October 1975. The information had been related to me by a retired military source who had served with the soldier in Northern Ireland in the late 1970s. According to this information, the incident centred on the recovery by the British Army of a small, diamond-shaped UFO at Clocaenog Forest.

When I finally had the opportunity to speak with the original source for the story and put to him the allegations I had heard, he gave me a most curious response: 'Look, Mr Redfern, I'm not saying I don't know what you're talking about. But I'm not saying I do either. If you want to know anything, ask the Army. Just don't ask me. I'm sorry to sound rude, but that's all I've got to say.'

Apparently, that was all that anyone had to say on the matter. Despite eventually tracking down three people involved in the recovery operation, I was unable to obtain anything conclusive. The matter remained one of mystery. And this trend continued throughout my investigations into several reported UFO-retrievals that had occurred in the United Kingdom in the late 1970s and early 1980s.

From ex-ATV man Roger Chambers, for example, there was the intriguing possibility that a UFO had been retrieved by the Royal Navy after having crashed into the sea near the Isle of Wight in 1978. As Roger told me, however, the authorities moved swiftly to ensure that the case received no coverage in the media. Similarly, Roger's response when I questioned him about the 'survivors' recovered at the site of the UFO crash at Rendlesham Forest in December 1980 was, 'Don't put my address down; I don't want a bullet in my head.' Roger, though, was not alone in having at his disposal information relating to crash-retrieval operations in the vicinity of RAF Bentwaters.

In 1988 I had periodic contact with Captain John E. Boyle, chief of the Public Affairs Office at RAF Bentwaters. In a letter, he told me that in the late 1960s and early 1970s, the 67th Aerospace Rescue and Recovery Squadron of the US Air Force just happened to be based at RAF Woodbridge (which was twinned with RAF Bentwaters and practically backed on to Rendlesham Forest), and in Captain Boyle's own words, 'provided stand-by rescue coverage for the American space flights'. He continued:

> Of course, they were never needed to provide emergency
> rescue actions, but at the time, the unit was trained and

available to rescue astronauts with their HH-53 and HC-130 aircraft.

In early 1988, the 67 ARRS was redesignated as part of the 39th Special Operations Wing, their primary mission changing from that of rescue to supporting US Special Operations forces. Their secondary mission remains that of search and rescue and they would provide any assistance necessary in future space missions.[1]

In addition, in 1994 it was revealed by now-retired Colonel Charles Halt of the USAF that at the time of the UFO incident at Rendlesham, a Lockheed C-141 Starlifter aircraft was seen to land at the base, and a team of 'special individuals' departed from the aircraft and headed straight into the forest![2]

Was this team of 'special individuals' the same one that was responsible for capturing the surviving crew of the UFO, as recalled by Roger Chambers? And if so, what part was played by the 67th Aerospace Rescue and Recovery Squadron, which was on stand-by to 'rescue astronauts with their HH-53 and HC-130 aircraft'?

I felt it was far too coincidental that the Rendlesham crash and retrieval had occurred in the vicinity of RAF Woodbridge – the very base that was designed to deal with just such an eventuality – and considered a possibility that had not previously been given much thought: perhaps the crash did not occur within the forest after all. Perhaps the craft had been recovered elsewhere by the 67th ARRS and was inadvertently 'dropped' within Rendlesham Forest while being shipped to RAF Woodbridge. This might be considered an extreme scenario, but as *A Covert Agenda* made clear, there was strong evidence to show that only a fraction of the true story surrounding the Rendlesham crash had leaked into the public domain. This case, I concluded, was going to run and run.

My research failed to uncover further significant information concerning crashed-UFO incidents within the UK during the

1980s; come the 1990s, however, the situation changed dramatically. From Jenny Randles I learned of a potentially important case that bore remarkable similarities to the Walthamstow episode of early 1964 involving the bus driver Bob Fall.

It was July 1991, Jenny revealed, and the source, Mr 'M.L.' of Cheadle, Staffordshire, was visiting friends in the area of Churnet Valley, east of Stoke on Trent. At 10 p.m. M.L. saw an unusual object fall from the sky in the Ipstones area. As was the case with Bob Fall in 1964, the object was described as metallic in appearance, rather like aluminium, and was 'ten feet long, cigar-shaped and very bright'. The witness, Jenny added, wasted no time in contacting Cheadle Police.

Come daybreak the police began a search of the vicinity, concentrating on an area of woodland where the object was seen to descend. It was evident that the matter was being treated seriously when a police helicopter was drafted in to lend assistance.

Jenny revealed that no object was ever found, but the police search did locate something of interest – an area of newly broken branches that gave the impression that something had crashed through the trees from above.[3]

For three years following the incident at Ipstones, the UK was apparently free of crash-retrieval operations. At approximately 11 p.m. on 26 September 1994, however, all hell broke loose when an unusual-looking aeroform crash-landed on the runway at the highly sensitive RAF station at Boscombe Down, Wiltshire.

Numerous theories were put forward to explain what had crashed: a UFO, a top-secret 'Stealth' aircraft, or one of the elusive 'flying triangles' that had been seen in abundance in UK skies in the late 1980s and 1990s. Claims and counterclaims abounded.

What was most interesting to me, however, was the location of the crash. RAF Boscombe Down had, I knew, been implicated in the UFO puzzle for more than thirty years. Prior to the publication of *A Covert Agenda*, for example, I had come across the account of Sheila Lamprey of St Austell, Cornwall, who in October 1963 had seen a strange aerial spectacle in the vicinity of Lostwithiel and Liskeard.

In a letter to the Air Ministry, Mrs Lamprey wrote:

I happened to look up and saw some kind of high flying delta wing jet plane, leaving a long vapour trail, and beside it, parallel and travelling at exactly the same speed, some kind of red flying object about quarter the size of the plane . . . it veered suddenly away from the jet, at tremendous speed, sent out two booster flashes and sped even faster away and upwards in an arc. It boosted out two more flashes which gave it more speed upwards and out of my sight.

Please understand, I am not enquiring into any secret flying object. I have never seen anything like this before. It has been on my mind, and I would like some reassurance that you know all about this.

In scanning the Air Ministry's files on Mrs Lamprey's encounter, I noted that one Flight Lieutenant Bardsley had ventured that the sighting was probably connected with activity that originated, intriguingly, with RAF Boscombe Down.

But that was not all. One full month before the Boscombe Down crash, a possibly significant UFO encounter had occurred in the immediate area. The case had been investigated by Paul Fuller, who forwarded details on to me:

On August 14th, at 23.15 BST, two witnesses observed and photographed two 'piercing' white lights low over the northern sky from their home in Southampton. The lights were side-by-side, very close together and about the size of a pentop 3mm in diameter held at arm's length.

For several minutes the lights remained stationary, allowing one of the witnesses to grab his AW818 camera, wait for the flash to warm up, and then take a single photograph as the lights began to move towards his location.

Rather oddly, his camera then jammed and subsequently two of the frames revealed pinpoint damage on the negatives. Over a period of 2 minutes the lights then began to move southwards – away from the Salisbury/Boscombe Down area – and both witnesses observed the 'craft' as it flew directly above their home. The second witness reported seeing an oval-shaped light grey object with six red lights positioned around the perimeter as it passed overhead. Both witnesses heard a 'deep resonating' sound unlike that of an ordinary aircraft.

What makes an unusual case into an important case is that one of the Southampton witnesses underwent pre-pilot training at RAF Cramwell/Cosford flying Bulldogs, a few years previously. During the initial phase of the UFO sighting he attempted to rationalise the lights as those of a hovering Harrier or helicopter. However, this interpretation was ruled out by the object's subsequent appearance and its peculiar noise.

But that was not the only UFO encounter that plagued the area in the weeks leading up to the crash at Boscombe Down. Back in the late 1980s, I had begun subscribing to a publication put out by a newspaper clipping agency, who would forward me up-to-date copies of articles on UFOs culled from all manner of newspapers and magazines throughout the country.

Among the batch of clippings that reached me in late 1994 was one pertaining to an incident that occurred just weeks before the crash, and right on RAF Boscombe Down's doorstep. As the *Salisbury Times* of 23 August 1994 put it:

A green flying saucer hovered beside the A303 at Deptford last week – according to a lorry driver who rushed to Salisbury police station in the early hours of the morning. The man banged on the station door in Wilton Road at 1.30 a.m. on Thursday after spotting the saucer suspended in mid-air. 'He was 100 per cent convinced it was a UFO,' said Inspector Andy Shearing.

The man said it was bright green and shaped like a triangle with rounded edges. It also had green and white flashing lights. Other drivers had seen it and were flashing their car lights at him. A patrol car took the lorry driver back to the spot but there was no trace of the flying saucer. Inspector Shearing said police had been alerted about similar sightings in the same area in the past.

And then there was the crash itself. The first real indications that something truly extraordinary had occurred came from two respected sources: *Air Forces Monthly* magazine and the *Sunday Telegraph*. Based on the information reported by both journals, I was able to construct a picture of the events in question.

At approximately 11 p.m. on 26 September 1994, a small, twin-tailed aeroform crash-landed on the runway at RAF Boscombe Down, whereupon an emergency containment operation was put into place. As luck would have it, at around the time of the crash, a number of aviation enthusiasts in the area had been listening in on 'airband' radios, and were aware that something unusual had occurred.

The following day, several of those same enthusiasts drove to Boscombe Down, whereupon they were quickly apprehended by local police, who had set up roadblocks to keep away prying eyes. Before being ushered away, however, a number succeeded in catching a glimpse of the disabled craft, which was situated at the end of the runway, and, aside from its twin tail fins, was completely covered with tarpaulins. *Air Forces Monthly* continued:

Shortly after the crash an unmarked, civilian registered (CIA operated?) Boeing 737 and a similarly anonymous

DC-8 visited and two days later the wreck was loaded on to a C-5 Galaxy and flown to Air Force plant 42 at Palmdale, California. The secrecy surrounding the incident has led to speculation that the aircraft involved was a TR-3A, the existence of which the US Government has yet to officially acknowledge.

Since the TR-3A was rumoured to be a roughly triangular-shaped craft, there was a strong possibility that it was also a TR-3A that was seen in the early hours of that August morning near the A303, which runs very close to RAF Boscombe Down. However, things were not as cut and dried as they seemed.

George Wingfield, who was educated at Eton College and had worked for the Royal Greenwich Observatory and at IBM UK Ltd, had the following to say on the case:

> If what the lorry driver saw in August was a Black Manta [the nickname supposedly given the TR-3A] it must have a vertical hovering capability similar to the Harrier and also be able to operate silently. Despite much speculation, no one has ever suggested such capabilities for the TR-3A, and at present we can only regard what was seen at Deptford as an 'unidentified flying object'.

I pondered on Wingfield's statement: if the craft seen by the lorry driver on the A303 was something other than the TR-3A (and I could not discount this possibility), then what of the very similar vehicle that crashed at RAF Boscombe Down? Was it an unidentified or an identified flying object?

Working on the possibility that the aeroform could have been an advanced aircraft, Paul Fuller and the two witnesses to the initial encounter of 14 August 1994 made their own enquiries at the Ministry of Defence.

'I have studied your report, and have spoken to our defence advisers and can tell you that there were no unusual radar traces in the Southampton area,' said a Ministry spokes-woman, Kerry Philpott.

Paul considered this a somewhat ambiguous statement and queried Kerry Philpott further. '[R]ather than state that I was unaware of any aircraft that could be responsible for this sight-ing, I said that on speaking to our air defence advisers I ascertained that there were no unusual radar traces in the Southampton area,' Paul was informed.

'Of course,' explained Paul, 'both these replies could be con-strued as an admission that a radar trace was detected, and that that trace represented a known aircraft.'

In a letter to *3rd Stone* magazine, Kerry Philpott wrote:

In response to your enquiry I am not aware of an aircraft crash on Salisbury Plain on the evening of 26th September. However, I am aware of a press report alleg-ing a crash at Boscombe Down airfield on the same evening. Staff at Boscombe Down have confirmed that there was no crash on the 26 September and the only fly-ing which took place out of Boscombe Down that evening was the launch of two Royal Navy Sea King heli-copters in support of an Exercise.

I was eager to see what Paul Fuller would make of this. 'Again,' said Paul, 'even this brush-off could be misleading if the alleged crash actually occurred five minutes into 27 September. Ultimately we are left in an unsatisfactory situation.'

We were indeed. In March 1997, however, a solution was at hand.

Air Forces Monthly, who had been responsible for breaking the story in the first instance, had conducted an in-depth, two-and-a-half-year investigation, and in March 1997 claimed, 'The Boscombe Down incident aircraft is designated ASTRA [which is] an acronym for Advanced Stealth Technology Reconnaissance Aircraft. No doubt most controversial of all, the ASTRA is believed to be the Mach 5+ hypersonic SR-71 replacement most commonly referred to until now as Aurora.'[4]

I saw no reason to doubt what *Air Forces Monthly* had to say: their extensive research had led to the publication of a highly detailed ten-page article on the crash. But there were still questions to be resolved. What was the mystery craft seen hovering near Boscombe Down only weeks before the crash? And what was it that led Police Inspector Andy Shearing to comment that 'police had been alerted about similar sightings in the same area in the past'?

I concluded that even if the object that crashed at Boscombe Down was the ASTRA, there were still far more exotic craft being flown from the base. As with the TR-3A, there was no indication that the ASTRA had the ability to hover in the fashion described by the lorry driver at Salisbury. Beyond any shadow of a doubt, there were bizarre things afoot at RAF Boscombe Down.

My interest in crash-retrieval reports in the 1990s was further piqued when, only a month after the recovery operation at RAF Boscombe Down, yet another mystery device plummeted to earth. This time the location was an isolated field at Hepton Hill, just north of the Cotswolds. I quickly sought out the witnesses.

The date was 31 October 1994, and, according to residents of both Church Lench and Norton, a 'barrel-like object' was seen to descend at speed into the field, which was quickly sealed off by the military – who went on to issue strong warnings to all those who attempted to access the location.

With astonishing haste, the strange object was loaded aboard a Royal Navy lorry, which departed for destinations unknown. Questions had been put to the Royal Air Force and the Fleet Air Arm: both issued a strong denial of any involvement in the crash and subsequent recovery operation.

One witness who was able to confirm the crash, however, was Paul Brooke of Norton, who likened the object to a 'forty-gallon drum'.

'There were several fire engines and lots of police there,' recalled Brooke. 'The area was cordoned off and people were stopped from entering the field. Then at about eight that night [the object] was taken away by a Royal Navy vehicle with a police escort at the front and back.'

But perhaps the most significant (not to mention carefully phrased) statement came from Inspector Mike Rowlands of Eversham Police:

> I can't categorically say that it did not happen, but my investigations have revealed that it was a bale of straw that was on fire and which was put out by the fire brigade. The reports of something falling from the sky may either be hoaxes or somebody may have seen something and come to the wrong conclusion.

'Do they think we are mad around here?' countered Paul Brooke.

Needless to say, the case died a quick death as far as the media were concerned, and on my one visit to the area in 1995, I was able to add little more to the basic facts. The incident was shrouded in secrecy. The arrival on the scene of the military, however, was enough to convince me that whatever was found within that field back in October 1994 was far more than a mere bale of straw! Either that or, with the Cold War at an end, the military had been assigned some very odd tasks![5]

In late 1996 a case surfaced that contained all the ingredients I had been searching for: credible witnesses who were willing to speak on the record; confirmation from officialdom that something unusual had taken place; hard-to-deny evidence of strange, aerial activity in UK airspace; and a massive military operation designed to seek out and recover a mystery object that had impacted off the coast of Scotland.

It was early October when the first ripples of something

bizarre began to appear. Those same ripples, however, were to remain with me throughout the month.

As was often the case when important UFO sightings occurred (particularly those in which the military was implicated), people who had seen my name referenced in books and magazines would telephone me with the details; and by utilising such a network, I generally got to hear of any new and important cases practically immediately.

Therefore, when on 7 October I was informed that a major UFO incident involving the RAF had occurred in East Anglia, I made it my business to look into what had taken place.

The next day I had in my possession a copy of an official transcript of fascinating conversations involving Royal Air Force personnel at RAF Neatishead, Norfolk, and RAF Kinloss, Scotland, the civilian police at Skegness, the coastguard at Yarmouth and the crew of a North Sea tanker. The conversations had taken place in the early hours of 5 October and, as the transcript showed, dramatic events were unfolding.

0314 Skegness police: 'We can see a strange red-and-green rotating light in the sky directly south-east from Skegness. It looks strange as it is stationary and there is no aircraft sound in the area.'

0326 RAF Kinloss: 'Northwood have a radar contact bearing 221 degrees at 16 miles. It looks to be stationary and there is no way of determining its height but it must be quite a size to be visible from Skegness.'

0331 RAF Kinloss: 'Neatishead now confirms a couple of radar contacts in the area but no height; they seem to be stationary. There are definitely no military aircraft in the area and no notified civil flights should be there.'

0346 Conocoast Tanker: 'We have these lights on visual. Now they are flashing red, green and white. Cannot identify it as an aircraft as it looks stationary and it is approximately one mile high.'

Yarmouth Coastguard: 'Did you see from which direction it appeared?'

Conocoast Tanker: 'No. It just appeared and is stationary.'

0353 RAF Kinloss: 'Neatishead say it could be caused by the weather.'

Conocoast Tanker: 'I don't think so as we have visual contact.'

RAF Kinloss: 'Well, Neatishead and Northwood report that there is no transponder on this object and therefore no means of interrogation. It is obvious that whatever it is it does not want anyone to know that it is there. Also Neatishead report its position as directly over Boston.'

0408 Conocoast Tanker: 'It is still stationary and flashing red, green, blue and white. It looks very high, north of us, and there is no engine noise.'

0417 Yarmouth Coastguard: 'Skegness, can you get video footage as the RAF are very interested and may require it later.'

0427 RAF Kinloss: 'Neatishead are keeping a log of what looks like clutter on the radar.'

0445 Yarmouth Coastguard: 'Conocoast, can you give us an update?'

Conocoast Tanker: 'We can see two lights flashing green and red.'

0501 Yarmouth Coastguard: 'Give us both bearings of the two lights.'

Conocoast Tanker: 'There is one stationary light at 345 deg true and the other at 160 true. The lights are both visible with the naked eye and both exhibit the same characteristics flashing red, blue, green and white.'

0517 Boston Police: 'We can still see the light. It is towards the south-east and seems about 40–45 degrees in the sky. It is just a bright light to us.'

0521 RAF Kinloss: 'Neatishead are running a trace on this and cannot explain it. If they are helicopters they are fast approaching the end of their endurance as it is well over two hours since the first report let alone how long they were up there before they were actually sighted.'

0552 Conocoast Tanker: 'We can still see the lights, and they are on their original bearings and flashing the same colours but they seem higher and dimmer.'

0708 RAF Neatishead: 'We had a report from Northwood that a civil flight had also reported strange lights in the area. They fit exactly what was seen from the ground, multi-coloured, flashing, stationary lights.'

0731 RAF Northwood: 'This echo is still on our screens and we cannot explain this at all apart from it being a meteorological phenomenon but then again we have visual sightings also. The civilian flight that reported these lights as a flare was six miles away at the time. All very strange.'

1109 RAF Neatishead: 'The object still has not moved. London radar and Waddington can also see it.'

1920 Anglia Radar: 'There is nothing there now. We are of the opinion that it was the Boston Stump.'

Needless to say, the official release of this fascinating exchange was an unprecedented event, and the case received extensive media coverage.

'We are trying to prove that it does not represent any sort of security threat and that it was not an aggressive intrusion into our airspace,' said a Ministry of Defence spokesman, Nigel Sergeant. 'This is one of the bigger sightings recently and has caused quite a bit of interest.'

Sergeant was not wrong. In the days following the encounter, both the MOD and the RAF were deluged with enquiries from the press.

'We have not been able to offer an explanation,' said Flight Lieutenant Keith Sweatman of RAF Neatishead. 'The number of independent reports we have had suggest there is something to follow up. We will be investigating thoroughly.'

I followed the debate closely, and was most intrigued (and somewhat puzzled) to see that within seventy-two hours a solution to the encounter was in hand.

'We now know', began Flight Lieutenant Sweatman, 'that the radar trace was Boston Stump – the church tower at Boston. And the weather people said that the coloured lights in the sky coincided with an electrical storm over the Wash.

'You do get weird experiences with electrical storms, and they can produce lots of different colours.'

There was no doubt in my mind that Sweatman's view was expressed sincerely. I well recall, at the height of the controversy, a lengthy conversation that my colleague Irene Bott had with Keith Sweatman and the impression I gained was of someone who appreciated the complexities of the case and who did his utmost to come up with a satisfactory explanation. I was not convinced, however, that the official explanation was the correct one.

First, the visual encounters reported by the crew of the *Conocoast* were not isolated. Oddly, however, very little media attention was given to the additional reports, several of which negated the theory that the unexplained lights were the result of an electrical storm.

Of those reports, one that impressed me was that of Dorothy Hinchcliffe of Skegness: 'I was lying in bed looking out of the window and saw a very, very bright, sharp light going at quite a speed towards Gibraltar Point.

'It was about three a.m. I saw this thing steaming along. It was too bright to be an airplane. It had a very bright light which streamed along so smoothly. You just don't know what's out there.'

Yet another report filed on the same evening as that of the *Conocoast* came from a very credible source: the police at Addlethorpe. I chased down the facts. According to Police Sergeant Mick Slowey, a report had been received from one of their officers who was on patrol at Addlethorpe at the time and had seen 'a red boomerang-shaped object with a green light over the top of it, which seemed to be out at sea'. Sergeant Slowey concluded:

> There was obviously something there, but no one seems to know what it was. For it to be there for so long is very strange. I like to keep an open mind about things, and personally, I don't think the MOD will be able to find a rational explanation for it. I live right near the sea, actually, so I wish I'd seen it myself!

There was also the account of the Barton family, who were on a boating holiday at Burgh Castle on the Norfolk Broads. At 6.30 a.m. on 5 October both Mr Barton and his son noticed two 'white, cigar-shaped objects which stood motionless in the sky' and which remained there for a considerable time.

I was as certain as I could be that, despite the RAF's assertion that the strange lights were due to natural weather phenomena, that theory could in no way account for the seemingly structured object viewed by police at Addlethorpe. And what of the Boston Stump?

When I first heard that the RAF had made a determination that the unusual radar plots had been put down to the Boston Stump, my first question was what the hell is the Boston Stump?

As Keith Sweatman had noted, the Stump is a two hundred-foot-tall church tower which overlooks the town of Boston, Lincolnshire; and as Nick Pope noted, 'Under certain meteorological conditions, radar systems can pick up very tall objects around some radar heads.'

Nick was keen to point out, however, that:

Radar operators are very familiar with this phenomenon. In other words, if this was the explanation, it would surely have been suggested immediately.

The biggest problem with this explanation is that it fails to take account of the fact that the object was seen by dozens of police at Skegness and Boston, the crew of the *Conocoast*, and the civil aircraft. And to the best of my knowledge, church towers don't fly a mile into the sky and start flashing!

Nick had hit on the major flaw in the RAF's explanation: everyone in the vicinity, even the military, was well acquainted with the Stump – when I passed through Boston on my way to interview the ex-ATV man Roger Chambers in 1996, I could not fail to see it looming over the town. If the Stump was responsible for the radar returns, why did it take a full three days before anyone in officialdom came up with the answer? Could someone not have made such a determination at the time the events were occurring? As was the case with many of my research associates, I was far from happy with the explanations of the military.

I was amused to see that the locals, too, were far from convinced by what the RAF and the Ministry of Defence were alleging.

'It seems that the Boston church known as "The Stump" is not on dry land after all,' wrote one reader of the *Eastern Daily Press*. 'In fact, it is situated somewhere in the North Sea, or the Wash, or the North Norfolk coast, or at Yarmouth, or even floating in the sky miraculously above the A47 in Norfolk.'

I was convinced that behind closed doors the military was cringing quietly. But what was it that convinced me that the

Norfolk encounters were connected with a crash-retrieval operation?

Although the sightings reported by the RAF, the police at Addlethorpe, the crew of the *Conocoast* and various members of the public took centre stage as far as the media were concerned, an important factor was missed by practically all those who looked into the controversy: the encounters of 5 October 1996 in Norfolk were not isolated.

Only one week previously, a UFO 'triangular [shaped] and orange in colour' was seen over Walthamstow; and also in that week, at least two people had reported unidentified aerial activity in the Metheringham area of Lincolnshire.

'It was pouring with rain and just after midnight,' said one of the witnesses. 'All of a sudden there was this bright white round light which hovered over the car. When I stopped the car it disappeared.'

But it was in the period 25–26 October 1996 that things really began to hot up. At approximately 4.50 p.m. on 25 October, a security engineer, James Mason, was driving in the vicinity of Kings Lynn when his attention was drawn to a 'blue light' that appeared in his rear-view mirror. Thinking that he was being flagged down by a police car, Mason pulled his car over to the side of the road and got out. He initially thought that the light had vanished:

> My car lights went off and on again. I looked up and realised this light had gone overhead, and was about two hundred yards in front of me and about one hundred feet in the air. It wasn't flashing; it was spinning. It looked like a Catherine wheel. I was so freaked out I turned back and came back on a different road, and then went down Bethel Street Police Station to report it.

Three days after James Mason's encounter at Kings Lynn, I received a veritable deluge of telephone calls, all pertaining to a series of events that had occurred over the course of the preceding forty-eight hours on the Isle of Lewis off the northwest coast of Scotland. The callers were unanimous: some form of airborne object had exploded over the Outer Hebrides. Witnesses spoke of seeing unusual aerial activity, and the military had organised a hasty operation to recover 'something' from the harsh Highland seas.

As was the case in February 1964 and January 1974, a wave of country-wide UFO encounters had been followed by the crash (and possible retrieval by the military) of an unknown object. There was no time to waste. I plunged headlong into the heart of the mystery.

It was clear from studying the evidence that something of major importance had occurred: from approximately 4 p.m. onwards on 26 October 1996, the Isle of Lewis had been well and truly flung into the crashed-UFO controversy.

'At first,' said Norman Macdonald, a fifty-seven-year-old joinery contractor at the Port of Ness, 'I thought it was a firework. Then I saw three flashes and heard two further bangs. I rushed into a local shop and took the staff and customers outside. They also saw the dense smoke spiral. That was about four-ten p.m.'

Over the course of the following few hours, both the Royal Air Force and the local police received numerous telephone calls from anxious Lewis residents, all of whom had either witnessed an aerial explosion or had seen peculiar flashes of light followed by debris plunging into the sea. The response of officialdom was immediate.

On learning that the military had taken steps to identify the source of the mystery explosion, I fully expected that some form of search-and-rescue operation would have been put into place. However, I was totally unprepared for the sheer scale of that operation. Someone, somewhere, was anxious to know what it was that had come down in the Outer Hebrides.

As I sought to determine fully what had taken place, I spoke with numerous official sources: the Ministry of Defence Press Office, the early-warning station at RAF Fylingdales, the coastguard, the police and a variety of media contacts. It was clear that a major incident had occurred.

The coastguard confirmed the many reports of strange aerial lights and, more interestingly, the presence of an aerial 'smoke trail' near the Isle of Lewis at the time of the explosion some ten miles long. The military, however, provided a more remarkable revelation.

In speaking with both the MOD and the RAF I was amazed to learn that a massive operation had been coordinated to deal with the encounter. In a search that cost no less than £200,000 and covered an area of some 300 square miles, an armada of ships and numerous aircraft were dispatched to the scene with the utmost haste: an RAF Nimrod aircraft packed with sophisticated detection equipment scoured the vicinity for no less than ten hours on two sorties; the coastguard helicopter from Stornoway flew two four-and-a-half-hour operations; a Royal Air Force helicopter from RAF Lossiemouth conducted an intensive search; and a flotilla of ships and boats, including the Stornoway-based tug the *Portosalvo*, numerous lifeboats from Lochinver, and a variety of fishing boats also lent assistance to the military. In addition, both the coastguard and the police mounted shore patrols in Ness, on the Butt of Lewis. Officially, nothing was found . . .

Was it possible, I wondered, that decaying space debris was responsible for the strange lights and the subsequent aerial explosion at the Isle of Lewis? A quick telephone conversation with RAF Fylingdales put paid to that theory: there was no possibility that a satellite or rocket in Earth orbit had re-entered the atmosphere in the vicinity of the Outer Hebrides, I was informed.

What of the possibility that a meteorite was the culprit? Simon Riley, District Staff Officer for Stornoway Coastguard, said that while meteorite activity was not out of the question, 'we have also not ruled out space debris'. He elaborated: 'Part of the problem has been to get a fix on where this accident happened. All the people involved in the search have worked very hard, some around the clock, and extensive enquiries have been made but nothing has been found to give a positive explanation. It is very puzzling.'

The Northern Police Constabulary was equally baffled: 'Officers were busily involved in the investigation. But it's a real mystery. It's very, very odd.'

Only days after the attempted 'recovery' operation occurred, I was forwarded a stash of material concerning an official inquiry into the Isle of Lewis events by none other than the Sandia National Laboratories in New Mexico, USA.

Sandia's interest ran deep (staff there even contacted the Armagh Observatory in Northern Ireland for assistance), and appeared to centre on ascertaining the time at which the incident occurred. The Ministry of Defence man Nick Pope, who had taken a deep interest in the Outer Hebrides encounters, gave me some information about Sandia: 'The facility operates spy satellites, and their line of enquiry strongly suggested that they were trying to search back through spy satellite imagery to see whether the UFO had been captured on film.'

What Nick did not state, however, and which I knew full well, was that Sandia had a long history of involvement in the UFO subject in general, and in the crashed-UFO issue in particular. There were the many rumours surrounding the crash and retrieval of a UFO at the El Indio–Guerrero area on the border of Texas and Mexico on 6 December 1950. In *The FBI Files*, I had revealed that on precisely that date, the Bureau had gone on full alert on a matter that was definitely UFO-related; and in addition to that, there was a reference to both Sandia and the El Indio UFO retrieval in a classified UFO document made available to the investigator and nuclear physicist Stanton T. Friedman:

> On 6 December, 1950, a second object, probably of similar origin, impacted the earth at high speed in the El Indio–Guerrero area of the Texas–Mexican border after following a long trajectory through the atmosphere. By

the time a search team arrived, what remained of the object had been almost totally incinerated. Such material as could be recovered was transported to the A.E.C. facility at Sandia, New Mexico, for study.

I had also been able to secure via the US Freedom of Information Act a fascinating document dating from 1980 that, once again, implicated the Sandia National Laboratory in the UFO controversy. Pertinent sections of the document read:

On 11 Aug 80, Russ Curtis, Sandia Security, advised that on 9 Aug 80, a Sandia Security Guard related the following: At approximately 0020hrs, he was driving East on the Coyote Canyon access road on a routine building check of an alarmed structure. As he approached the structure he observed a bright light near the ground behind the structure. He also observed an object he first thought was a helicopter. But after driving closer, he observed a round disk-shaped object. He attempted to radio for a backup patrol but his radio would not work. As he approached the object on foot armed with a shotgun, the object took off in a vertical direction at a high rate of speed.

In view of the above, Sandia's interest in the Isle of Lewis crash was of great interest to me, particularly when only days later a large-scale military exercise began just off the coast of Scotland and relatively close to where the mystery object was seen to crash. For me, this was too coincidental.

Nick Pope, also, recognised the significance. Commenting on the crash report and the subsequent military manoeuvres (which involved no fewer than thirty-two warships, seven submarines and eighty aircraft), Nick stated at the time, 'Rumours began to circulate that the whole incident might centre on the crash and subsequent recovery of a top-secret prototype aircraft or unmanned aerial vehicle such as the rumoured Aurora or HALO.'

This was the second occasion on which the Aurora (supposedly at the cutting edge of US aviation technology) was rumoured to have crashed within the confines of the UK; however, the Isle of Lewis incident followed directly on from the huge wave of UFO sightings around the country that essentially began with the infamous episode of the Boston Stump.

Could the Aurora have been responsible for all of those many and varied UFO encounters that occurred throughout

From: Andrew Bates, Secretariat (Air Staff)1a
MINISTRY OF DEFENCE
Rm 7249, Main Building, Whitehall, London SW1A 2HB

Telephone (Direct dial)   0171 218 6437
(Switchboard)   0171 218 9000
(Fax)   0171 218 2680

Mr J Dillon

Your reference

Our reference
D/Sec(AS)57/3
Date
18 November 1996

Dear Mr Dillon,

 Thank you for your letter to the my colleague Miss Philpott, about the reported incident in the vicinity of the Western Isles on 26 October. As the Section within Secretariat(Air Staff) that deals with Flight Safety and Search and Rescue (SAR) issues, your letter has been passed to this office and I have been asked to reply.

 As you are aware, following reports to the authorities of an alleged explosion in the air, an extensive search of the area was carried out by the RAF and the Coastguard SAR. This search was later called off after it became clear that no aircraft had been reported overdue.

 With regards to your request for information, Sec(AS)'s involvement in this incident only concerned the deployment during the search phase of military SAR assets and we have no evidence to support any of the media theories about the cause of the incident.

 I hope that this outlines the position.

Yours sincerely,

Bates

In 1996, the Ministry of Defence denied that a UFO had impacted off the coast of Scotland on 26 October of that year.

October 1996? I considered it highly unlikely. But if not Aurora, then what?

Contrary to what was being admitted officially, information given to *UFO* magazine suggested that some form of object was, after all, located during the huge search-and-rescue operation. The recovery occurred at approximately 8 a.m. on 27 October when the crew of an RAF Nimrod aircraft (callsign Rescue 11) reported to RAF Kinloss that a positive sighting of something had been made. Quite what that 'something' was has never been made public. The military was unswerving: 'Nothing was found; the entire incident remains a mystery.' Perhaps they should have admitted to being 'stumped' . . . [6]

CHAPTER NINE

THE KEEPERS OF THE SECRET

WHEN SPEAKING WITH FELLOW UFO INVESTIGATORS, I WAS
often told that the accounts of retrieved UFOs and dead alien
bodies held by British authorities simply could not be true.
Why? More often than not I was told that it would be nigh-on
impossible to keep concealed matters of such extraordinary
magnitude. The secret would inevitably leak out.

Aside from the fact that such 'secrets' *had* leaked out (and
are herein contained!), those making such pronouncements
had simply not seized the opportunity to acquaint themselves
fully with the evidence.

Time again I had argued with colleagues that if anyone
wished to make a definitive statement about the British
Government's involvement in the UFO puzzle, they simply
could not do so from the comfort of their front room. It was
vital to go out into the real world and acquaint oneself with the
various official departments that were involved in investigating
UFO sightings and encounters; it was important to understand the workings of the defence and intelligence communities; and, most crucially, I would tell associates: 'Get down to
the Public Record Office and see for yourselves the official files
on the subject that are now coming to light. But more importantly, take a look at the vast amount of data stored there to

which we aren't being given access! Have you ever stopped to consider what the material might tell us?'

Despite my attempts to spur on people, however, I found that the number of UFO investigators who had delved deeply into the world of the British Government's involvement in the UFO subject was depressingly small. Certainly there were respected researchers such as Tim Good, Graham Birdsall and Jenny Randles, who had spent time trying to determine the extent to which British authorities were implicated in the issue of unidentified flying objects, but most colleagues remained woefully ignorant of the evidence. And, oddly enough, several other acquaintances who claimed to have unearthed vital information that could have furthered our cause steadfastly refused to make it publicly available. I thought to myself, Small wonder that the veil of secrecy surrounding the subject has remained practically intact for almost half a century!

Paradoxically, however, this tended to work in my favour: from my point of view, if I was going to access the true facts surrounding the British Government's knowledge of crashed-UFO incidents, it was far better to do so in an environment where I could work quietly and carefully. More importantly, it made the possibility that my activities would become a matter of official record less likely! At this stage in my investigations, the last thing I wanted was for the doors of secrecy to become firmly closed to me.

I felt that I had secured enough data to support my notion that a number of UFOs had crashed on UK soil and had been retrieved under cover of the utmost secrecy. I now had to determine (a) who was responsible for keeping this information under wraps; and (b) where the debris and bodies were being stored. I would start with the 'who' and take my lead from the United States . . .

As I knew from my research for *The FBI Files*, official interest in the UFO subject on the part of the US Government and military dated back to at least the late 1940s. The US Air Force, for example, had initiated three investigative projects:

Sign, Grudge and Blue Book. The Air Force's findings were clear, as Captain John E. Boyle, chief of the Public Affairs Office, USAF, told me in 1988:

> The US Air Force did investigate UFO sightings from 1947 to 1969. During that time, over 12,500 reported sightings were investigated; the vast majority, about 95 per cent, were explainable. They were caused by such natural phenomena as meteors, satellites, aircraft, lightning, balloons, weather conditions, reflections of other planets, or just plain hoaxes. Of the very few that remained unidentified, there was no indication of a technology beyond our own scientific knowledge, or that any sighting could be considered an extraterrestrial vehicle. Most importantly, throughout Project Blue Book, there was never a shred of evidence to indicate a threat to our national security.[1]

As impressive as this statement sounded, however, I knew it could not be considered the final word on the subject. Aside from the astonishing fact that in 1969 one Brigadier Bolender wrote in an official Air Force memorandum, '[R]eports of unidentified flying objects which could affect the national security are not part of the Blue Book system', documentation released under the terms of the American Freedom of Information Act proved conclusively that the US Air Force was not alone in collecting and investigating UFO data.

By the time I wrote *The FBI Files*, literally thousands of pages of once classified UFO material had been released into the public domain by a host of official agencies, including the CIA, the FBI, the Atomic Energy Commission, the National Security Agency, the Defense Intelligence Agency, the Department of State, and the intelligence arms of the Army and Navy.

And as that mass of evidence showed, many of the investigations undertaken by the above agencies were carried out under cover of overwhelming secrecy and without the knowledge of those Air Force projects: Blue Book, Grudge and Sign! The CIA's files, for example, showed that the Agency was monitoring UFO activity on a worldwide scale; documentation declassified by the Defense Intelligence Agency told of attempts by military pilots to blast UFOs out of the skies; the National Security Agency's papers warned of the potential threat posed by alien civilisations; and the FBI went as far as to monitor members of the US public who claimed contact with extraterrestrial creatures. In other words, the Air Force's statement, which had previously been considered final, had been invalidated. As the investigator Stanton Friedman put it, 'Everybody and his brother was in the UFO data-collection business!'

However, as thorough as the intelligence-gathering techniques of the FBI, DIA and NSA were, tantalising rumours suggested that hidden deep within the US intelligence community there existed a high-powered group that was strongly implicated in UFO investigations, and to which even agencies such as the FBI and the NSA were denied access. That group came to be known as the Majestic 12 or MJ-12 – a select body comprising (among others) the first four Directors of Central Intelligence, the first US Secretary of Defense and a number of leading American scientists.

Stanton Friedman and other researchers, such as William Moore, Jaime Shandera and Tim Good, had all undertaken outstanding research to try to crack the secrets of Majestic 12 – secrets that appeared to centre on the retrieval, containment and analysis of an alien spacecraft and bodies found in the Roswell, New Mexico, area in July 1947.

Shandera and Good had both received copies of seemingly official papers (though they were later pronounced bogus in some quarters) referencing the establishment of a covert investigative body shortly after the Roswell crash; Moore had received coded messages from insider sources that ultimately led both him and Shandera to locate in the National Archives an officially released document that referred to Majestic 12;

and Friedman, who could be considered the key investigator of Majestic 12, had visited numerous government archives and interviewed a wealth of official sources. Friedman's conclusion? UFOs were real. Majestic 12 was real. And the Roswell crash was real.[2]

In addition to the research of the civilian UFO community, in late 1988 even the FBI got into the act. In *The FBI Files*, I revealed that Bureau agents had taken a keen interest in both the Roswell event and the Majestic 12 group, but their efforts were ultimately thwarted by the barriers of secrecy. Referring to the Majestic 12 papers released to Tim Good and Jaime Shandera, the Bureau commented, 'We've gone knocking on every door in Washington with those MJ-12 papers. All we're finding out is that the Government doesn't know what it knows. There are too many secret levels. You can't get a straight story. It wouldn't surprise me if we never knew if the papers were genuine or not.' I knew precisely how that FBI agent felt . . .[3]

Reviewing the information that had been collated on Majestic 12 by Friedman, Moore, Shandera and Good, I noticed how eerily it paralleled my own research here in the United Kingdom. The US Air Force's official position was that extraterrestrial spacecraft were not visiting the Earth; and yet buried incredibly deep within the American intelligence community was the immensely powerful Majestic 12 group, which was withholding from the public, the media and the scientific community prime evidence of UFO reality: the long-deceased alien bodies and wrecked spacecraft recovered at Roswell way back in the 1940s.

Likewise, the official stance of Britain's Ministry of Defence on UFOs read very much like that of the US Air Force:

The MOD and HM Forces are concerned with the security of this country, and we look at reports of unexplained aerial observations solely to establish if there is any evidence which would suggest that the UK's air defences have been compromised in any way, or whether some form of physical threat is perceived to exist. If we are satisfied that there is no evidence which indicates the existence of a threat we make no attempt to investigate further or involve ourselves in establishing the precise nature of the sighting/phenomena. I should say, however, that to date it remains the case that we have no evidence to suggest that any threat has been posed to the security of this country by 'UFOs'. We accept that there will always be some sightings that appear to defy explanation, and we are open-minded on these as essentially it is outside our remit to investigate further.

As straightforward as the MOD's position seemed, it could not account in any way, shape or form for the many accounts I had received relating to UFO-crash incidents in the United Kingdom.

The conclusion was inescapable: somewhere within the UK there existed an equivalent of the United States' Majestic 12. Then there was the daunting question of where to look: the intelligence agencies MI5, MI6 and the Government Communications Headquarters at Cheltenham? The Army? The Navy? The Air Force? The Ministry of Defence? The Home Office? The list seemed endless. Nevertheless, I had to start somewhere.

If there was a British equivalent of Majestic 12, or 'MJ-UK' as I dubbed it, I reasoned that in all probability the group (a) liaised to some degree with its American counterpart on matters of common concern; and (b) could be staffed only by 'the elite of the elite'. My first move was to speak with the man who for three years investigated UFO encounters for the MOD's Secretariat of the Air Staff: Nick Pope.

In a London wine bar in early 1997, I came clean with Nick: I accepted that during his term with Sec(AS)2A he did indeed get to see a wealth of UFO data, largely submitted by members of the general public (but occasionally by military sources, too); however, based on the evidence presented in *A Covert Agenda*, I could not accept that he saw all of the truly outstanding material. Somewhere in the UK, I explained, it was my belief that there was a whole 'museum' of UFO artefacts, debris, alien bodies, and perhaps even relatively intact space vehicles stored far away from prying eyes.

With my cards on the table, Nick and I discussed the controversy: Roswell, Majestic 12, UFO-crash reports in the UK, and a bewildering number of claims of conspiracy and cover-up. Of extreme interest to me were Nick's opinions on the incident at Roswell in July 1947. Did he subscribe to the theory that what was recovered was an extraterrestrial vehicle? He would not commit himself.

As far as Roswell is concerned, I would describe myself as on the fence. My views on this keep changing, I must admit. I'm not one of these people who have a fixed, definite view and sticks to that, no matter what. A year ago, I was probably 80 per cent-plus convinced that the Roswell incident did happen, and did involve the crash of an extraterrestrial spacecraft. And I based that primarily upon the testimony of Jesse Marcel.

It seems nonsensical to me that people of his calibre would mistake something truly exotic for a weather balloon, when by the very nature of who they were, they operated weather balloons and saw them on a daily basis.

But now, I'm having a few doubts about Roswell. Let's say our RAF, in an overseas exercise, lost an aircraft in a crash over an undiscovered part of Papua New Guinea. We wouldn't simply leave the plane there: we'd go in and get it back; we'd need to do all sorts of tests to see why the plane crashed.

But the problem I have with Roswell is I'm having doubts that a crash would occur and the aliens, if indeed the object was alien, would simply let the wreckage lay strewn across the desert for us to recover. But maybe the story's more complicated. It's so difficult to say.

'I know you're aware of all the controversy surrounding Majestic 12,' I said to Nick. 'What are your opinions? Do you feel that there is such a group in the United States that has overall control on issues such as Roswell?'

Difficult to say. If Roswell did involve a genuine crash of an extraterrestrial craft, then it's certainly likely that a study group would have been set up, and Majestic 12 is as likely or unlikely a name as anything else. Now, I've never seen any official documents with Majestic 12 written on them; and I've never come across any domestic UK interest in anything called Majestic 12 or remotely similar.

However, access to what the Americans were, and are, up to is incredibly difficult. I'll give you an example . . . When I was with the Secretariat of the Air Staff, I was aware that so many of the good-quality cases had taken place in the States, and because I wanted to tap into the expertise of the Americans, I attempted to make contact with my opposite number. This was fairly early in my posting.

I approached the American Embassy in London and asked to be put in touch. They drew a blank, and said, 'Sorry, since the Blue Book was closed down in '69, we don't do this any more. Maybe one or two things go on at a local level involving the public relations staff on a US air base, but there's no governmental involvement on this.'

I'll be honest with you, I didn't like that answer and . . . I won't say I didn't believe it, but I was a little sceptical. So I tried again. This time I tried the British Embassy in Washington, who again drew a blank. Same answer. Now, a few months later, I was on a course in London, and I ran across a US Marine colonel. He said that he couldn't believe there wasn't some sort of study group. He said,

'Leave it to me. I'll find out who it is you need to talk to.' A few weeks later, I got a call from this guy. His reply was, 'Gee, I've looked long and hard, but I've drawn a blank.'

'Do you feel', I asked Nick, 'that the reason you were unable to turn up anything substantial relative to ongoing US involvement in the UFO subject was because, quite simply, there was no involvement, or was it because you were specifically being denied access to a Majestic 12-type group?'

Nick thought for a moment:

If the Americans do have a covert involvement, a Majestic 12 group which is conducting research and investigations, then for me not to get access, it must be wrapped up pretty tight.

There is evidence, of course, that the Americans are far more involved in this – to this day. The whole business of documents on UFOs, wholly or partially withheld under the Freedom of Information Act, is an important part of coming to that conclusion. There is evidence that we've not been told the whole story. Quite why that is, I don't know. Quite why the British aren't briefed, I don't know. But somebody once asked me why the Americans would keep us in the dark, given that we're both in NATO and have a special relationship, and I said, 'Well, that's easy; I'll give you several reasons: Burgess, Philby, Maclean and Blunt!'

'Technically,' I put it to Nick, 'if there is a Majestic 12 group, would it not be a breach of law not to inform you of the facts, given the Anglo-American relationship?'

That's an interesting point. You'd have to ask a lawyer; however, I suspect that I'd have to look at the wording of the replies I got from the Americans. From my knowledge of the way bureaucracies work, you never say 'never'. You have to look incredibly carefully at the way something is phrased. In the parliamentary questions in *Hansard*, for example, you'll see phrases like 'We are aware of no such approach' rather than 'There has been no such approach.'

'But would it be fair to say that you weren't satisfied with the replies you got from the US Government?' I asked.

'No, I wasn't satisfied, but there were only so many hours in the day and there were only so many doors I could knock on.'

'You say you weren't satisfied. Do you believe that what you were being denied access to was evidence of extraterrestrial reality?' I pressed.

I think we have an extraterrestrial presence. But sometimes I wonder if that's what the Americans are really covering up. They may simply be covering up their embarrassing lack of knowledge. If structured craft of unknown origin are routinely penetrating very heavily defended airspace, who do you say it is? You can't say it's the Russians because you don't want to admit that they're more advanced than you; and you can't say it's extraterrestrial. So, maybe you just state the party line. The bottom line may be that they genuinely don't know.

I'll say this, however: I'm sure that within America there are people at an official level who at the very least suspect strongly that there is an extraterrestrial presence here. Whether there are people who are covering this up or not, I'm not sure.

Since Nick had been in the employ of the Ministry of Defence since 1985, I wanted his opinion on whether a secret of the magnitude of that allegedly held by Majestic 12 could be concealed effectively for decades.

Difficult but not impossible. Nothing's ever impossible if you keep the numbers of those in the know small enough, and if you have a big enough incentive for keeping it secret.

The counter-argument is, of course, that the atomic bomb was, one would think, the most important secret of the late 1940s, but the Soviets got that one within a few years. The difference is that that was the result of targeted intelligence. The Soviets knew the Americans had the atomic bomb; they had a particular goal in mind. If the Soviets didn't know there had been a crash of an extraterrestrial spacecraft, if they weren't aware of anything other than someone had made a mistake and it was just a weather balloon, there would have been no targeted intelligence. You can argue yourself round in circles on this.

I then steered the conversation round to the most important issue, at least from my point of view:

Nick, you've related to me your attempts to liaise with US counterparts on the UFO subject; you maintain to this day that you weren't satisfied with the replies you received from the Americans; and you've given sound reasons why the existence of a Majestic 12-type organisation in the US cannot be ruled out. Is it not possible that somewhere within the UK there is a British equivalent of Majestic 12, and the division in which you worked was specifically denied access to the really important evidence: the retrieved craft, the bodies, the debris and so on?'

A wide grin came over Nick's face:

I've been asked this before, and I always come back to the same point: I served three years in Secretariat Air Staff, and I was dealing with the most important data of all – the witnesses telling me their stories. I think in three years, if there had been someone standing unseen behind me doing something like my job, I would have got a whiff of something; I would have got a few hints here and there. The fact that I didn't leads me to suggest that all this business about men in black, secret covert departments, is just a mixture of conspiratorial nonsense and urban myth.

I do not believe there is any evidence to support the crash of any extraterrestrial craft in Britain. I have not seen it, put it like that. If people want to put documents before me and suggest that I talk to witnesses, then I'm happy to do so. But all I can say to you, now, is that to date I have seen no evidence to support these UK crash theories.

My view is that if there has ever been the crash of an extraterrestrial craft, then Roswell is it. I've yet to see any convincing evidence other than Roswell.

Had I perhaps presented Nick with the material I had been able to obtain pertaining to UFO crashes on mainland UK, his position might have altered somewhat. But, at that juncture, I considered it best to remain relatively tight-lipped. I was at a crucial stage in my investigations and could not afford to jeopardise matters by 'spilling the beans' too soon. However, I still had several questions for Nick . . .

In 1996 his book, *Open Skies, Closed Minds*, was released amid a wave of media publicity, and I was interested to know what the reaction was to its publication and to Nick himself.

As far as the UFO lobby is concerned, some of them have seen me as the messiah who's going to lead them to the promised land; some of them have perceived me as the 'cigarette-smoking man' from *The X-Files*; some of them have seen me as some upstart who has simply cashed in on the job that I did to make a fast buck; and I think some people in UFO research see me as some Johnny-come-lately who just swanned into the Top Ten! It's fair to say that there has been a bit of jealousy. It simply depends on whom you ask. But my postbag is almost completely in favour.

I'm not in this for approval. I'll call it like I see it. If people don't like that, that's tough.

'How was the book received in official quarters?' I wondered.

Among the RAF, certainly, the response was very favourable. It had been clear to me for many months that within the ranks of the RAF there were people who had seen UFOs, very often from their cockpits while flying fast jets.

There was a body of knowledge within the RAF about visual sightings tracked on radar; about aircraft being intercepted; about aircraft being overtaken at high speed by UFOs. The RAF has far more of a belief in UFOs than the Civil Service does: mainly because they've seen them!

I've had people come up to me in the corridors of power and say, 'Well done, mate; it's about time someone got the debate going on this. We know they're out there.' Sometimes I get the impression that there's a sort of climate of acceptance among the RAF, certainly. Almost an undeclared war, I sometimes like to say. The RAF encounter UFOs very frequently.

I could not agree more, and yet I knew that when he served with the Secretariat of the Air Staff, Nick got to see very few official UFO reports submitted by the RAF. He put this down to 'the military being a very conservative culture'. However, I had uncovered a credible body of evidence (as is described in the following chapter) that such reports were being syphoned off before reaching Nick's office.

The big question, however, was what was the Ministry of Defence's response to Nick's book? 'Let me take a toilet break,' replied Nick when I brought up that question. It hadn't unnerved him that much, had it? A couple of minutes later, he was back.

I had a lot of opposition to the book. There is a standard procedure at the MOD for publications clearance, and I submitted my manuscript in accordance with that. Funnily enough, after the Gulf War I was involved in publications clearance myself; not least on General Sir Peter de la Billière's book *Storm Command*. I didn't anticipate there being any problem, because I'd deliberately made sure, of course, that there wasn't any classified information in there. I'd seen that there'd been some very close-to-the-knuckle books on the Gulf War which had got through without any problem, so I thought mine would go through with just a nod and a wink.

I was absolutely amazed to receive a letter back: 'Your manuscript is totally unacceptable to the MOD and quite beyond amendment.' I should say that this was due to one or two very narrow-minded people who really had no knowledge or interest in the subject, and who wouldn't have acknowledged the reality of it if one had landed in their back garden!

I responded: 'If you cast your mind back, I think you will recall that the Commander in Chief of British Forces in the Gulf, General Sir Peter de la Billière, wrote, submitted and got approved a book on the Gulf War.' There is no bar to using your official experiences to write a book, as long as you don't have classified information, and as long as you get it cleared. At the end of the day, the two or three people who were making life difficult were basically told to stop being so 'effing stupid'!

Eventually, the book was cleared, and I sought and obtained blanket clearance to do all sorts of interviews, articles and lectures to promote it. I knew that my position was defensible.'

I wound up the interview: 'What's your opinion on the subject as a whole, with one book under your belt and another on the horizon?'

For a moment, Nick considered his answer:

Well, I think we live in interesting times. I think there is better evidence than there's ever been of, I believe, an extraterrestrial presence. MPs have been taking more of an interest in this than ever before. Serious media coverage is increasing, with defence correspondents, as opposed to feature writers, beginning to get involved.

I think we're moving in the right direction. As far as the phenomenon itself is concerned, I think it's evolving; but that may simply be that people are more willing to come forward with their sightings. It's a circular argument.

Undoubtedly, we've got better information and better evidence than we've ever had before. But whether that's because the phenomenon has evolved and accelerated, or whether it simply reflects the fact that people are more free and easy about coming forward in the current environment, it's almost impossible to say.[4]

I thanked Nick for his comments and observations. We downed the last of our drinks and headed off into the cold London evening.

Most of the following day was spent analysing what Nick had imparted to me. His comments, particularly those relating to the crashed-UFO issue, were invaluable.

Nick's inability to determine exactly what was going on in the USA, for example, was very illuminating. 'I wasn't satisfied' was his to-the-point statement when commenting on the denial from US authorities that there was any present-day interest on their part in the UFO subject. There was no doubt in Nick's mind: 'There is evidence . . . that the Americans are far more involved in this – to this day.'

And what of those tasked with concealing the greatest secret of all: Majestic 12? Could physical evidence of extraterrestrial infiltration in our society be concealed effectively? Bearing in mind his twelve years with the Ministry of Defence, I considered Nick's carefully delivered words: 'Nothing's ever impossible if you keep the numbers of those in the know small enough, and if you have a big enough incentive for keeping it secret.' Crashed and recovered UFOs, I opined, were indeed 'a big enough incentive' . . .

Despite Nick's belief that the existence of a Majestic 12-type organisation in the USA was a very real possibility, he could not bring himself to accept that a similar group existed within the United Kingdom. I found that odd.

Nevertheless, taken as a whole, Nick's comments convinced me that the department in which he worked – the Secretariat of the Air Staff – was not a part of any such MJ-UK group. I would have to look elsewhere.

Nick Pope may have failed to obtain official confirmation from the Americans that they were still implicated in the UFO mystery, and he may have been denied access to both Majestic 12 and any British counterpart; however, there was evidence to show that Nick's proactive involvement in the UFO subject, and his repeated attempts to determine the truth of issues such as the Roswell event, had attracted the attention of some hidden MJ-UK group.

Occasionally, I would hear from research colleagues bizarre (and largely unsubstantiated) stories concerning Nick Pope's 'real' involvement in the UFO subject on behalf of the MOD. Even Nick himself acknowledged this in *Open Skies, Closed Minds*: 'Many within the world of ufology probably regarded me as just "the man from the ministry", as likely as not up to my eyeballs in crashed UFOs, dead aliens and cosmic cover-ups.'

And so it was that I initially took little serious notice when a most strange tale was told to me concerning, of all things, Nick Pope's dustbin!

UFO activity in the vicinity of RAF Boscombe Down dates back to the late 1940s, as Rita Hill, formerly of the Royal Air Force, has revealed.
(Rita Hill)

The Home Office, London. Far below RAF Rudloe Manor, there exists an off-limits facility which falls under the jurisdiction of the Home Office. Home Office involvement in the UFO mystery is extensive and dates back to the early 1960's.
(Nicholas Redfern)

According to various sources, the runway at RAF Cosford was the scene of a UFO retrieval in December 1963. As late as 1997, information continued to surface with regard to tell-tale 'burn marks' left by the UFO at the scene. **(Nicholas Redfern)**

In December 1963, a UFO was seen to briefly touch-down near an aircraft hangar at RAF Cosford, Shropshire. A bulky case file on the incident exists at the Public Record Office at Kew. **(Nicholas Redfern)**

Cannock Chase, Staffordshire, was the site of a UFO crash in early 1964. The incident was monitored by British, American and Soviet intelligence operatives. According to those with intimate knowledge of the affair, three dead alien creatures were recovered from within the wreckage of the UFO. **(Nicholas Redfern)**

Within hours of the UFO crash near Cannock Chase in 1964, one Harold South managed to secure a number of photographs of the object. As a result, he was interrogated at length at Bloxwich Police Station and his camera and film were both confiscated. **(Nicholas Redfern)**

In 1970, a crash-retrieval operation occurred when a Royal Air Force Lightning jet plummeted into the North Sea following its encounter with a UFO. **(Nicholas Redfern)**

According to a former British Army source who was interviewed by retired police sergeant Tony Dodd, in 1974, alien creatures recovered from a UFO crash site in North Wales were transported, in the utmost secrecy, to the Chemical and Biological Defence Establishments at Porton Down.
(Matthew Williams)

The Government Communications Headquarters at Cheltenham. In 1989, staff at GCHQ were responsible for monitoring intelligence data pertaining to a reported UFO crash in South Africa. **(Nicholas Redfern)**

In 1994, a still-unidentified aerial craft crash-landed at the top secret Boscombe Down. Was the craft a UFO or a top secret military vehicle of a highly advanced design? The jury is still out.
(Matthew Williams)

The Public Record Office at Kew. In 1996 official documentation confirming the involvement in UFO investigations of the RAF's Provost and Security Services was removed from the shelves of the PRO under circumstances which to this day have not been fully resolved. **(Matthew Williams)**

In 1996, staff at RAF Rudloe Manor admitted that their heavily guarded underground complex contained 'floor spaces equivalent to 12 full-size football pitches'. Is Rudloe Manor the final resting place for the various crashed UFOs recovered by British authorities since the Second World War? **(Matthew Williams)**

In late 1996, UFOs were tracked on radar at RAF Neatishead, Norfolk. shortly afterwards an unidentified object impacted off the Isle of Lewis and became the subject of a major military search and retrieval operation. **(Nicholas Redfern)**

In 1996 the late Martin Redmond MP raised questions in Parliment with respect to the involvement in the UFO subject on the part of the Government Communications Headquarters (GCHQ). The Government declined to comment. **(Nicholas Redfern)**

Can crashed UFO secrets be successfully concealed? 'Nothing's ever impossible if you keep the numbers of those in the know small enough, and if you have a big enough incentive for keeping it secret.' Nick Pope, Ministry of Defence, 1997.
(Nicholas Redfern)

From within the Ministry of Defence's Main Building at Whitehall, covertly-operated departments carefully monitor UFO activity in Britain's airspace. **(Nicholas Redfern)**

The telephone rang: it was a fellow whose name I was vaguely aware of in research circles. According to him, several months previously Nick Pope had woken early one morning, and on looking out of his bedroom window had seen two men (dressed entirely in black, no less!) rifling through the contents of his dustbin.

As the story went, Nick leaped downstairs, flung open his front door, bounded down the drive, and in the words of the caller, 'gave both of them a good kicking'! Nick, by now furious, had demanded to know what was going on, and after repeatedly questioning the two, was told that their presence was part of a GCHQ-sponsored surveillance of Nick's activities: he was getting too close to the truth and had to be stopped!

'Well, that's all very interesting,' I said, diplomatically bringing the conversation to an end. Try as I might, I could not resist the urge to ask Nick if there was any truth to the story . . .

'Oh!' Nick laughed out loud. 'I know what this is all about! A piece had appeared in the *Guardian* Diary some time ago saying that my rubbish had been "interfered with" – which in fact it had! But it didn't quite happen like that chap said.'

Nick explained. It was the day after the Easter Bank Holiday in 1995. As was his usual routine, he had placed his rubbish bin outside his house ready for collection. However, he had forgotten that the previous day had been a Bank Holiday, and that the rubbish was due to be picked up one day later than normal.

As I say, I'd forgotten this, and put mine out on the normal day. You know how it is when you put your rubbish out, everyone thinks: what does he know that I don't? So, it ended up that in our little bit of the close everyone had put their rubbish out because I had got the wrong day.

But when I got back home in the evening, my rubbish had been collected but everyone else's was still standing there! I mentioned this to one or two people, who said, 'Well, you know, it's obvious: some agency has been collecting your rubbish as part of a surveillance operation, and has been doing so on the official collection day so as not to arouse suspicion. But like you, on this occasion they got the wrong day: they collected your rubbish, thinking the real refuse collectors would be along soon, and you'd never notice.'

Now, at the instigation of a friend, I wrote a sarcastic little note and put it in the next batch of rubbish . . .'

'What did the note say?' I asked, amused at the way all this was turning out.

'Well, I wrote, "To whom it may concern: Bet you didn't think they'd have you doing this when you joined up. Bet you thought it would be more glamorous; lots of running around with guns. Still, everyone has to start somewhere. Apologies for the remains of the Indian takeaway!" '

Both Nick and I could see the funny side to this escapade, but there was a serious angle to be addressed, too.

'So who did you think was responsible? Some government department?' I asked.

'If it was anything sinister, I think it was probably journalists, as opposed to anything more spooky,' was Nick's reply. 'However,' he added with a touch of humour, 'if I find as an appendix to your book a commentary on my pizza-eating habits, I think I'll have narrowed down the suspect list!

'This hasn't happened to me since,' Nick elaborated, 'but it's been suggested to me that this is because of my note and the whole thing being referred to in the *Guardian*. It rather sort of smoked them out.'

Was the matter as innocent as Nick Pope suggested? Or was even he the subject of a government-orchestrated monitoring operation? I made additional enquiries.

Among those to whom I spoke on the matter of official surveillance operations was Matthew Williams. Although Matthew was well known in the UFO field as the editor and publisher of *Truthseekers* magazine, it was less well known that he had served for a number of years with Customs and Excise – first with the Personnel Division and later with the Criminal Investigations Unit.

Without mentioning Nick Pope by name, I gave Matthew brief details of the facts related to me by Nick. Had he come across anything similar during his Customs and Excise days?

Absolutely all the time. If there was someone who was under surveillance, we would find out from the local council which day was 'bin day', then we'd turn up very early in the morning on that day and collect the rubbish just like the bin men would. Doing it the same day as the official collection usually means you don't create suspicion. The whole contents of the rubbish would then be brought back to the offices, and then there was the task of having to go through it all! We were usually looking for evidence of drug taking.

But the thing is, this was standard practice for many government departments. And a lot of those departments would send their 'cream' over to us to be trained.

Matthew then related something that made the existence of a super-secret MJ-UK organisation seem all the more plausible.

Normally during surveillance operations, you'd be given background information on the person you were investigating; however, occasionally orders would come down from on high to carry out a surveillance of someone's house or place of business, or whatever. In these cases, you would never know on whose behalf you were carrying out the surveillance. Or why. You would just report back to the office and the information would be referred back to whoever it was that had requested the surveillance. These operations were known as 'secret squirrelling' operations, and they would basically allow the security services to carry out their investigations without getting their hands dirty.

The whole thing is, it could mean that those directly involved in carrying out surveillance operations on people in the UFO community aren't the security services, the 'men in black', or MJ-12, but are just some local civil servant who doesn't really know what he's investigating – that keeps everything really secret.[5]

Despite Nick Pope's belief that the matter was of little consequence, I now found it difficult to dismiss the probability that his proactive stance with respect to the UFO issue had attracted the attention of MJ-UK. But how could I determine the existence of such a group? And, more importantly, how could I get closer to accessing its secrets?

Surprisingly enough, establishing that there were other military and Civil Service branches that investigated UFO encounters beyond the division in which Nick Pope worked was a relatively simple task.

In *A Covert Agenda*, for example, I had devoted a chapter to the UFO activities of the MOD's Defence Intelligence Staff (DIS), and was able to state conclusively that as late as 1992, the DIS was receiving from its US counterpart, the Defense Intelligence Agency (DIA), official briefings on the UFO issue – briefings that suggested the DIS was surveying UFO activity on a worldwide scale. Yet Nick Pope had hit a brick wall when he tried to initiate something similar. Whatever the DIS had learned about the nature of the UFO problem, it evidently felt that informing Nick Pope of the facts was not a high priority . . .

There was also the undeniable involvement of the RAF's Headquarters' Provost and Security Services (see Chapters 10 and 11), and tantalising rumours surrounding MI5, MI6 and GCHQ. But it was hard facts with respect to the crashed-UFO issue I was after. If I could prove that any (or indeed all) of the above agencies were implicated in the retrieval of alien spacecraft, then I was a step closer to identifying the member-ship of MJ-UK.

I decided to start with MI5 and MI6. Among those who had attempted to force the British Government to reveal the full extent to which MI6 (the agency responsible for collecting overseas intelligence data) was implicated in the investigation of UFO encounters was Martin Redmond MP. On 16 October 1996, he bravely brought up the matter in Parliament:

> Martin Redmond: To ask the Secretary of State for Foreign Affairs if he will list by month for each of the last ten years, and this year to date, the number of occasions that MI6 has monitored unidentified flying objects investigations; and if he will make a statement.

> David Davis: I shall write to the hon. Member shortly. Copies of this letter will be placed in the Libraries of the House.

Forty-eight hours later, Martin Redmond had his response: 'As you may know,' wrote Malcolm Rifkind, the Foreign Secretary, 'it has been the long-standing policy of successive Governments not to comment on the operations of the intel-ligence and security agencies. I intend to maintain that policy.'

While Martin Redmond did not ultimately obtain the data he had requested, Rifkind's response was curious. If MI6 had no involvement in the UFO issue, a swift denial would have sufficed. No such denial was forthcoming. And I knew that there were other reasons for believing that MI6 was heavily involved in UFO investigations -- even in those investigations that extended to reports of crashed and recovered UFOs.

Timothy Cooper's name was one that was widely known in UFO research. A California-based investigator, he had a deep interest in reports of recovered UFOs – not least because his own father, who had been in the employ of the US military back in the 1940s, was on one occasion given access to a lengthy, top-secret report dealing with a crashed UFO, complete with alien bodies.

In addition, Cooper had forged contacts with a number of retired military personnel who had been implicated in highly classified issues in the 1940s, and had been given access to a variety of seemingly genuine US Government documents dealing with both crashed UFOs and Majestic 12.

From my point of view, the most important document was one dated 19 September 1947 and purportedly written by the Director of US Central Intelligence, Rear Admiral Roscoe Hillenkoetter. The document stated:

> The recovery of unidentified planform aircraft in the state of New Mexico on 6 July 1947, ten miles northwest of Oscura Peak, and a debris field 75 miles northwest of the Army's 509th Atomic Bomb Group, Roswell Army Air Field, is confirmed. A subsequent capture of another similar craft 30 miles east of the Army's Alamogordo Army Air Field on 5 July 1947 has convinced the Army Air Forces that the craft and wreckage are not of US manufacture.
>
> The research scientists at the Air Forces Research and Development Center, Wright Field, are utilizing their test facilities and a new biological laboratory in an on-going study program. The offices of the JRDB, FBI and the State Department are assisting the Joint Intelligence Committee in acquiring any intelligence from MI5 and MI6 on possible Soviet long-range reconnaissance aircraft/missile research and development tests.

If both MI6 and MI5 (Britain's own intelligence-gathering organisations) were involved tangentially in determining the origin of the objects found in New Mexico in early July 1947, I considered it most likely that both would have received some form of briefing from the Americans.

I scanned the relatively small body of data on MI6 that was

available at the Public Record Office, but was not surprised to find that there was no reference to MI6 involvement in the New Mexico crashes; however, I was able to make one interesting observation.

According to the document made available to Timothy Cooper, initial investigations in 1947 centred on the possibility that the retrieved craft were Soviet in origin, and it was with this in mind that both MI5 and MI6 were brought into the fold. In that year and also in 1948, I learned, the Air Ministry's Directorate of Scientific Intelligence (DSI) was implicated in determining what advances the Soviets had made with respect to, and I quote from the relevant file titles, 'aircraft design and production'. Were the DSI's studies initiated at the request of MI6? Timewise, this was not out of the question.

Of course, MI6 was (and is to this day) a vast body, and I could not accept that the whole organisation would have been exposed to data pertaining to the New Mexico crashes. A more reasonable scenario was one that saw selected people entrusted with the facts on a strict 'need-to-know' basis.

Once again, Nick Pope's words on Majestic 12 echoed in my head: 'Nothing's ever impossible if you keep the numbers of those in the know small enough . . .'

MI5 and MI6 aside, Martin Redmond made similar enquiries in Parliament in 1996 with respect to the work of the Cheltenham-based listening station: Government Communications Headquarters (GCHQ). Again, Redmond received from Malcolm Rifkind a tight-lipped 'no comment' response.

As with MI5 and MI6, however, there was a body of evidence that linked GCHQ with reports of crashed UFOs. Several years previously I had received a copy of a document that I had been advised originated with GCHQ and that appeared to relate to a UFO-crash story that was notorious in research circles.

The content of the document was certainly scant, but briefly referenced a 1989 UFO incident that occurred in South

Africa. My enquiries into this case led me to believe that the crashed-UFO story (which involved a highly detailed account of how the UFO was 'shot down' by elements of the South African military, and was subsequently shipped off to the USA along with its crew of two alien creatures) was in fact a strange, but certainly successful, cover story that had been put into place to mask an entirely different, yet no less sensational, event: the illegal transfer of nuclear technology from US authorities to the South African Government!

This, however, was hardly the issue: from my point of view the leaked document suggested that Government Communications Headquarters at Cheltenham were going to extraordinary lengths to ensure that they were fully conversant with the facts, even to the extent of intercepting classified US military and intelligence telex messages going back and forth from the States to South Africa.

CONFIDENTIAL

TELEX - FACSIMILE COPIER - CABLE REQUEST

Date: Originator   MESSAGE TO BE SENT TO
0G03°0   C.I.A.   Location: V.A.
               C/I   Telex No. & Answer Back: 6371840001
                                   Fax Telephone No. N/A
MESSAGE NUMBER   Cable Address   N/A
34G705°0   Room   Extn.
               3Rc - 1c 0-4

Client Name   Secondary Desc.   Client/Account Code
G.R. DAVIS   ---------- ----   6570887

Message approved by   Copy to be sent to (if not originator)   Room
WEBSTER W.   CIA/NSA/DIA   ----- -

Special Instructions (including destination details of any copies which are to be sent)

TREAT WITH CAUTION - CLASSIFIED - TOP SECRET

     G2, ONI, Q43. ATTN: UFO SIGHTING AFTER
     UFO INCIDENT IN SOUTH AFRICA, 7 MAY
     198°.

     INCIDENT IS REGARDED AS OF INTEREST,
     INFORM OSI OF POSSIBLE PLOY.

A Government Communications Headquarters (GCHQ) paper relating to a crashed-UFO incident in South Africa in 1989.

What was GCHQ's interest in crashed UFOs? Staff there were saying nothing; however, despite my having repeatedly supplied GCHQ with copies of the document at issue, on no occasion was anyone within the organisation willing to state with authority that the material was bogus . . .

That being the case, what else did GCHQ have on its files about recovered UFOs? Again, only a deafening silence issued forth from Cheltenham. But I had other means at my disposal . . .

Among those with whom I spoke on the GCHQ–UFO link, one name stood out beyond that of anyone else: Robin Cole. Born and bred in Cheltenham, Robin had a long-standing interest in the UFO issue, and in 1997 authored a first-class paper on GCHQ's involvement in the investigation of UFO encounters. More significant to my investigation, however, Robin was acquainted with several sources who, in his own words, 'had close links to GCHQ'. And so it was that in October 1997 I supplied Robin with a copy of the purported GCHQ report on the 1989 UFO crash on South African soil.

'When you get a chance, Robin,' I said to him, 'show this to your sources, will you? Let me know what they have to say.' I did not have to wait long . . . On 20 November Robin gave me some fascinating information.

Basically, what I did was wait until I met them in a social situation. I said, 'I've got something that might be of interest to you. See if you can shed any light on it.'

I produced the document, and he was a bit taken aback when he saw it, and said, 'How the hell have you got hold of this?' I said, 'Well, I don't know if I can reveal the source.'

He looked at it. He couldn't be a hundred per cent sure the document was what it was alleged to be, but said that the layout looked good. He said that if he could have a look at the original, he'd be able to tell immediately as they use specially formatted paper at GCHQ.[6]

Unfortunately, I did not have access to the original document, only a photocopy; however, the comments of Robin's GCHQ source convinced me that the document was real and that GCHQ was no stranger to the crashed-UFO controversy . . .

With MI5, MI6 and GCHQ all potential players in MJ-UK, I now turned my attention to the military. Again, I was able to unearth some fascinating evidence.

Among those who could shed light on what selected individuals in the Royal Air Force knew about crashed-UFO events was Paul Stokes, who had served with the RAF in the 1950s and 1960s. In particular Stokes recalled an experience that occurred during his service days at RAF Horsham St Faith.

On one evening Stokes (along with several other people, including a flying officer, a sergeant, a flight lieutenant and a warrant officer) was ordered to attend a meeting held in an office of 245 Squadron's hangar. Overseeing the meeting was a wing commander, who informed the select group, 'There is a rumour going around some of the other camps at the moment that the Americans have captured a flying saucer and have the occupants and the craft in a secret hangar somewhere in the States. This is not true and if you hear this story on this camp you are to stop it immediately. It's nonsense; do you understand?'

'Yes, sir!' was the unanimous response and the meeting was brought to a close.[7]

Scanning Stokes's account, however, I wondered what could be so important about crashed-UFO rumours that high-ranking RAF officers wanted them quashed at all costs? If the rumours were without substance, then they were essentially of no consequence and certainly not something that would have concerned someone of the rank of wing commander. I therefore had to assume that there was some substance to the matter, and that senior Royal Air Force officers knew that this was the case.

A similar account from one Richard Newman caught my attention. Newman's information was certainly scant, but interesting none the less.

He told me his girlfriend's brother had at one time served with the British Army and had received some form of official briefing on the UFO crash at Roswell in 1947. Try as I might, I was unable to extract much more pertinent data, and suspected strongly that this was due to a reluctance on the part of both Newman's girlfriend and her brother to speak out.

Nevertheless, I passed the few facts I had uncovered to Stan Friedman, and was present at Quest International's UFO conference in Solihull in 1996 when, during the interval, Stan had the opportunity to interview first-hand Newman's girlfriend. Although she was unable to add much to the basic facts, she confirmed the accuracy of the information that had been imparted to me, and, more importantly, confirmed that the briefing given to her brother had occurred prior to the release of any of the published books on the Roswell case.

By far the most important account of British military knowledge of crashed UFOs, Majestic 12, MJ-UK and a host of related matters, however, came from the investigator Jenny Randles . . .

CHAPTER TEN

THE SOLDIER'S STORY

ALTHOUGH IT HAD BEEN REPORTED WIDELY IN BOTH UFO literature and by the media at large that Tim Good had received copies of the still-controversial Majestic 12 documents in early 1987, it was relatively unknown that a very similar offer of such documentation had been made to Jenny Randles some months previously by a source connected to the British Army. Jenny gave me the details in March 1997.

I got a phone call from a complete stranger asking me if I was the writer Jenny Randles. This would be late October 1986. It was a very strange conversation; it was a very hesitant call and not the kind of thing you would expect from anybody full of confidence.

I assumed at first that it was just a UFO witness who was reluctant to talk about a sighting, as they sometimes are, and was just testing the water before they ventured into it.

But after I confirmed who I was, he said that he had some information which had been given to him by his superior officer – a major – in the British military forces, and he needed to see me to talk about it. Was I willing to do so at a prearranged location?

I said to him, 'That's fine; but I want someone to come with me.' He was reluctant, and said so. I pointed out to him that if he wanted the meeting on that day – which he did, in fact, more or less within an hour or two – I couldn't get there because I don't drive and therefore I needed someone to come with me. He reluctantly accepted that. This wasn't only true, it was a very useful excuse for me to have someone else there.

Jenny explained that she made arrangements to meet the mysterious caller at a public house at Eccles, some ten miles from where she was then living. Jenny then quickly telephoned a colleague, Peter Hough, and both set off in Peter's car. On arriving, they walked into the pub. It was a busy lunchtime and the pub was swarming with customers.

We had no idea who we were looking for. We just assumed that he would find us. We went and sat down and at first we thought that no one was coming because no one immediately came up to us. But shortly after, this guy walked up to our table.

He was, I would say, in his late twenties; there was nothing strange about him particularly. In fact, Peter and I were surprised by the credibility level of that particular afternoon because we hadn't gone with any great expectations, to be perfectly honest.

He said that he'd hesitated before coming over because he'd been given a photograph to identify me, and it was one taken about ten years earlier in which I had much longer hair and which had been used in the book *UFOs: A British Viewpoint*.

He sat down, we talked, and he went through his entire story. We must have spent about three or four hours going through it, and Peter and I both took about twenty pages of notes each. He was very forthcoming; he

never failed to answer a question and was certainly convincing in that regard.

'Robert', as I'll call him, said that until early 1985 he
had served with a particular British Army unit. But
towards the end of his tour of duty, his commanding
officer – the major – had befriended him and several
others within the unit over the space of a few months.

In retrospect, although it wasn't obvious at first, what
his CO was doing was sounding them out for interest in,
and awareness of, UFOs.

Jenny told me that this included a discussion of a UFO seen
by sources within the Brazilian military, and various cases
within the United Kingdom in which anomalous objects had
been tracked on radar during Army exercises.

His CO would say things like, 'What do you think about
this case? Have you read about that incident in the
newspaper?'

And the CO seemed to home in on not those who
were interested, but on Robert, primarily, it appeared,
because of his lack of enthusiasm for the subject. He was-
n't entirely dismissive, but was willing to listen without
being too critical.

It was some months into this whole scenario when
Robert's CO showed him a photograph of what looked
like a UFO, and he asked him for his comments on it,
while at the same time informing him that the UFO had
been tracked on radar, and had been seen both from the
ground and from a commercial airliner. 'Well,' Robert
replied, 'you can fake anything these days.'

'What if I were to tell you that things like this have
been tracked on radar and chased by aeroplanes?' said
Robert's CO. 'What if I were to tell you that they've also
been recovered and we've got bodies, and things like
that?'

Robert replied, 'Well, I'd need to see evidence to prove that.'

At that time, his CO didn't say anything more and just let it drop.'

Some months went by, and things only really took off when Robert was leaving his tour of duty in the Army and was getting ready to go into civilian life. It was at this stage that Robert was told by his commanding officer that he had some information which he wanted Robert to get out to the world at large. It was too dangerous for the CO to do it, and he had decided that Robert was the person to trust with it.

Robert's CO told him that, while in America, he had become friendly with a US Air Force officer stationed at Wright-Patterson Air Force Base in Ohio. This man had been serving as a records officer, and had accidentally intruded into top-secret US Government UFO files while he was doing some repair work on the computer system. The result of this was that he had discovered these UFO records and had managed to print out over six hundred pages of material.

He recognised the significance of what he'd got, and managed to spirit it away without anybody knowing. However, he evidently triggered some sort of alarm and was eventually found out and was subsequently arrested. Although the files weren't recovered, he was sure that they ultimately would be, and before he was hauled before a court martial, he decided that he wanted the British CO to take the files out of the country.

He told the CO where to get the material, how to pick it up, and to get it out of the US quickly because he didn't think it would be there for much longer. The CO did pick it up, and did bring the files back to Britain without detection.

But shortly afterwards, this computer operator died

before the court martial in what was alleged to have been a car accident involving drunk driving.

The CO said he was always suspicious of this and thought it was a set-up.

'And what was contained within the files?' I asked.

Before going into detail, Jenny explained to me that at that point in his dealings with his CO, Robert had not yet personally seen the files, and that remained the case until he left the British Army in 1985.

Ten weeks before he telephoned Jenny, however, Robert was invited to a reunion with his CO and once again the issue of the mysterious files surfaced . . .

Robert's CO explained that he was due to take on a new position within the British Army and he needed to offload the UFO files. Was Robert the man for the job?

Robert could see his CO's predicament and agreed to help. The files were at a specific location and Robert was given instructions on how to pick them up. On doing so, Robert finally had the opportunity to peruse their contents. Jenny continued the story.

It was blatantly obvious to both Peter and I that much of what the files referred to was the Roswell crash. Robert said that there was mention of a UFO which had crashed somewhere in the western United States in 1947, and that wreckage and bodies were found.

Robert wasn't saying this in an overenthusiastic way: it was all done very methodically and matter-of-factly. And that was one of the most convincing aspects of what he was telling us. But you could hear the awe in his voice, as if he'd never come across any possibility like this before.

There was lots of material about Roswell, including photographs of the UFO and of the aliens; and one of the most detailed files was an autopsy report on one of the bodies recovered from the Roswell crash. Robert remembered the name of the doctor who had written it. His name was Dr Frederick Hauser, a name I'd never seen connected with UFOs in any way whatsoever.

Robert said that there was a very detailed account that was mostly filled with medical jargon about the autopsy which he didn't understand, and there was a photograph of this entity with a slit right down the middle from the neck to the navel.

I asked Jenny if Robert had made any specific comments about the nature of the aliens.

One of the first things Robert said was that the aliens were very human-looking. He said that the head was completely bald, but the most unusual feature of the face was the nose, which was almost flush into the face – almost unnoticeable.

He couldn't tell from the photographs, but the autopsy report made it clear that the beings were slightly smaller than average human size – about five feet in height.

In addition to this, Robert said that the other biggest single file in the report was one with a rather disturbing title: 'Elimination of non-military personnel'. He said that this was a document discussing the ways in which witnesses who had come into possession of too much information on UFOs were silenced.

And although this sounds very much like something out of a spy film, from his detailed discussion of a number of case histories in the file, the one tactic that was used most often – particularly with people in influential positions – was to offer them high-paid jobs in government departments. They had pretty much determined that, where money was concerned, people usually comply.

But there was a discussion of the so-called 'men in black' – people going around warning people about national security and intimidating them into silence.

However, Robert told us that this tactic was only used on those whose instability was considered to be significant enough that, if they ever told their story publicly, it would not be considered credible.

For all that, if all else failed there was one final option: 'termination'. Although this tactic wasn't employed too frequently, those charged with carrying out such dubious activities were well trained to ensure that any 'UFO-related deaths' appeared to be due to suicide or accident.

Could Jenny tell me anything else about what both she and Peter Hough had learned from Robert?

There were also a number of other specific case histories, including a case which, Robert said, involved a UFO which had crashed somewhere in England in 1980. Robert couldn't remember where exactly in the country this was supposed to have been, but he said that there were definitely photographs of the object and it was incredible. It was at night; it was a disc; and it was surrounded by lights.

Some of the things that Robert said about it suggested the Rendlesham Forest case. For example, he said that the crash was in connection with a military base which was near by. That's why it was covered up so effectively.

With the details of the files in hand, I asked Jenny to recall the rest of that afternoon's events.

Robert told us that, for his own protection, he'd separated the material into about twenty or thirty piles so that there was no complete document anywhere. In other words, if anyone found any one batch of material, it wouldn't make much sense because everything was scattered about in different locations in his house.

Robert decided that he would have to think about

what to do next. So Peter and I arranged to meet him about a week later at a covert location – which was actually a country park in the middle of nowhere – where the documents would be handed over to us.

We were suspicious because Robert hadn't brought with him to the pub one scrap of paper to support his case, but he was very credible. Come the day of the meeting, Peter and I went to the park, but Robert failed to turn up, which was not exactly a great surprise to us.

A few days later I was surprised when Robert wrote me a letter. In it he alleged that in the week between our meeting at the pub and when we were supposed to be handed the documents, he had been contacted by what he termed his 'former employers', and that they had taken him to a military base somewhere in southern England. He didn't say much more than that, but specified that they had interrogated him for forty-eight hours. The military were clearly aware of everything that had happened, including our meeting in the pub. And they knew all about the six hundred pages of documentation, which they ordered him to hand over, pointing out that he had a wife and children and it was they who would suffer if he didn't.

Apparently, Robert was told that the files were nothing more than a prank on someone's part, and they were to be transferred to a US Air Force base in England before being flown back to America, where they were to be destroyed.

Robert's letter was full of apologies, saying things like 'I know this means now that you will never believe a word I said. There is nothing I can do about that. But I am telling you that I am going to spend the rest of my life trying to prove that this is true, and if I ever get proof I will contact you. All I can do is ask you to think of me kindly. But I have to think of my family. They have to be my priority.'

Essentially, that was Jenny's remarkable tale. But was Robert genuine? Did he have fleeting access to top-secret government files pertaining to crashed UFOs and alien autopsies? Or was he just a clever hoaxer? Despite the fantastic scenario that Robert described, I learned from Jenny that there were firm grounds for believing that the basics of Robert's account were factual.

Jenny had explained that, at the close of their meeting with Robert in the pub in Eccles, both she and Peter took steps to ensure that as Robert drove out of the pub car park, they were in a position to note his car registration number.

> We did this so that we could use a friend of ours in the police force to track Robert down. As a result of that, during the intervening week between that meeting and when we were supposed to meet with him in the park, we were actually able to do quite a bit of digging into Robert.
>
> It turned out that what he told us proved to be correct. The name he had given us was his real name; he lived where he said he lived; he had recently been in the Army; and his car had been registered in the area he worked in precisely the same month that his Army career had come to an end.
>
> We even used a bit of subterfuge to get to speak with his employers. In fact, we lied through our teeth and pretended that we were making enquiries about Social Security matters!

There were other aspects of the case, too, Jenny revealed, that suggested that Robert had indeed been exposed to sensitive military-and government-originated UFO data.

First, there was the significant fact that Robert advised Jenny and Peter that the military files referred to the aliens as 'extraterrestrial biological entities', or 'EBEs'.

This, I knew, was extremely significant: the reason being that this was precisely the same terminology used in the

Majestic 12 papers published by Tim Good several months after Jenny's interview with Robert; however, the key point was that in the latter part of 1986, EBE and extraterrestrial biological entity were most certainly not terms with which the civilian UFO research community was acquainted. If Robert had not had the opportunity to see such files, from where did he pick up the specialised terminology?

In addition, Jenny told me that persistent digging on the part of a US research colleague, Benton Jamison, had uncovered the illuminating fact that Dr Frederick Hauser – the man who Robert maintained had authored a lengthy report on the autopsy of one of the aliens recovered at Roswell in 1947 – had indeed served with the US military in the 1940s in a medical capacity. Again, if not from genuine documentation, from where did Robert glean the name Frederick Hauser?

And from my point of view, I considered it significant that Robert had alluded to his commanding officer's intimate knowledge of a UFO incident in which the Brazilian military was involved. As explained in Chapter 1, the Brazilian military was apparently aware by the 1950s that a UFO had crashed within the UK at some point prior to that time, and this suggested to me that the two nations collaborated to a degree on the UFO issue.

But that was not all. While Robert's recollections of the references in the file to the 'elimination of non-military personnel' were most disturbing, they were not without precedent.

There was the journalist Dorothy Kilgallen, who in the 1950s had been informed of the analysis by British scientists and airmen of a recovered UFO. The result? Death from acute ethanol and barbiturate intoxication in November 1965 . . .

There was the actress Marilyn Monroe, who had learned of a 'secret effort by US and UK governments to identify crashed spacecraft and dead bodies'. The result? Sudden death one day after both she and Dorothy Kilgallen were referenced in CIA documentation leaked to the investigator Milo Speriglio . . .

There was US President John F. Kennedy, who was reportedly unhappy about the overwhelming secrecy surrounding the UFO issue. The result? Death in Dallas, Texas, on 22 November 1963 – the circumstances of which were never resolved fully . . .

And there was the information imparted to retired police sergeant Tony Dodd concerning a source 'who knew the full story of the Lightning crash' in the North Sea in 1970. The result? Death in Germany in unusual circumstances . . .

In other words, this aspect of Robert's account, despite its seemingly incredible and dark nature, did hang together.

Finally, there was one other issue that I felt merited both investigation and comment. In listening to what Jenny Randles had to say about her experience with Robert, I was particularly interested in what happened to Robert after the initial meeting in the pub at Eccles.

Robert, she said, had been contacted by his 'former employers' and was duly escorted to a military base in southern England for interrogation. While Jenny was not told the name of the base, she knew that it came under the control of the British military as opposed to a facility that fell under the jurisdiction of the Americans.

This was interesting. As we'll see in Chapter 10, in the early to mid-1990s, I had carried out an intensive investigation of a Royal Air Force base that was rumoured to be heavily involved in the UFO issue: RAF Rudloe Manor, Wiltshire – home of the RAF's Provost and Security Services (P&SS).

Most pertinently, in 1994 I learned from Flight Lieutenant Andy Woodruff, who at the time was stationed at RAF Rudloe Manor, that of those P&SS personnel trained in the field of counter-intelligence (CI), their investigations 'cover any matter affecting the security of the Royal Air Force and range from losses of classified documents to major espionage cases'.

In view of this, was Rudloe Manor the base at which Robert was interrogated? I considered the probability to be high: the crux of Robert's case centred on 'losses of classified documents'.

While all of this data certainly seemed to confirm that Robert was precisely whom he claimed to be – an ex-British Army source who had had occasion to view an extraordinarily important file dealing with recovered UFOs – there was a distinct possibility that Robert was himself the unwitting player in a subtle disinformation ploy on the part of the military.

As Jenny rightly pointed out to me, several aspects of the affair stretched credulity to the limit. Referring to the records officer at Wright-Patterson Air Force Base who uncovered the files in the first instance, Jenny told me:

This is one of the parts of the whole story which I find totally unbelievable. He had discovered these UFO records and had managed to print out over six hundred pages without anybody noticing, which I think would have taken ages. And anyway, wouldn't you rather just make a disk of it?

Then he managed to get this material away from Wright-Patterson without anyone knowing – despite the fact that he had apparently triggered an alarm of some sort. And then Robert's CO somehow miraculously got all of this material out of the country and back to Britain.

And why would Robert's superiors need to interrogate him for two days to get him to hand over the files? Presumably they could have simply marched into his house on a pretext of national security and removed them.

I think that Peter and I more or less mutually decided between ourselves that the most likely explanation was that Robert had been set up by someone, and that he really did have this documentation. If it was a hoax, then Robert certainly wasn't guilty of it. And I'd probably still have to say that today.

In retrospect, it's fairly obvious from the detailed notes we took of what Robert told us that what he was describing was very similar to the Majestic 12 documents which

Tim Good released in 1987, and the appendices to those documents which have still never surfaced. It's clear from those MJ-12 papers that have been released that those half a dozen pages are just the tip of the iceberg, and there were masses of other data which were never released.

The MJ-12 documents surfaced in May 1987. Tim Good had received them at some point after our meeting with Robert, and published them – more or less at the last minute – in *Above Top Secret*.

I thought that what was happening was this: someone had first approached Moore, Shandera and Friedman with these papers, and because they'd sat on them for a couple of years and hadn't published them, they had given up on them. It was not unknown in October 1986 that I was then writing *The UFO Conspiracy* – which dealt with government investigations of UFOs – and that maybe they were hoping that by feeding this story to me, I'd publish it in *The UFO Conspiracy*.

But when Peter Hough and I started to make enquiries and checks, someone, somewhere, got cold feet and the offer was withdrawn. When we didn't pass the test, Tim Good was the next option; he was writing *Above Top Secret* at the time and didn't ask as many questions. I should stress that this is surmise, but it was curious the way it all came about.

'Is it significant', I asked Jenny, 'that these documents surfaced at the time that people such as yourself and Tim were writing books that dealt with government and military investigations of UFO encounters?'

'I'm sure it is,' Jenny replied quickly. 'I'm absolutely certain that the MJ-12 documents are disinformation.'

I continued: 'But was the offer of these papers an attempt to assist the civilian UFO research community, or was it to knock our credibility?'

I think the latter. The fact that the MJ-12 papers were released to people in strategic positions — and by that I mean people who could relate the account in a book — was important. The whole point was to discredit the question of delving into the UFO phenomenon.

I personally believe that there is a covert government investigation of UFOs within both the UK and in America. But I think that this happens because the powers that be don't actually know what's going on. I think that they're trying to find out as opposed to already having found out.

'Has Robert ever surfaced again in the past ten years?' I asked.

No. His name has never cropped up anywhere; I've kept a very careful watch. I have actually written him a couple of letters — the last time being about five years ago — but he's never answered. I've chosen not to publish his name simply because, if he's telling the truth, I don't want to get him into trouble. But if I ever need to prove all this, I can prove the existence of Robert's letter, and, of course, I had Peter Hough with me when I met with Robert.

Another thing to bear in mind which I think is possibly significant and which has maybe been overlooked is that the paperback version of *Skycrash* [the first published book devoted solely to the UFO crash at Rendlesham Forest in December 1980] had been released just a few weeks before I was approached with this offer of the files. Now, in the paperback, there was a whole new chapter addressing the possibility that the UFO crash story was a smokescreen for something else — possibly a nuclear missile or a Russian satellite. Perhaps this might have alerted someone to the need to destabilise me in some way. If they could make me look less credible, people might take what I had to say less seriously.

I'll give you an example. When *From out of the Blue* –
my second book on the Rendlesham Forest case – was
released, I remember it was reviewed by Nigel Watson in
Fortean Times magazine. In that book, I had mentioned
my experience with Robert and the files, and Nigel homed
in on this and said, 'Jenny is taking ludicrous stories like
this seriously,' and dismissed the whole book as a consequence of that! So, in other words, even in that one
instance, if this was a disinformation exercise, it worked!

I think there is a fascinating story to be unravelled
here. But because of our Official Secrets Act, we're never
going to unravel it successfully in this country.'[1]

Over a period of several days, I reviewed time and again the
evidence as it had been related to me by Jenny. Despite the fact
that Robert had surfaced more than a decade previously, I
noted that there was one aspect of his account that had a direct
bearing on a series of events that unfolded in the 1990s. I took
a close look at my interview notes with Jenny . . .

According to what Robert had to say to Jenny about the
nature of the autopsied aliens he had seen in a number of still
photographs, the creatures were: (a) 'very human-looking'; (b)
'completely bald'; and (c) 'slightly smaller than average human
size – about five feet in height'. Finally, there was the interesting observation that one photograph seen by Robert showed
an 'entity with a slit right down the middle from the neck to
the navel'. In 1986, this information was interesting. Come
the 1990s, however, it was crucial.

Robert's description of the various 'alien autopsy' photographs he had viewed in 1986 sounded very much like still
shots taken from a remarkable piece of film footage that, in
1995, had been released by Ray Santilli. Although rumours
had long circulated within the UFO research community to
the effect that this film existed when it surfaced it was greeted
by a massive wave of media publicity.

The date was 13 January 1995. Reg Presley, lead singer with

the pop group the Troggs, was interviewed on the BBC television show, *Good Morning with Anne and Nick* (Anne being Anne Diamond, and Nick being Nick Owen), and disclosed that he had recently viewed a sensational piece of film showing the autopsy of one of the alien bodies found at Roswell, New Mexico in July 1947.

Naturally the UFO research community swung into action, and I recall that my telephone became red hot over the course of the following two to three weeks. What did I know? 'Not a lot' was my honest reply: I was as much in the dark as everyone else. Nevertheless, I followed the debate closely, particularly when it became clear that the film was due to receive a public airing. But under what circumstances had the film been acquired?

It transpired that the footage was held by Santilli, described by the *Daily Mail* as 'an English entrepreneur whose business is making videos'. As Santilli himself later clarified:

As a result of research into film material for a music documentary I was in Cleveland, Ohio, USA in the summer of 1993. Whilst there I had identified some old film material taken by Universal News in the summer of 1955. As Universal News no longer existed[,] I needed the film to investigate the source of the film and was able to determine that the film was shot by a then local freelance cameraman. He had been employed by Universal News because of a Film Union strike in the summer of 1955. The cameraman was located, following which a very straightforward negotiation took place for his small piece of film, i.e. cash for three minutes of film. Upon completion of this the cameraman asked if I would be interested in purchasing outright very valuable footage taken during his time in the forces. He explained that the footage in question came from the Roswell crash; that it included debris and recovery footage and, of most importance, autopsy footage.[2]

Since later pronouncements from Ray Santilli slightly contradicted his original account of how he came to acquire the
film, he conceded: 'I still maintain that the story of the film's
acquisition is true. Certain non-relevant details were only
changed to stop people getting to the cameraman.'

With that in mind, how did the film surface into the public
domain and what exactly did it show? I turned to the Ministry
of Defence man, Nick Pope (who was invited to a select viewing of the film at the Museum of London on 5 May 1995), and
over drinks in a London wine bar in January 1997 sought out
his recollections of both the film and the day's events. Nick
told me:

> I'd heard rumours for some time, over a matter of
> months, I think, that there was this film doing the rounds
> that purported to show an autopsy, or a number of autop-
> sies, from the so-called Roswell crash. I'd had a number
> of discussions with Philip Mantle [council member of the
> British UFO Research Association, and probably the first
> UFO investigator to view the film], and I believe it was
> Philip who invited me to the British premiere at the
> Museum of London on 5 May 1995.
>
> I went along not really knowing what to expect, but I
> suppose with a feeling of excitement that I might be
> about to witness something important. And I knew that
> whether it was real or whether it was fake, this was going
> to be a big story; I certainly had no doubts about that.
>
> I won't say that I was keeping a low profile at the
> Museum of London, but I was certainly not advertising
> my presence. I wasn't, like a number of people, wearing a
> name badge or going out of my way to speak to the
> media.
>
> Well, I turned up; there was a lectern at the front of the
> auditorium and there was a kind of expectant atmos-
> phere. I was expecting Ray Santilli, whom I'd heard about
> but not met, to introduce the film in some way. But to

my surprise, and I think to the surprise and disgust of just about everyone there, there was no introduction: the film simply started and then stopped.

I don't have a particularly strong constitution, and I would say there was a kind of awkward atmosphere. I could smell the sweat and the distaste at one point. Everyone had gone in a light-hearted mood, particularly the journalists. They were thinking, This is a Friday; there's a little bit of a party atmosphere.

But that mood didn't last that long; a rather shocked hush fell over the auditorium. Afterwards, the lights went out and people were expecting an announcement. That announcement didn't come. Now, one or two of the journalists recognised Ray Santilli at the back, and in a fairly aggressive and angry way, they surrounded him and started firing questions. I recall that he was almost physically picked up and escorted from the room by his minders or his commercial backers, whoever they were. There were certainly some people there who didn't want him placed in a position where he had to answer the questions that were being fired at him: 'Where did you get this?' 'Who took it?' 'Can we speak to the cameraman?'

Nick also had a number of perceptive comments to make with respect to the 'guest list' at the screening of the film.

The invitation policy was interesting in itself because it's been the subject of some debate. A lot of the key figures who one would have expected to have been invited – and mainly I'm talking about Stanton Friedman – I don't think ever received invitations. I don't think Timothy Good received an invitation, and I'm fairly sure Jenny Randles didn't. Of course, in the months and years since, accusations and counter-accusations have flown about this, and about why that might have been.

Commenting on the graphic nature of the film, Nick added, with a smile on his face, 'I think there were a few people afterwards who headed for the toilet before they headed for the complimentary wine and sandwiches, shall we say.'

And what was Nick's assessment of the content of the film?

There was something lying on the autopsy table, and it wasn't human . . . probably around five feet, perhaps a little less. It was essentially humanoid, with a bulbous, hairless head. The eyes seemed slightly larger than ours . . . the nose and mouth were basically humanoid . . . and the mouth was frozen in an expression of horror. The torso looked muscular, especially the upper arms and thighs. It had six fingers on its hands and six toes on its feet. The upper [right] leg appeared to be seriously injured, and the [right] hand almost severed at the wrist. These, presumably, were injuries sustained in the crash.

But was the film genuine?

I'm certain as I can be that it's a fake. For a number of reasons; primarily the story that we're supposed to be believing simply doesn't make sense. If this really was the most highly classified operation in the world, classified higher than the hydrogen bomb, it's inconceivable that this cameraman would have been left to his own devices to develop these films, and that bits of them would simply not have been recovered from him and that he would have sat on it for nigh on fifty years. The story is more full of holes than a piece of Swiss cheese.[3]

I had to agree, but I was niggled by the fact that the 'Santilli footage' seemed to be remarkably similar to that batch of still photographs seen by Jenny Randles's British Army source (Robert) in 1986.

I was also impressed by the fact that Philip Mantle had

apparently viewed footage (also held by Ray Santilli) of another seemingly alien autopsy.

As Philip told it, the date was 28 April 1995, and the location, Ray Santilli's London office:

> The alien is humanoid, almost human looking with an enlarged abdomen, two arms, two legs, but it has six digits on each of its hands and feet. There is no hair visible anywhere; the head is slightly enlarged but it has a nose, mouth, ears and two dark eyes. Female genitals are also visible.
>
> The alien's body is cut open and various organs are removed and placed in various receptacles.
>
> The people conducting the autopsy are completely covered in protection suits of some kind and unfortunately the faces of these individuals are not visible.[4]

Although Ray Santilli later went on to explain that this film was not disseminated because of the graphic dissection of the creature's genitals, it had to be said that the original and much-publicised footage did not stand on its own: there was this backup.

Although Santilli's account of the way in which he obtained the film was often viewed with suspicion, I did not gain the impression that he was in any way knowingly perpetrating a hoax. Jenny Randles held a similar view: 'Let me emphasise that, personally, I think Ray Santilli comes over as a sincere, puzzled guy – not as a hoaxer. A man who simply bought a product in good faith and tried to market it without being too obstructive to research.'

A number of other researchers with whom I discussed the film held like-minded opinions, and ventured the possibility that Ray had simply invented out of thin air his claim to have purchased the film from a retired US military cameraman in order to give the film some provenance.

On the face of it, this seemed reasonable: after all, the bone of contention with many people was not the film itself (which if a hoax was a damned good one), but the identity of the elusive cameraman. At least three colleagues went a stage further and suggested that the film had been given to Ray by an anonymous intelligence source as part of a government-sponsored programme designed to get the general public thinking about the issue of alien life forms.

Working on the possibility that the release of the film was with the consent of a governmental (or, more likely, quasi-governmental) agency, was it possible that the same film released by Ray Santilli in 1995 (aspects of which may have been viewed by elements of the British Army in 1986) was also circulating among other government and military agencies throughout the world?

I determined to approach both Ray Santilli and Philip Mantle directly. Speaking with Ray, I considered him to be an amiable guy, who was fully aware of both the pros and cons of the film. And, as Ray impressed upon me, if the film had been a hoax, it could only have been created by a respected special-effects company – such was its quality. I agreed. As Ray also pointed out, no one had come forward with a 'how we conned the world'-type story, which would surely have been snapped up for a high price by a national newspaper. There was only silence. But what of the Army link to the film?

In discussion with both Ray and Philip, I learned that neither had heard rumours to the effect that stills from the film were possibly in the hands of the British Army in 1986; however, both confided in me that a number of sources (some with official connections) had viewed the film prior to Ray's release of it in 1995. Both, for example, related to me the accounts of Dr Hoang-Yung Chiang of the National Research Centre for Biotechnology in T'ai-pei, Taiwan; and the Japanese UFO researcher Johsen Takano, who had on occasion advised the Japanese Government on the UFO issue.

As Philip and Ray confirmed, both Takano and Hoang-Yung had admitted seeing the film prior to Ray's release of it:

Takano had apparently seen it when a copy was taken to Tokyo by a CIA courier for official viewing by members of the Japanese Government; and Hoang-Yung had occasion to view it while on a visit to the CIA's headquarters at Langley, Virginia.

Philip added that yet another source had come forward: Sergeant Clifford Stone of the US Army, who in 1969 was stationed at Fort Ley, Virginia, where he was part of a nuclear/biological/chemical accident (NBC) quick reaction team.

According to Stone, while on a visit to Fort Belvoir, Virginia, in that same year, he had fleeting access to an auditorium where a bizarre film was being shown. As Stone recalled, the film was packed with footage of UFOs of all shapes and sizes; in addition, there were shots of a number of unusual corpses . . .

'When I saw the Santilli tapes, I saw the [still] pictures first,' recalled Stone. 'They were haunting, because they took me back to this day in 1969, to these movies . . . There were bodies that looked very, very, very close to that one. And there were alive ones, also.'[5]

There was also the curious account of Richard C. Doty, who in the 1980s had served with the US Air Force's Office of Special Investigations (OSI).

'Several months ago I called Richard Doty,' Stan Friedman told me in November 1995. 'He said that he thought he had seen some autopsy footage that sounded like the Santilli stuff back in the early 1980s. He and the others at OSI knew it was not real because they knew what alien bodies really looked like.'[6]

This was interesting. Despite the fact that Doty (who had long-standing dealings with a number of American UFO investigators, including William Moore, who was deeply involved in the Roswell investigation) maintained that the body in the Santilli footage was something other than alien, his testimony (and that of Sergeant Clifford Stone) suggested strongly that the film was not of recent manufacture and had not been faked in the 1990s (as had been postulated in some quarters) by sources known to Ray Santilli.

But if the body was not of alien origin, then what on earth was it? William Moore suggested that the 'aliens' seen in the various autopsy films were sufferers of Turner's Syndrome – a distressing genetic disorder – who had come from a remote village in Brazil. Moore revealed that his information strongly suggested that the film released by Ray Santilli dated from approximately 1960 – not from 1947.

Moore went on to elaborate that the footage was shot, somewhat opportunistically, by a 'B-grade' science-fiction film-production company who intended using it as the centrepiece of a feature film to be made at a later date. Moore further added that, assuming his information was valid, certain persons within the field of counter-intelligence had been aware of the existence of the film for perhaps twenty years, and that the possibility had been discussed of its being utilised for disinformation purposes. That idea, Moore learned, was ultimately rejected because the footage was considered too incredible to be credible . . .[7]

On first hearing William Moore's revelations, I felt that he was truly on to something; however, even this ingenious theory was not without its problems – not least because a number of eminent sources were maintaining that the body could in no way be considered human.

Dr C.M. Milroy, a senior lecturer in forensic pathology, for example, said of the footage, 'The scalp was shown being reflected anteriorly, having been cut in a standard autopsy manner. The skull was then shown being sawn with a hand-saw across the front of the skull, though the backwards cuts and removal of the skull cap were not shown. What appeared to be the membranes covering the brain (dura) were shown being cut and removed.' Dr Milroy was careful to add, 'However, the appearances were not those of a human brain.'[8]

This was something that had been echoed by the *Daily Mail*, which had taken a lot of interest in the film: 'An organ is removed that is the size of a human liver, but not the shape. No intestines can be discerned and its internal arrangements do not seem to resemble anything human. It has no belly button – every human does, except some separated Siamese twins.'

In other words, there was strong evidence to support the theory that the body was indeed non-human in origin. But what of the statements of the ex-AFOSI man Richard Doty and William Moore?

In *Alien Contact*, Tim Good noted that Moore had readily admitted that, having developed a number of contacts in the US intelligence community, he 'may have been fed false information'; and, as Tim also noted, Richard Doty was a specialist in the field of counter-intelligence.[9]

Admittedly, I found it difficult to gauge anything conclusively from the autopsy film; however, there was one interesting aside. You'll recall from Chapter 8, which dealt with the crash of an 'unknown' off the Outer Hebrides in late 1996, that, among those who took an interest in determining what had taken place, one was the Sandia National Laboratories in New Mexico – and Sandia's involvement in the crashed-UFO issue was provocative. And when on 9 August 1980 a security guard caught sight of a UFO in the vicinity of Sandia, who prepared the official documentation surrounding the incident? None other than Richard Doty!

With this information in hand, I naturally wanted to know what Jenny Randles thought of the similarities between the film released by Ray Santilli and the still photographs described by Robert in 1986. Jenny told me:

Bear in mind, October 1986 was years before the autopsy film surfaced. In fact, the connections with the autopsy film and with what Robert told Peter Hough and me are chillingly similar. One of the impressions that you get from the alien autopsy footage is that the body is very human-like; and is around five foot in height. I have to say, it struck me as soon as I saw the footage that this was very similar to what Robert had described.[10]

Regardless of whether those photographs seen by Robert back in the mid-1980s were still shots from the 'Santilli footage', I felt that my quest had succeeded in uncovering illuminating, if fragmentary, evidence to support the notion that there was far more to the film than a mere Hollywood-created special effect.

Taken as a whole, the testimonies of the former US Air Force Office of Special Investigations operative, Richard Doty, Sergeant Clifford Stone of the United States Army, Dr Hoang-Yung Chiang of the National Research Centre for Biotechnology in Taiwan, the investigator Johsen Takano, and Jenny Randles and the enigmatic 'Robert' all suggested that the film had been in existence for years – if not decades – and that elements of the intelligence communities of a number of countries, including the USA, the UK and Japan, were aware of the existence of the film.

On numerous occasions I deliberated on the evidence I had obtained: somewhere with the United Kingdom there existed an above-top-secret committee that operated under the tightest security and that had full access to the facts surrounding the UFO crash at Roswell in July 1947, Majestic 12 and the many crashed-UFO incidents that had occurred on mainland UK. Second, that committee appeared to be staffed by elite members of MI5, MI6, GCHQ and the military. And third, for half a century the truth had remained buried under a mountain of unverifiable facts, half-truths and outright denials.

More interesting to me, the experience of Jenny Randles suggested that MJ-UK, whatever its make-up, was not beyond playing a few mind games of its own. The process of offering Jenny classified files on crashed UFOs and dead aliens, and then 'pulling' them at the last moment, indicated some form of 'dangling carrot' operation. But with what purpose in mind?

My best 'guesstimate' was that the operation was orchestrated officially and designed (a) to ascertain how the average man or woman in the street would react when confronted with extraordinary UFO data; (b) to determine the most profitable way to release officially that same data if circumstances dictated; and (c) to continue to confuse the civilian UFO research community by spreading among it fantastic tales that were sure to fracture the already fraught lines of communication. MJ-UK was indeed a subtle entity. But I was closing in: I had the group locked firmly in my sights and had gone some way towards exposing their activities.

The late Dr Eric Walker (a graduate of Harvard who had held such prestigious positions as the President of Pennsylvania University, the Executive Secretary of the Research and Development Board, and the Chairman of the Institute for Defence Analysis) had already sought and discovered some of the truth about Majestic 12 and their acquisition of crashed UFOs and alien bodies. On 8 March 1990 he described the group as 'a handful of elite'; adding the highly significant fact that: 'They are not all Americans . . .'[11]

CHAPTER ELEVEN

RUDLOE MANOR: UFO HQ?

HAVING SATISFIED MYSELF THAT THERE WAS INDEED A British equivalent of the fabled Majestic 12 organisation, my next step was to try to determine from where the group operated. Nick Pope's inability to uncover any official ongoing interest in the UFO issue in the United States effectively convinced me that the Secretariat of the Air Staff was not a part of any such group, as did his comments on the crashed-UFO controversy in general. However, this did not rule out the possibility that somewhere within Whitehall there were those 'in the know'; and the rather terse responses given to Martin Redmond MP when he tried to access any UFO files generated by GCHQ, MI6 and the Defence Intelligence Staff, suggested that British authorities were far more deeply implicated in UFO investigations than had previously been thought possible. But with such an abundance of UFO debris in their possession, where were those tasked with maintaining the secrecy storing all of this invaluable evidence?

I tried to think logically: the location would almost certainly be under the jurisdiction of the military; it would need to be totally secure against infiltration (the security would be formidable); and it would have to be a facility of considerable size to allow adequate investigations of the retrieved vehicles (and very possibly alien bodies, too) to take place. It transpired that there was one location in particular that fitted the profile perfectly: RAF Rudloe Manor – home of the RAF's Headquarters Provost and Security Services.

In UFO research circles, Rudloe Manor was legendary. Rumours that top-secret investigations into UFO encounters were undertaken from the Wiltshire base had circulated for years: Graham Birdsall of *UFO* magazine had uncovered details in 1979; and eight years later, the whole controversy surrounding Rudloe Manor spewed forth when Tim Good's *Above Top Secret* was published. Graham Birdsall recalled:

Late one evening back in 1979, I received a telephone call from a friend of long-standing which was to rank as one of the most important messages I have ever received whilst researching the subject of UFOs.

The call came from Oxford, and my source and the information that was passed directly to me [were] to remain secret for a number of years. It concerned the location and activities of an establishment which was to be revealed publicly for the first time in Timothy Good's book *Above Top Secret*.

I wish to make it absolutely clear that I was not the sole source of the information on RAF Rudloe Manor that Timothy Good details in his book, but my information enabled him to complete the jigsaw in a puzzle that he was very close to solving at the time. I was one of two independent sources which revealed the whereabouts of an official Ministry of Defence establishment that handled UFO reports, and possibly much more.

This establishment was not in London, but in Wiltshire, some one hundred miles away from Whitehall and the publicly known MOD department that supposedly dealt with all UFO reports.[1]

Tim Good's information, I knew, was no less provocative, and centred on the possibility that Rudloe Manor was up to its neck in UFO investigations; and furthermore that the Whitehall office in which Nick Pope worked was essentially kept 'out of the loop' when it came to accessing the British Government's truly guarded UFO data.[2]

As intriguing as Tim's discoveries were, however, no one appeared willing to go on record with respect to the Rudloe Manor–UFO allegations, and the entire matter remained one of those interesting, yet ultimately frustrating, rumours that surface time and again.

However, if there was indeed some substance to the rumours, I wanted to know; and if Rudloe Manor was the final resting place for those many UFOs retrieved by British authorities since the mid-1940s, then I was damn well going to find out. If there was documentation, I would find it; if there were witnesses, I would locate them and encourage them to speak on the record; and if I came across actual evidence pertaining to recovered UFO debris and extraterrestrial biology? Nothing short of a full public disclosure would suffice. But first, what was so special about RAF Rudloe Manor?

To the unsuspecting, Rudloe Manor appeared on the surface to be a Royal Air Force facility with no great relevance to anything in particular. But this was far from the case . . .

When I first learned in 1996 that Martin Redmond was planning to ask a substantial number of UFO-related questions in Parliament, I naturally wondered whether he would be drawn into the controversy surrounding Rudloe Manor. He was. On 17 October 1996 the following exchange (recorded in *Hansard*) took place:

Mr Redmond: To ask the Secretary of State for Defence what work is currently undertaken at RAF Rudloe Manor; what work was undertaken in the last ten years; what was, by rank, the establishment for the last ten years; and if he will make a statement.

Mr Soames: I will write to the hon. Member and a copy of the letter will be placed in the Library of the House.

Eleven days later Nicholas Soames responded to Martin Redmond's questioning, and revealed some eye-opening facts about Rudloe Manor. In a two-page letter (a copy of which was supplied to me by Sarah Pepin of the House of Commons Public Information Office) Soames wrote:

RAF Rudloe Manor consists of a parent unit and five lodger units:

No 1 Signals Unit – providing voice and data communications for MOD, RN, Army and RAF establishments throughout the country;

Detachment of 1001 Signals Unit – operating the UK military communications satellite system. No 1001 SU comprises several sites, one of which is located at RAF Rudloe Manor;

Headquarters Provost and Security Services (UK) – a RAF unit commanding the six geographical P&SS Regions within the UK;

Headquarters Provost and Security Services (Western Region) – providing specialist Police and Security support to all RAF establishments within the West Midlands, the West Country and South and Mid Wales;

Controller Defence Communications Network – a tri-service unit controlling world wide defence communications.

Information on the establishment of the Station is not available for security reasons in the form requested. However, I can tell you that it comprises 557 Service and 225 civilian personnel.

As Nicholas Soames's letter showed, Rudloe Manor played a central role in maintaining Britain's defensive capabilities. Even so, Soames's response was cautious. As far as the Defence Communications Network was concerned, for example, I had been able to determine that its headquarters (code-named 'Burlington') was situated 120 feet underground and was capable of housing no fewer than 55,000 people in the event of a national emergency.

Second, the information provided by Soames on the RAF's Provost and Security Services was little more than scant. As I had learned directly from staff at Rudloe Manor, the P&SS was a functional element of the RAF Police and had jurisdiction in areas such as counter-intelligence, security vetting of personnel, crime and disciplinary matters, and the issuing of passes, permits and identity cards. And Rudloe Manor was also home to yet another department: Flying Complaints Flight . . .

'Complaints from Members of Parliament or the public about military aircraft may be tasked by the Ministry of Defence to the Flying Complaints Flight for investigation,' I was informed by Rudloe Manor in 1994. 'Complaints range from damage to property, injury to persons or livestock and sonic booms, to allegations of flying indiscipline.'[3]

According to information imparted to Tim Good, however, Flying Complaints Flight had a far more significant task, too. 'I had access to every top-secret file there was, except low flying, because they dealt with UFOs,' Tim was advised by a former senior noncommissioned officer who served as an investigator with the Provost and Security Services. 'We could get in anywhere,' Tim's source added, 'but not in that department. I remember they used to have an Air Ministry guard in the passage; you couldn't get past them. We could see the Provost Marshal's top-secret files, yet I couldn't get into the place dealing with UFOs.'[4]

Again, this was not lost on Martin Redmond: 'To ask the Secretary of State for Defence if a lodger unit housed within his Department's Flying Complaints Flight specialises in unidentified flying object investigations; and if he will make a statement.'

In a 28 October 1996 response, Lord Howe stated firmly, 'I can confirm that there is no unit within the Flying Complaints Flight (FCF) based at RAF Rudloe Manor (or anywhere else) specialising in investigations into unidentified flying objects. I should add that despite continuing misunderstandings about the role of RAF Rudloe Manor in alleged "UFO" investigations, the Station is not and never has been involved in this way.' Not everyone, however, was in agreement with Lord Howe's assertion . . .

Although it was not until late 1996 that Martin Redmond began to address seriously the issue of covert involvement in UFO investigations on the part of both the P&SS and FCF at Rudloe Manor, my own research began in the early part of 1994. At that time, the only data at my disposal was that contained within Tim Good's books; and as interesting as their revelations were, Tim's sources declined to go on record. I would have to start from scratch. First stop: Nick Pope.

In speaking with Nick in April 1994, I was pleased to see that he was well informed on a variety of UFO-related issues, including the allegations surrounding RAF Rudloe Manor. He, however, was not convinced that anything of substance lay behind them, and maintained that it was out of the question to suggest that a separate division at Rudloe Manor was getting to see top-secret UFO data to which he had no access. However, I had not forgotten that Nick remained unaware that the Defence Intelligence Staff was receiving briefings on the UFO subject from US Intelligence until I presented him with the proof. Nor had I forgotten the curious affair of Nick's 'disturbed dustbin'. Although undoubtedly an event with its humorous side, this too served to illustrate that there were things afoot about which Nick simply had no knowledge. I had to try another approach.[5]

Shortly after meeting with Nick Pope in April 1994, I received from the Public Record Office two files of UFO documents that dated from the early 1960s and originated with an old and long-defunct Ministry secretariat known as S6. I began to leaf through the mass of papers.

On reading the files, I was somewhat disappointed to see that none bore a security classification, and all seemed relatively innocuous 'light in the sky'-type reports.

However, I was suddenly stopped dead in my tracks. I blinked and swallowed hard. Staring me in the face was an eleven-page document that fully affirmed the rumours surrounding Rudloe Manor. The document was dated December 1962 and concerned a series of unexplained UFO encounters at Chilliswood Farm, Taunton. According to the records, on several occasions in the late summer and early autumn of 1962, Chilliswood Farm was regularly visited by at least one unknown intruder. The main witness was Anne Henson, then a sixteen-year-old schoolgirl: 'On August 30th 1962 between 10.30 p.m. and 10.55 p.m. I opened the window in my room which faces N.N.E. and saw a diminishing star-like object with red and green coloured flames coming from it. It was slightly larger than the average star, [and] it appeared to be round.'

She elaborated and revealed that the phenomenon made a number of return 'visits' to the farm, the final occasion being on the night of 18 October.

Looking through her statement, I noted that Anne Henson had mailed a detailed letter outlining her sighting to RAF Chivenor, whereupon it was forwarded immediately to the officer in charge at Chivenor: Wing Commander C.M. Gibbs, OBE, DFC. Quite why Miss Henson's letter warranted the attention of a wing commander was not made clear from the file; however, I was amazed to see that Wing Commander Gibbs quickly solicited the assistance of none other than the RAF's Provost and Security Services at Government Buildings, Acton!

Prior to their arrival at Rudloe Manor in 1977, the P&SS operated out of an Acton office, but this was the first time I had come across actual documentation linking firmly the Provost and Security Services with the UFO issue. More importantly, it was also from Government Buildings in the 1960s that Flying Complaints Flight operated. This was a major breakthrough.

As I continued to scan the report, I noted with mounting interest that one Sergeant J.W. Scott, an investigator with the Provost and Security Services' Special Investigation Section, was assigned to the case, and made a number of visits to Anne Henson's home. Although Sergeant Scott failed to see the curious aerial object for himself, he duly prepared a three-page report on the case that was immediately classified 'Staff Confidential' and was channelled through to his superior, the Deputy Provost Marshal at the Acton office.

Curiously, instead of immediately forwarding the report to S6 (which was effectively the original version of the office in which Nick Pope worked), the Acton office spent some considerable time deliberating on what should be done with the report. Ultimately, I was able to ascertain that S6 did receive a copy of the report in question – albeit after a protracted delay of several weeks.[6]

More importantly, I was also able to link conclusively the Special Investigation Section at Acton with Flying Complaints Flight. In a 7 December 1996 interview with Neil Rusling, the Treasurer of the Royal Air Force Police Association, it was explained to me that 'Flying Complaints Flight is part of Special Investigation; it's part of the Special Investigation set-up at HQ P&SS. Acton was HQ P&SS UK, which is now at Rudloe Manor. It's just a matter of knowing where these places are.'[7]

On first examining the 1962 report, I considered the situation into which I had plunged. For years, the rumours surrounding the involvement of the P&SS and Flying Complaints Flight at Acton and later at Rudloe Manor in UFO investigations had been denied firmly. And yet, I was now in possession of officially released RAF documents that negated completely those very same denials! Then I had a sudden thought: perhaps the documents had not been released officially, after all.

I recalled the experiences of the American investigators Bill Moore and Jaime Shandera. Both had been officially informed that the US Government had no knowledge of a Majestic 12 group; however, a perusal of a number of files at the National Archives on the parts of both Moore and Shandera did apparently uncover one decades-old document referencing Majestic 12.[8]

Since the document discovered by Moore and Shandera was almost certainly 'planted' by someone who wanted the existence of Majestic 12 to become a matter of public record, I had to consider the possibility that the document I had uncovered (which, remember, was completely at variance with the British Government's stance that the P&SS had no involvement in the investigation of UFO encounters) was likewise planted – possibly by someone attached to Britain's very own Majestic 12! As time progressed, that possibility became an almost certain fact.

With this unprecedented evidence in hand, I realised that the potential was there to crack once and for all the long-standing rumours surrounding both the Provost and Security Services and Rudloe Manor. There was no time to waste: if the document was a plant to draw attention to the fact that the P&SS were heavily involved in UFO investigations, I had to act quickly lest the entire file be withdrawn when its contents became apparent to those tasked with maintaining the secrecy.

I had no choice: I would approach the Provost and Security Services directly with the evidence I had secured from the Public Record Office. This, I hoped, would serve two purposes. First, it would force an official admission out of the P&SS that they were implicated in the UFO mystery; and second, any form of positive response from the P&SS would contribute greatly to my quest to determine the extent of their involvement in the subject. And if I was going to go straight to the P&SS, I would settle for nothing less than an official response from the Director of Security and Provost Marshal himself: Air Commodore J.L. Uprichard.

On 28 April 1994 I sent Air Commodore Uprichard a copy of the 1962 report I had found within the PRO files, and a letter requesting clarification of the UFO-related activities of the P&SS.

One week later, a letter arrived at my home. It was from the Air Commodore.

> The Royal Air Force Provost and Security Services organization is a functional element of the Royal Air Force Police with responsibility for investigating alleged criminal offences and security breaches within the Service. As part of that remit, the Flying Complaints Flight investigates alleged breaches of the United Kingdom Low Flying System.
>
> The 1962 report to which you referred is a rare example of an alleged UFO sighting being treated as a low flying incident and investigated accordingly. Routinely, we neither investigate nor evaluate such reports.[9]

Air Commodore Uprichard's response was invaluable. Although he maintained that such investigations were 'rare', his letter confirmed the authenticity of the 1962 report, and provided a link between that same UFO investigation and Flying Complaints Flight. Only weeks into my enquiries, I had uncovered the crucial evidence that for years the UFO research community had been striving to locate.

But this was only the beginning. I had been able to prove that the Provost and Security Services were implicated in UFO investigations more than thirty years ago, but what of the present day? I spoke with both serving and retired military sources, a number of whom were able to supply me with both information and guidance. But by far the most important source was Jonathon Turner.

It was late September 1994 when I first liaised with Turner. I was intrigued to see that for ten years he had served with the Royal Air Force as a medic; when I spoke with him he was still officially 'on reserve'. Nevertheless, he was willing to divulge what he had uncovered about Rudloe Manor's involvement in the investigation of UFO encounters.

When he was stationed at RAF Lyneham, he learned that a number of pilots based there had seen UFOs while on flying operations; however, details of those encounters were not recorded in the flight logs. Instead, details would first be channelled through to the relevant squadron commander, then to the base commander, and ultimately through to . . . RAF Rudloe Manor.

'If the P&SS considered [the sighting] a matter of national security,' Turner added, 'they would interview the pilot and crew, who would be reminded to keep quiet about the UFO, under the Official Secrets Act.' So much for the MOD's assertion that UFOs are not covered by the OSA, I thought.

And Turner himself was fully aware of the possible ramifications that could conceivably result from speaking out publicly. Stressing that the RAF 'regards UFOs seriously', he informed me, 'I have no objection to you using the information I supplied to you [and] you may use my name if you wish, but I would like your advice of possible legal action from the MOD, or unwanted visits from P&SS to my home. This may seem a bit paranoid but all this is new to me and I look to you for guidance.' As I informed Turner, I felt that he was unlikely to feel the effects of any form of backlash because any action on the part of the Ministry of Defence or the P&SS would only add further weight to Turner's disclosures. The best course of action on their part was to sit tight, seethe quietly, and hope the whole controversy would quickly die away. Needless to say, the controversy did not die away.[10]

As I revealed in *A Covert Agenda*, my investigations into Rudloe Manor also turned up cryptic revelations concerning the tracking by Flying Complaints Flight of mysterious and decidedly unidentified objects in Britain's airspace using what was known as the Skyguard radar system. Again, it appeared that Rudloe Manor was the British Government's very own 'UFO HQ'.

With so much data pertaining to Rudloe Manor, the P&SS, FCF and their involvement in UFO investigations at my disposal, I felt duty bound to inform Tim Good (who was almost single-handedly responsible for initially publicising the various rumours surrounding Rudloe Manor) of the advances I had made.

And so it transpired that on a sunny morning in September 1995, I travelled down to Tim's home town of Beckenham with a copy of the original manuscript for *A Covert Agenda*. We agreed to meet at Beckenham Railway Station and then made our way to a nearby restaurant for lunch.

After scanning the material, Tim asked if he could make use of a small section of it in his forthcoming book, *Beyond Top Secret*. I agreed, and in return Tim put me in touch with his (and soon thereafter my) literary agent: Andrew Lownie. Then a most strange thing happened.

Soon after Andrew was working hard to sell *A Covert Agenda* (which disclosed a great deal about the involvement of Rudloe Manor in UFO investigations); Tim's *Beyond Top Secret* was looming on the horizon with yet more 'Rudloe revelations'; Nick Pope's book was soon to be published; and the media were latching on to the fact that UFOs were a serious defence issue.

Suddenly (and quite out of the blue), the Ministry of Defence made a stunning admission. In response to a letter from the researcher Chris Fowler, an MOD spokeswoman, Kerry Philpott, wrote on 14 December 1995:

Your letter mentions the role of RAF Rudloe Manor. Rudloe Manor is the Headquarters of the RAF Police, which does serve as a focal point, amongst other things, for flying complaints. In the past, Rudloe Manor was indeed the RAF coordination point for reports of 'unexplained' aerial sightings. However, once received they were simply forwarded to Sec(AS)2 for appropriate action. Nowadays Rudloe Manor, along with other RAF stations, forward such reports directly to this office. I can confirm that RAF Rudloe Manor does not carry out any research into 'UFOs' or any related matter.

After years of denial and obfuscation, here was the evidence. Chris Fowler quickly contacted Tim and supplied him with a copy of Kerry Philpott's letter. Tim noted in a 7 January 1996 letter to Chris:

This is certainly the first time the MOD has officially admitted that Rudloe Manor used to be the RAF's 'coordination point for reports of "unexplained" aerial phenomena'. Nicholas Redfern has been pursuing this line of enquiry for a number of years, and one ex-RAF officer informed him – quite openly – that at one time such reports were sent to RM . . .

You have done well in eliciting this response from the MOD, and I have written to Miss Philpott to ask the exact period when this coordination point was active. I'll let you know the result. Unfortunately, there is as yet no official confirmation that RM was ever used for conducting secret research into UFO reports, as confirmed for me by several sources. But we are making progress.

We were indeed making progress. At a drinks party at Andrew Lownie's flat on 24 January 1996, Tim supplied me with a copy of a letter he had received from Kerry Philpott stating that Rudloe Manor served as the RAF's 'coordination point' for UFO reports until 1992.

However, I was convinced that behind the MOD's statement there lay far more than was being officially admitted. For example, the timing of the MOD's letter to Chris Fowler was crucial: it had surfaced at the very time that both Tim and I were on the verge of releasing to the public crucial data on Rudloe Manor's UFO investigations. I considered this to be an attempt on the part of the MOD to limit the potential 'damage' to the Ministry's public stance that both my book and Tim's would cause.

Indeed, it appeared that the MOD's 'admission' was something of a red herring. Although Kerry Philpott's letters to both Chris and Tim were interesting, I noted that she was at pains to point out that Rudloe Manor and the P&SS had no active involvement in UFO investigations, aside from operating as a point of coordination from where UFO reports could be dispatched to her office: Sec(AS)2A.

Unfortunately, this was totally at variance with the data I had been able to obtain. The 1962 report I had located at the Public Record Office showed conclusively that the Provost and Security Services were conducting their own investigations: in that instance, the officer assigned to the case, Sergeant Scott, had even made several personal visits to the home of the witness!

Then there was the ex-RAF medic, Jonathon Turner, who was able to state conclusively that Rudloe Manor was carrying out its own UFO investigations, and, more importantly, those same investigations appeared to revolve around sightings reported by the military that were subject to the Official Secrets Act. Turner was certain: 'All UFO reporting is carried out at the Flying Complaints Flight, which is a smokescreen for UFO investigations.'

Perhaps most importantly of all, however, according to Kerry Philpott, Rudloe Manor served as the RAF's coordination point for UFO reports until 1992, and would routinely forward any such reports to Sec(AS)2A. And yet, Nick Pope, who had the responsibility of examining all incoming UFO data at Sec(AS)2A between 1991 and 1994, had no knowledge that Rudloe Manor fulfilled such a function (he felt the stories concerning Rudloe Manor were little more than myths); and in late 1996 he went on to inform me that during his tenure, he could not recall any UFO reports arriving at his office from Rudloe Manor in the 1991–92 time frame. In view of Nick's astonishing statement, where were all Rudloe Manor's UFO reports going? I suspected strongly that they were not going anywhere: whatever secrets Rudloe Manor had learned about UFOs, it was determined to keep them strictly 'in house'. Kerry Philpott's disclosure was, at best, far from satisfactory. But the real surprise was to come later in 1996.

When in May of that year I was asked by the BBC to take part in a forthcoming episode of its documentary series on the paranormal, *Out of this World*, I felt that this was an ideal opportunity to make public for the first time the 1962 P&SS UFO report on which I had been working quietly for approximately two years. First, it would allow the public to see that there was indeed some substance to the allegations surrounding the Provost and Security Services; and second, Matthew Williams, who had undertaken an inordinate amount of research into what was taking place at Rudloe Manor, was also due to be featured in the programme, and this would give us the perfect excuse to hit the MOD with a 'double whammy'.

The *Out of this World* team was impressed with the Provost and Security Services document I had obtained, and this proved to be the central point of my interview, which was conducted by the reporter Chris Choi. Similarly, the segment in which Matthew was featured was equally impressive, and showed both him and Choi being questioned by security staff at Rudloe Manor. Most remarkably of all, one of those same security staff let it slip in an unguarded moment that he was fully acquainted with *Out of this World*'s activities, in spite of the fact that the series had not yet aired.

When it became clear to the UFO research community that I had been able to secure the release of an official P&SS document on UFOs, I was inundated with letters from colleagues enquiring how they, too, could obtain a copy. I pointed out that copyright restrictions enforced strictly by the Public

Record Office prevented me from making copies, and I suggested that anyone interested in examining the document for themselves should make a visit to the PRO where it was readily accessible. Or was it? Back to Chris Fowler, who wrote about his experiences at the PRO:

> On August 27 and 28 1996 I visited the Public Record Office in Kew, along with Matthew Williams, Richard Conway and Sue Dilworth in search of released documents relating to UFO sightings and investigations that had been released under the thirty-year ruling. In particular we were after a document, AIR 2/16918, which contained a [report] concerning a UFO sighting in the 1960s that was investigated by the Provost and Security Services. This document had been brought to light by researcher Nick Redfern who had discovered it previously and featured it when he was on an episode of the BBC series on the paranormal: *Out of this World.*
>
> We arrived at the Public Record Office ready with the reference number of the said document which we had got in advance from Nick. After signing into the PRO, we went straight away to the reference room and ordered the document on the computer for viewing.

Approximately twenty minutes later, however, the document had not surfaced. Enquiries revealed that the file was at the PRO's 'Photo Estimates' division where, presumably, copies were being made for another interested party. Chris's account continued:

> We asked if it was possible to view the document and get a copy of it. On doing so, we discovered that it wasn't in Photo Estimates, after all, and had apparently gone 'missing'. The staff there were quite helpful, and one informed us that it had been missing since May [when filmed by *Out of this World* in early June, I had used my own copy

From Group Captain J Rose OBE MIISec RAF

**Headquarters Provost and Security Services
(United Kingdom)**
Royal Air Force Rudloe Manor Hawthorn
Wiltshire SN13 OPQ

Telephone Hawthorn (01225) 810461 ext 5600
fax 5721

N Redfern Esq

Please reply to
The Officer Commanding
Your reference

Our reference
PSS/260/8/Air
Date
28 Feb 96

Dear Mr Redfern

COORDINATION OF ALLEGED UNIDENTIFIED FLYING OBJECT SIGHTINGS

Thank you for your letter dated 30th January 1996 which Air
Commodore Uprichard passed to me as Officer Commanding, Provost and
Security Services (United Kingdom). The matters referred to in the
report which you enclosed with your letter occurred in 1962. I am
sure that you will appreciate that it is difficult for me to
provide definitive answers to all of your questions as the vast
majority of correspondence and documentation dating from that era
would have been destroyed many years ago.

I can confirm that Flying Complaints Flight, which is part of
Headquarters Provost and Security Services (United Kingdom) (HQ
P&SS(UK)), was responsible for coordinating reports of unexplained
aerial sightings until 1992. I have not been able to determine the
date on which Flying Complaints Flight began to fulfil this role.
Please note, however, that Flying Complaints Flight only moved to
RAF Rudloe Manor (with the rest of HQ P&SS(UK)) in 1977. RAF
Rudloe Manor itself would have had no role in the coordination of
unexplained aerial sighting reports prior to the arrival of HQ
P&SS(UK). Indeed, it is likely, although we are unable to confirm
this, that Flying Complaints Flight coordinated such reports whilst
at the previous location of HQ P&SS(UK) at Acton.

Flying Complaints Flight would have received reports regarding
unexplained aerial sightings from members of the public as well as
from RAF witnesses. They would merely have forwarded these reports
to the Secretariat (Air Staff) at the Ministry of Defence and no
further action would have been taken either by Flying Complaints
Flight or by any other HQ P&SS(UK) personnel. It is probable that
reports would have been retained by Flying Complaints Flight for a
limited period of time before routine destruction.

*RAF Rudloe Manor denies that the Provost and Security Services investigate UFO
sightings and encounters. Declassified Air Ministry memoranda located at the Public
Reord Office tells a different story. In 1996 that same memoranda vanished under
circumstances that still remain unresolved.*

of the document]. This I found interesting: if the PRO knew that the file had been missing since May, why was it listed as being in Photo Estimates?

Why, indeed? Chris was far from finished:

On the following day, we arrived yet again at the PRO, and once again enquired with staff if the missing document had turned up yet. It hadn't, but we were told that it was still being searched for and was being treated seriously.

We were only spending half the day there, as we had to get back to Wales, so before leaving, once again asked if the document had been located. This time the staff member went and got the manager of the department. When we spoke to her, we explained about the document and told her that it had been featured on *Out of this World* recently. She then told us that they, the Public Record Office, had received a note from the Ministry of Defence requesting the document back.

The implications of the MOD's actions were readily apparent. Almost certainly the inclusion of the report on that decades-old UFO encounter investigated by the P&SS was a major source of embarrassment to the Ministry of Defence, and a determination had been made to withdraw the material from public viewing. Was the inclusion of that report in the file a bureaucratic mistake, or had it been planted by sympathetic sources? Either way, it made little difference since the entire three hundred-page file had completely vanished from the shelves of the PRO.

But who, specifically, within the MOD had requested that the document be returned? Chris told me that he had contacted Kerry Philpott at Sec(AS)2A and was informed, 'When enquiries were made the PRO's computer records showed that this file was held by the PRO's photo ordering department.'

Philpott added, 'Once an official file has been selected for permanent retention, and has been transferred to the PRO, it would be illegal for any documents contained on the file to be removed, or tampered with in any way by anyone.'

> I was surprised at this response after being told otherwise by the PRO [recalled Chris]. It's most likely that Kerry Philpott was telling the truth in her letter to me, as she was probably told by staff at the PRO that the document was in the 'photo ordering department', which is what they are still telling people who haven't found out otherwise.
>
> In early October [1996] I phoned the PRO myself and was put through to the manager. When I confronted her with what she had told us on 28 August, and with Kerry Philpott's reply, she confirmed that she told us they did have a note from the MOD requesting the document.

Chris continued to receive contradictory replies with respect to the exact location of the file for months; however, it failed to turn up. And there were still more remarkable revelations to come as Chris related:

> During November I received a phone call from Richard Conway as he was writing an article on our visit to the PRO for *UFO Reality* magazine. I filled him in on all the details, and as Richard was writing it up, we decided he should call the manager.
>
> Later that day, Richard called back and told me something that gave me a surprise. He had spoken to the manager and she had told him that she had made a mistake: they hadn't received a note from the MOD requesting the document! This after confirming the matter with me twice! It now seems that perhaps she told us something she shouldn't have back in August. Her superiors would by then have certainly been aware that a member

of staff had told members of the public that the MOD had requested the document because of my letter to Kerry Philpott.

That the manager did make an admission that the file in question had been requested to be returned to the MOD was something also supported firmly by Matthew Williams: 'She did say that; I was witness to that, and heard her with my own ears.'

'One thing is obvious,' concluded Chris, 'someone along the line is not telling the truth. It's also hard to imagine how someone could steal such a thick document from the PRO with all the security they have.'[11]

On 15 February 1997, I had the opportunity to speak with Richard Conway; by that date the file was still missing from the Public Record Office. That crucial piece of evidence, which fully confirmed that the Provost and Security Services were conducting their own UFO investigations, had vanished . . .

Although someone in officialdom had sought to obliterate any and all evidence of direct P&SS involvement in the UFO mystery, they had overlooked one crucial fact: I had secured my own copy of the file at issue some three years previously. Although I did not really entertain the possibility that the P&SS would go so far as to demand the return of my copy, I made additional copies and took steps to ensure that they were secreted at a variety of locations. Overreaction or common sense? Only time would tell.

There was another matter, too, over which the P&SS had absolutely no control: in late 1996, Anne Henson, the key witness involved in the 1962 UFO encounter investigated by the P&SS, surfaced publicly. Now fifty years of age, and the mother of three children, Anne had returned to live in the very farm where that historic encounter had occurred so many years before.

Her recollections of Sergeant J.W. Scott of the P&SS Special Investigation Section were intriguing. He had arrived on her doorstep armed with 'charts and compasses', Anne stated.

> The man stayed for a few hours, then left saying he'd be in touch. He left me with the impression that it would not be a good idea to talk to anyone about what we'd seen. If I did, he said, nobody would believe me anyway. I thought to myself, You know what it is and you're not telling me.'
>
> I think the MOD knew something was going on, but weren't sure what . . . and they just didn't want to admit it. It could have been a UFO – I can't see why there shouldn't be life on other planets.
>
> Now, whenever I'm outdoors, I have a look at the skies, and I wonder if it's up there, and whether perhaps I'll see it again one day.[12]

Then, in February 1997, there came a dramatic development. Among those who had attempted to force the British Government to be more forthcoming with its UFO files was Dr Colin Ridyard of Anglesey, who had taken a deep interest in the missing 1962 P&SS–UFO report on Anne Henson's encounter at Chilliswood Farm.

Dr Ridyard made enquiries with the PRO, and on 26 February was informed by Stephen Blades, the Reprographic Orders Supervisor at the PRO: 'This file is still unaccounted for [and the] relevant staff have been informed of this problem and have been made aware that a number of people are wishing to access the information in this file.'

Acting on this information, Dr Ridyard quickly contacted the MP Ieuan Wyn Jones – who had taken an interest in the UFO issue, and had on previous occasions asked questions in Parliament pertaining to UFOs. Having been briefed of the attempts of the investigator Chris Fowler to locate the file, Wyn Jones agreed to bring up the matter in Parliament.

At that time, matters began to heat up. On 13 March 1997,

the PRO denied to Dr Ridyard that the file in question had been withdrawn because of a 'censorship order'; while on 16 March Dr Ridyard countered, 'I dispute your sources of confirmation that [the file] is not unavailable because of any censorship order. Although not necessarily officially sanctioned, the fact remains that the document remains effectively censored under what can only be described as very dubious circumstances.'

The controversy continued. 'I can assure you that enormous efforts have been made already to locate this file,' Dr Ridyard was advised by Dr Elizabeth Hallam Smith, the PRO's Director of Public Services, 'and that these are continuing. This matter, which is one I am taking very seriously indeed, has caused me to review our rules for staff use of the records and I am introducing new and draconian measures to ensure that the risk of such misplacements is in future kept to an absolute minimum.'

Then, lo and behold, on 26 March there came a breakthrough. 'I am delighted to report that we have now located [the file] which had been misplaced in another box,' revealed the Public Record Office to Dr Ridyard. Was the matter at an end? Had the whole controversy simply been due to a filing error?

In no way did this statement explain satisfactorily the statements made to Chris Fowler by Vivienne Bales that the Ministry of Defence had requested return of the file. There was also the significant fact that the file had vanished at precisely the time when I intended publicising it on BBC TV's *Out of this World* programme. In other words, if I had not already secured my own copy several years previously, I would have been unable to demonstrate the extent to which the P&SS were implicated in the UFO mystery.

Moreover, in the latter part of 1996, the Public Record Office was closed for an in-depth stocktaking: the file remained missing. Indeed, it resurfaced (somewhat too conveniently, in my opinion) only when potentially embarrassing questions began to be asked in Parliament by Ieuan Wyn Jones MP.

Then on 15 April 1997 there came the elusive proof that I had been striving to locate: 'I can confirm', said I.D. Goode, the MOD Deputy Departmental Record Officer at the Metropole Building, 'that AIR 2/16918 was in MOD's hands last year and was returned to the Public Record Office on 9 November 1996.'

Goode's most significant comment, however, was saved until last: 'I regret that I can provide no further information as to what happened to the file after its arrival in the MOD.'

There were without doubt dark aspects to this affair that remained unresolved. Nevertheless, with the file now back in the public domain, the claim of the Provost and Security Services that they had no involvement in the investigation of UFO encounters was one that I had been able to demolish utterly.

Perhaps somewhat rashly, given what had already taken place with respect to the elusive document, I thought that would be the end of the matter. It was not.

Shortly after I.D. Goode confirmed, both in a recorded telephone conversation with Matthew Williams and in a letter, that the 1962 P&SS–UFO report had been removed from the Public Record Office and was 'in MOD hands' in 1996, it was announced by another Ministry of Defence spokesperson that this was an error! Goode was wrong: the file had not left the Public Record Office in 1996, after all, and was not therefore in the hands of the Ministry of Defence during the period of time that it was inaccessible at the PRO.

Needless to say, this affair was bordering on the farcical, and Chris Fowler, Matthew and I simply did not accept what the MOD had to say about the strange disappearance of Public Record Office file AIR 2/16918. As Matthew put it in a special *Truthseekers' Review* package in 1997:

We have got our MPs on to the case and they don't like the things they are being told and quite frankly they don't believe the MOD's new excuse for the missing file. We think we know why the file was removed from the Public Record Office and it has more to do with embarrassment over the secret UFO investigations departments being exposed than anything else.[13]

In addition to securing the views of Air Commodore Uprichard, the testimony of Anne Henson, the revelations of ex-Royal Air Force medic Jonathon Turner (not to mention exposing the strange tale of the missing Public Record Office file on the P&SS–UFO connection), I made further significant headway as I delved into the secret world of RAF Rudloe Manor.

In an effort fully to understand the workings of the Provost and Security Services in general, I sought out a number of retired and former RAF Police personnel whom I felt might be able to fill in a few blanks for me. One of those to whom I spoke was the aforementioned Treasurer of the Royal Air Force Police Association, Neil Rusling.

In December 1996, I learned that he had a most interesting background, and had served with the RAF's counter-intelligence section. 'I go no further, because I can't,' Neil replied when I asked him for details of the sort of work undertaken by counter-intelligence personnel. Nevertheless, he was able to assist me on the UFO angle.

Some six months previously, Neil had made a visit to RAF Halton. 'Being the Association Treasurer,' he explained, 'I still have a lot of contact with those that are still serving, and I was able to confirm that any UFO interest that the RAF would have would be done by the Flying Complaints unit.'

This was a significant revelation, particularly in view of Lord Howe's 28 October 1996 letter to Martin Redmond MP, in which Howe specifically denied that Flying Complaints Flight fulfilled any such function.

'Flying Complaints involvement – is that of today?' I asked Neil.

'As of today,' he replied firmly.

'That would be from Rudloe Manor?'

'That would be from Rudloe Manor, yeah.'

Neil was turning out to be one of the most important sources I had come across. Further questions crossed my mind.

'How would the Flying Complaints people pick up on a report?' I asked.

'Well,' Neil explained, 'the way that the RAF Police on stations would pick it up would be if somebody went and told them, or if somebody on the camp saw it, or if it was in close vicinity of an RAF station.'

'So, if a report was filed, and it went to the RAF Police, they would then forward it direct to Rudloe and from there it would be channelled to Flying Complaints Flight? Is that fair?'

'Yeah,' replied Neil. 'They might use a middleman at the P&SS Regional Headquarters, but all they would do would be to forward it on to the Flying Complaints people.'

'And Rudloe Manor would be the first port of call for such reports?'

Neil was certain: 'That would be the first port of call.'[14]

In addition to speaking with Neil, I felt that it was vital to obtain the opinions of Matthew Williams who had reported extensively on Rudloe Manor's operations in his *Truthseekers' Review* magazine.

What first led Matthew to believe that Rudloe Manor was no ordinary RAF base?

I'm telling you something now which breaks the Official Secrets Act. When I was with Customs and Excise, we would receive what were known as the Suspect Index Telexes – this would be 'flash traffic' which would say something like: 'Mr John Smith is coming into Heathrow; he's suspected of carrying drugs. Don't approach him. Inform us.'

Now, the 'us' we were to inform would sometimes be London Customs; sometimes it would be the Criminal

Investigations Unit; and sometimes it would say, 'Contact Rudloe Manor'.

Because of the high-level liaison between our departments and the security services, I was reasonably able to say that Rudloe and MI5 were linked. In fact, I've spoken with people who've told me that the security services both train and work at Rudloe.

And what of Rudloe's involvement with UFOs?

The first time I went down to Rudloe was in January 1994. I'd gone down with the [UFO] researcher Paul Damon. We were just having a look around the outskirts of the base, and were suddenly approached by armed guards who visibly threatened us. We told them, quite honestly, that we were interested in the UFO stories – we'd read Tim Good's *Above Top Secret*.

What was interesting was that the guard asked for our names, and made what was no more than a one-minute phone call from the guardhouse. Well, he came back and said our details checked out. But the speed with which they were able to do the check suggested that at Rudloe there is some sort of central computer where people's identities and personal details can be accessed immediately.

I knew that this was plausible: two years previously, Jonathon Dillon of the National Union of Journalists had spoken with a former RAF Police officer who informed him that Rudloe Manor employed personnel whose job it was to monitor both UFO researchers and RAF personnel with 'offbeat' hobbies – which included UFOs. Matthew continued:

Because Paul and I had received so much hassle at Rudloe, this really spurred us on; and this was one of the reasons why we spent so much time in the area speaking with the locals.

One of the things which came up was that there was a place at Rudloe which investigated UFOs. But a number of people, including people who worked there, said that UFOs were a taboo subject – you don't bring it up. One guy I spoke with was a flight lieutenant actually stationed at Rudloe. He had some interest in UFOs and asked his superior officer, a wing commander, what went on in the place which dealt with UFOs. The wing commander basically replied: 'I can tell you, or you can keep your job. What do you want to do?' Naturally he answered, 'I'll keep my job.'

Another guy who approached me worked in the command of the Defence Communication Network. His area was nuclear security – transporting nuclear materials and so on. He had access to top-secret data, and was sometimes allowed to action things, sometimes not. But he was never allowed to deal with UFO data. He had to give this data to very high-up sources. He didn't know what happened to the information, but he did know that there was somewhere at Rudloe which dealt with it all.

As well as that, I had a contact who was acquainted with people employed in the Defence Communication Network. They said that Rudloe has an extensive radar tracking system which extends to outer space; and there's apparently a huge room which is full of screens just monitoring Britain's airspace.

When I put this to the DCN, I got what I would call a 'shocked denial'.

One guy who worked at Rudloe told me that they had seen my [*Truthseekers'*] magazine and said, 'We know all about what you do.' When I asked him how he got to see the magazine, he suddenly went on the defensive. 'I didn't see it internally, if that's what you mean.'

He then came out with this implausible story about buying it on a street corner in Bath!

How did Matthew feel about Nick Pope's belief that the whole issue of Rudloe Manor was spurious?

I'll give you an example: the researcher John Holman sent a UFO report to Rudloe; it never reached Nick Pope. And this was in Nick's term at Sec(AS)2A. Nick always said that there could be no such thing as a cover-up because all the reports went to him. But we know that, with Flying Complaints Flight being the official coordination point, they got them first. What did they have that they didn't show Nick? To this day, he won't accept that he didn't get to see everything.

I was also particularly interested to know what exactly happened when Matthew went down to Rudloe Manor with the BBC's *Out of this World* team.

First, I should explain that at the base they have a number of unmarked cars which basically just drive around the area. On a number of occasions, I was stopped and questioned as to why I was there. One occasion, I was with Paul Damon and we stopped near the base – but in a car park; not right outside the main gates, or anything like that.

A car stopped by us. Immediately I recognised that it had been fitted with a 'covert aerial'. I recognised this from my Customs and Excise days because we used to fit them! Next minute, our car was surrounded by Ministry of Defence people. It was no surprise at all to me that they started asking a lot of questions. I said to one of the RAF policemen that I knew his vehicle was fitted with a covert aerial – the radios they used were basically secured to prevent anyone from listening in – and he gave me a little wry smile. Time and again, we would have these little confrontations.

But why should the level of security there be so much

higher than at other military bases? I'd visited RAF stations when I was with Customs and Excise, including RAF Lyneham. Lyneham is like Heathrow for the military, but Rudloe's security is way above that.

Through Customs and Excise, and documents I had access to, I learned that a lot of the function of Rudloe Manor revolves around military intelligence, basically: they liaise with C&E, police and Interpol amongst others. When I asked why all of this was so sensitive, I was told it was because of the other stuff – the UFOs. This was from people who worked there.

The BBC knew I was doing these investigations into Rudloe, and asked me to help with *Out of this World*: show them around the base perimeter, that sort of thing. When we arrived, we spoke with a guard who's normally stationed at the guardhouse. He'd been speaking quite freely with me and the BBC's Chris Choi about the size of the facility, how many people worked there, and being quite amicable. But the moment we mentioned the word UFO – which we left until last – he visibly shook and stopped in his tracks. His eyes widened, and he said, 'Sorry, I can't say any more.'

With that, he turned around and walked back inside the guardhouse. He then, over the Tannoy, made a call and another MOD policeman turned up. What was surprising was he said they knew we were coming, but they wished we'd let them know!

'How did you know we were coming?' Chris Choi and I asked. He just replied, 'We get to know about these things; we get our information.' When we again asked him how he knew we were coming, he simply said, 'I'm not going to discuss those sorts of things.'

The MOD chap then asked for some identification. Chris Choi didn't have any and all I had was my Barclaycard! I showed it to the guy. He looked at it, and said, 'Oh, yes! I know your name!' 'Oh, really?' I replied.

I started laughing and said to the camera, 'Did you catch that? He knows who I am!' But this is similar to conversations I've had with other staff at Rudloe: they all seem to know who I am.[15]

Like any good investigative journalist, I naturally wanted to secure support for Matthew's assertions. I had known Matthew long enough to determine that he was a credible source of data, but took the view that confirmation for what he had to say would prove to be beneficial to my work.

Having first checked that Matthew had indeed served with Customs and Excise in their Personnel and Criminal Investigations departments (detailed background data was made available to me with Matthew's consent), my next step was to evaluate his reference to high-level liaison between Rudloe Manor and Customs and Excise.

Following enquiries with Flight Lieutenant Andy Woodruff at Rudloe Manor, I received the following brief statement: 'The Flying Complaints Flight has the responsibility for RAF liaison with HM Customs and Excise.'

Not only was Rudloe undoubtedly working hand in glove with Customs and Excise, the division involved at Rudloe with the responsibility for undertaking such work was none other than Flying Complaints Flight – the people tasked with undertaking top-secret UFO investigations!

I then turned my attention to what Matthew had learned about the Defence Communication Network – specifically with respect to claims that at Rudloe there was housed an extensive radar tracking system that extended to outer space.

Again, this was not out of the question. For example, there was the proven fact that at Rudloe there existed 1001 Signals Unit, which was responsible for overall control of the United Kingdom's communications satellite system in near-Earth orbit!

Moreover, the Defence Communications Network at Rudloe had the responsibility for controlling defence communications on a worldwide scale. In other words, the DCN did have a keen interest in what was going on in the skies above our world.

I then turned my attention to Matthew's recollections of what occurred when both he and Chris Choi of the BBC were engaged in filming outside Rudloe Manor for the *Out of this World* television series. He fully confirmed that Matthew's version of events was correct. While engaged in some filming work with Choi at the Public Record Office, I asked him to recall his experiences at Rudloe Manor.

He and Matthew were chatting openly with one of the security personnel at Rudloe until the UFO issue was brought up . . .

A second security operative had let it slip to Chris and Matthew that he was fully acquainted with the activities of the *Out of this World* team; and perhaps most importantly of all, Choi was able to state authoritatively that the guard who examined Matthew's Barclaycard did make a statement to the effect that he knew who Matthew was! Matthew had passed muster.

Despite the high level of secrecy that surrounded Rudloe Manor's relationship with the UFO mystery, I had succeeded in getting all of my sources to speak on the record with one exception: a civilian carpenter who had been employed for a number of weeks to do repair work at Rudloe Manor in the early 1980s.

He explained that he made friends with several people at Rudloe and kept in touch with 'one or two' after completing his assignment. Over drinks one evening in a local pub, one of those friends quietly mentioned that several years previously, possibly around 1976–78, 'The Americans gave us a piece of metal from the Roswell crash and we've got it at the base.'

Unaware of what the 'Roswell crash' was, the carpenter asked for an explanation. However, when it became clear to the rather talkative airman that his words had fallen on essentially deaf ears, he declined to elaborate, saying only something to the effect of 'You'll find out one day, anyway.'

Several years passed before things became clear. As the carpenter explained to me, it was an evening in either 1987 or 1988: Tim Good was being interviewed on an ITV talk show hosted by the sports personality Jimmy Greaves; and during the course of the interview, and to the absolute astonishment of my source, Tim mentioned the crash of a UFO at Roswell, New Mexico, in 1947. The memories of that curious conversation in the early 1980s came flooding back.

'I wish I'd known then what happened at Roswell,' the carpenter concluded. 'I could have asked some more questions. But maybe this'll be of some help to you.'

I readily admit that attempts to chase this report back to the original military source who spoke with the carpenter proved immensely difficult, but I present the details as they were related to me primarily to demonstrate that the full Rudloe Manor–UFO controversy is one that is likely to continue for many years to come.

Further evidence subsequently reached me concerning Rudloe Manor and its link with the US intelligence community. From Paul Marks – a Surrey-based businessman – there came the intriguing account relating to a March 1997 discussion that took place while Marks was returning to the UK, having been engaged on business in Washington, DC. Marks told me:

I've established the exact date as 22 March. I was seated [on the aircraft] next to an interesting American whom I got chatting to.

After discussing my work, I casually asked him his line of business, to which he replied, 'US Government.' My interest naturally aroused, I then asked which branch, and to this he replied with words to the effect of 'Department of Defense, let's say.' He then proceeded to joke that he could tell me, but he'd have to kill me! Also, [he] mentioned in passing that he had several colleagues with him.

Somewhat sceptical and thinking I could be dealing with a Walter Mitty, I asked where in England he was staying, assuming it would be London. He replied that it was 'somewhere near Bath; we're working with some of your Ministry of Defence guys down there.' I then jokingly asked what interest the MOD have in that area, to which he replied, 'I'll be at an RAF base called Rudloe – ever heard of it?'

My point is this – why would an average American, unless he was really telling the truth, have heard of Rudloe and admit to working there. On the assumption that he really was US Government (which agency, I don't know, but take your pick), he hopefully assumed that there was no danger in telling me (an average Brit) and this might explain his lack of professionalism in actually mentioning the place. Little did he know that I knew the rumours about Rudloe's activities. But what on earth were they up to at that time that required several 'government' men to be travelling there?

What indeed? Rudloe's involvement in the UFO controversy seemed to be deepening. The next stop on my journey: the Home Office.

CHAPTER TWELVE

THE HOME OFFICE LINK

WHEN DARK RUMOURS BEGAN TO REACH ME TO THE EFFECT that the Home Office was deeply involved in the UFO problem, I was not, to be frank, overly surprised. As I was able to show convincingly in *A Covert Agenda* (not to mention in the previous chapter of this book), the publicly acknowledged division of the MOD that handled UFO reports – Secretariat (Air Staff) 2A – got to see only a mere fraction of the UFO data held by British authorities. More importantly, there was the highly illuminating fact that Sec(AS)2A rarely got to see any military-originated UFO reports of outstanding significance. With this in mind, the Home Office link was far from unexpected.

While rumours of direct Home Office involvement in the UFO subject had persisted for decades, the first account to which I gave any great credence came from Tim Good, who recalled an event from 1963:

A close friend of mine whom I have known since 1952 witnessed the landing of an unidentified flying object in Derbyshire in September 1963, and subsequently came into contact with its operators. Four years afterwards two men with Home Office identification cards turned up at my friend's flat and politely asked a number of questions which clearly indicated that they were familiar with aspects of the incident. When my friend refused to answer certain questions the men seemed pleased and eventually left. There were no threats; the men seemed perfectly normal in every way, and there was no follow-up. As in most such cases, nothing can be proven, but I am sure of my friend's integrity.[1]

Tim was able to make additional breakthroughs with respect to the Home Office angle in 1982, when in February of that year he conducted an eye-opening interview with a retired police inspector, in an attempt to determine if the UFO issue was subject to the constraints of the Official Secrets Act.

What I can say to you, [Tim was told] is that I know that the subject itself was the subject of a Home Office directive . . . There were certain specified telephone numbers: they turned out to be monitoring stations in relation to aircraft . . . So it was obviously radar that they were relying on there, and also somebody that they were relying on who had control of aircraft in the area.[2]

While conducting research into the available UFO files at the Public Record Office, I had always made a point of looking for any that might have possibly implicated the Home Office. I found none. I concluded that either the Home Office link was spurious, or, for reasons that I was unable to determine, it was a link that had to be denied at all costs. As time went on, and events unfolded, I had no choice but to go with the latter theory. I began to review the facts systematically.

There was Tim Good's friend who had been questioned by Home Office personnel in 1963; and there was the ex-ATV employee, Roger Chambers, who recalled that crucial film footage pertaining to the crash of a UFO on Cannock Chase, Staffordshire, in January 1974 was confiscated by Home

Office officials; similar footage pertaining to a UFO crash near the Isle of Wight in 1978 had the same fate.

I also recalled that several years previously Graham Birdsall, editor of *UFO* magazine, had informed me of the experience of George Wild, who had served as a senior prison officer at Armley Prison in Leeds. George had quietly let it be known to Graham that a 'senior Home Office prison official' had once let it slip that on the night of the UFO crash-landing at Rendlesham Forest in December 1980, high-level orders had come through to the nearby High Point Prison advising staff to prepare for a possible evacuation of the inmates due to a matter of national security.

Given the recollections of Roger Chambers that the 'crew' of the UFO that came down within Rendlesham Forest were retrieved by the military while still alive, I had visions of High Point Prison serving as a 'safe house' for these non-human visitors.

In late 1997, this aspect of the Rendlesham incident (and its possible tie-in with the Home Office) took an ominous and dark turn. On 23 October of that year, Lord Hill-Norton, Chief of the Defence Staff, 1971–73, officially raised in the House of Lords the question of unusual activities at High Point Prison in late 1980. The exchange ran thus:

> Lord Hill Norton asked Her Majesty's Government: whether staff at High Point Prison in Suffolk received instructions to prepare for a possible evacuation of the prison at some time between 25 and 30 December 1980, and if so, why these instructions were issued.

> Lord Williams of Mostyn: I regret to advise the noble Lord that I am unable to answer his question, as records for High Point Prison relating to the period concerned are no longer available. The governor's journal is the record in which a written note is made of significant events concerning the establishment on a daily basis. It has not proved possible to locate that journal.

*

It was Nick Pope who supplied me with a printed copy of this exchange; and although he did not subscribe to the idea that the British Government was engaged in a high-level conspiracy to keep top-secret UFO data under wraps, even Nick found it hard to accept that such an important piece of data as the 'governor's journal' could simply vanish without trace . . .

And there was another matter that was becoming clearer as time went on: all of those UFO events in which the Home Office appeared to play a role concerned either landed or crashed UFOs, as opposed to objects seen in the sky. I began to wonder if all of us in UFO research had for years been looking in the wrong place for tangible evidence of UFO reality. Everyone had been so busy battering on the door of the Ministry of Defence that they had overlooked the possibility that another agency could be responsible for overseeing the really crucial data. Then something struck me.

I recalled that some years previously I had read a small newspaper article concerning the various 'emergency planning' procedures that the Home Office had in place to deal with a variety of potentially calamitous events, including chemical spillage, nuclear war, inner-city rioting . . . and the crash on UK soil of artificial satellites and rockets.

I knew from previous research that, with the phenomenal increase in the number of satellites being put into Earth orbit by agencies such as NASA and the European Space Agency, the probability was that one such satellite would eventually plummet to earth and crash on a heavily populated area.

From the US State Department records on Project Moon Dust, which I had secured via the Freedom of Information Act, I knew that rocket and satellite debris was falling to earth with alarming regularity. More importantly, however, it seemed logical to me that if, as was the case, the Home Office had established guidelines to deal with crashed space satellites, then those same guidelines could equally apply to crashed UFOs. If I could prise out of the Home Office information on its handling of recovered satellite debris, then I was possibly one step closer to finding out what it knew about retrieved UFOs.

I telephoned the Home Office and asked to be put through to the press office. I explained the situation: I was interested to know what would be the Home Office's response if a large, metallic object, such as a satellite, crashed on the UK.

I was put through to a very helpful gentleman who informed me that the responsibility for monitoring satellite movements over the United Kingdom is predominantly the domain of the tracking station at RAF Fylingdales, Yorkshire. If it appears likely there is a possibility, however remote, that a satellite in a decaying Earth orbit might impact on the UK, Fylingdales have standing orders to inform the Ministry of Defence, who in turn are obliged to keep the Home Office informed. This is what the press officer told me in December 1996:

> The Home Office has responsibility for emergency planning, which obviously isn't specific, necessarily, to satellites. But the situation is they only really become a matter for the Home Office in effect when they've landed, because that's when the emergency services come into play. For example, there was one recently – a Chinese satellite which came down. That was one we were kept well informed of and were aware of. We were advised of the expected time it was going to land and all that kind of stuff.
>
> We don't really take much actual action; our side would be more the policy angle; ensuring that all the right contingency plans are in place.

And it was made very clear to me that if, God forbid, a nuclear-powered satellite were to crash on the UK, this would be treated as a major incident, involving in all probability the armed forces, the three emergency services – police, fire and ambulance – and the MOD. I thanked the man for his help.[3] Next stop: RAF Fylingdales.

'You want the Space Information Officer,' I was advised by the switchboard operator at RAF Fylingdales when I detailed my quest. A few moments later, the SIO was on the line. He outlined the situation:

We track satellites all the time. When there are predictions for satellite decays, and this is maintained by US and UK authorities, if there is one which is potentially going to cause problems, the Ministry of Defence and the Home Office are the people who get involved. We would just track it and keep these people up to date with what was happening with the satellite at the time. The Home Office and the MOD do all the coordination.

Accurate predictions as to where something is going to crash are very difficult: it depends exactly on what the satellite's doing – if it's rolling or if it's got high drag in one part or another. It also depends on what angle it enters the upper end of the atmosphere.

There are experts that are able to calculate to within an hour or so when it's coming down. We can advise the MOD of the position of the satellite, how it's moving, whether it's speeding up, slowing down, or whether it's changing its attitude or whatever.[4]

After listening to what both the Home Office and RAF Fylingdales had told me, it became obvious that both were well prepared to deal with the tracking and retrieval of practically any space object, be it a satellite or a UFO. And there was that significant statement from the Home Office's press office: 'they only really become a matter for the Home Office when they've landed'. That clinched it for me.

In addition, the comments of RAF Fylingdales with respect to predicting the potential crash site of a plummeting space vehicle went some way towards explaining how the military had been able to secure the crash sites at Cannock Chase and on the Berwyn Mountains in January 1974 so quickly. I was making real progress. And there was another matter, too.

In 1993 the US Departments of Defense and Energy began declassifying a large number of once secret documents concerning the satellite-tracking of large meteoroids hitting the Earth's upper atmosphere. Records revealed that between 1975 and 1992 the infrared and optical sensors mounted on Department of Defense-operated space platforms had recorded a total of no fewer than 136 fireballs entering the atmosphere. Furthermore, at least three of those events had occurred over Scotland and Ireland and, as *The Times* noted, 'The Ministry of Defence is understood to have been briefed about the nature and frequency of the blasts.'[5]

In other words, in addition to the tracking operations undertaken from RAF Fylingdales, British authorities were receiving information pertaining to objects entering the Earth's atmosphere via the Americans. Small wonder that the crashed-UFO issue was wrapped up so tightly in official secrecy.

It appeared clear to me as I conducted my investigations that, of those UFO-crash incidents in which the Home Office was implicated, there was one common link: radiation.

In the 1974 incident at Cannock Chase, for example, at least one witness to the crash died in Cotteridge General Hospital of radiation sickness with alarming speed; and then there was the UFO incident at Rendlesham Forest in December 1980 . . .

On a number of occasions I had discussed the Rendlesham UFO crash with Nick Pope, and was specifically concerned that Nick had been unable to uncover any documentation that detailed what action had been taken by the MOD at the time of its occurrence. While Nick did not judge this to be anything sinister, I had long been of the opinion that his inability to access any British-based documentation on the case was due to the fact that, quite simply, he did not have a 'need to know'.

Despite this, Nick did have one piece of important evidence at his disposal: an official report filed at the time by the Deputy

Base Commander at the nearby RAF Woodbridge –
Lieutenant Colonel Charles Halt (USAF). As Halt's memorandum made perfectly clear, at the reported crash-landing site
of the UFO, significant radiation readings were recorded by a
team of US Air Force personnel under his jurisdiction. This
was not lost on Nick. He told me:

> Of course, I've made no secret of the fact that I've tried to
> reopen the investigation into [the Rendlesham Forest
> incident]. I took the raw data from Colonel Halt's memo
> and gave it to the Defence Radiological Protection
> Service, and they came back and said, words to the effect,
> 'What the bloody hell happened there?' The radiation
> was ten times normal; that was sufficient to confirm that
> there was something very strange at the landing site.
>
> I've spoken to Halt and he's furious! A very high-pro-
> file event happens in a very significant part of the
> country; he makes a report, and effectively seventeen
> years later he's waiting for his response. And, not surpris-
> ingly, he's a little bit hacked off. I would be.[6]

If the Home Office's involvement in crashed-UFO incidents was indeed centred largely on the retrieval and containment of highly radioactive objects, then where was the
evidence stored? Healthwise, simply to lock away such
material in an aircraft hangar or warehouse seemed decidedly
risky. Far more likely, I considered, was the possibility of an
off-limits chamber buried deep underground where the risk of
radioactive contamination would be minimal. But where?
Early in 1997 came a breakthrough.

On the evening of 16 January I attended the monthly meeting of Irene Bott's Staffordshire UFO Group and met with
Matthew Williams, whom I arranged to interview the following day. I discussed just about anything and everything with
Matthew, including the issue of Home Office involvement in
the UFO subject. It transpired that Matthew had an interest-

ing tale to tell that tied the Home Office in directly with, of all places, RAF Rudloe Manor!

Matthew explained that, while conducting research into a mass of tunnels and caverns that extended under Rudloe Manor and the surrounding area (some of which were held by the military), he had come into contact with Dr Steve Neads, who ran the Shepton Mallet Caving Club.

They're experts in the mines; they know the whole area. On a number of occasions, they reached an area where the military tunnels start, and on one occasion there was somebody there – a military man. He asked what they were doing, and they replied, 'We're the caving club.'

He then said, 'If you're interested, perhaps we can get you a tour.'

From the way I understand it, on occasion, at their discretion, the military will allow people to see a little bit more of the tunnelling system if they have a valid reason. I suppose it's good for local public relations.

Now, some time later, they were contacted by someone from Rudloe Manor who then made a formal offer and said, 'Come along; we'll take you down.'

They met with a person of a certain rank and they were taken down an elevator shaft and down into various tunnels where there was heating and lighting, corridors and space, and so on. They were also taken on a tour of the old quarry area, which is supposed to be more of a derelict area, because it's where the quarrying was finished and there was no clean-up operation afterwards.

Although they had a good tour, it was made clear that there were other parts of the tunnels which were out of bounds due to the high security which existed there. Apparently the police who looked after the heavily restricted areas operated independently from the normal RAF Police who patrolled Rudloe Manor, and the two didn't liaise in any way or fashion.

As I remember it, these other guys weren't military police, but were a separate security force; and the people who worked at Rudloe Manor didn't know what went on in that higher-security area. They only knew that it was a lot more up to date; it was a lot more well developed; was a lot deeper underground; and that it was controlled by the Home Office.

'So,' I put it to Matthew, 'the implication is that deep under RAF Rudloe Manor, where classified investigations into UFO activity have been taking place for years, there is a heavily guarded area of tunnels and caverns that falls under the jurisdiction of the Home Office?'

'Yes, absolutely,' replied Matthew.[7]

Was there a link, UFO-wise, between what went on at Rudloe Manor and that ominous Home Office facility buried far beneath the surface of the base amid myriad imposing caverns and tunnels? Both Matthew and I agreed that such a place would have served as a perfect storage facility for contaminated, or radioactive, crashed-UFO debris. Not only was the area closed to the public (and, it should be remembered, to the majority of the staff at Rudloe Manor), but the likelihood of anything hazardous escaping from such a deep level was exceedingly slim.

Nearly one and a half years after beginning my investigation into the Home Office's purported involvement in the UFO mystery, I wondered if I had at last located the British Government's equivalent of the USA's rumoured 'Hangar 18': a 'cosmic museum' filled to the brim with all manner of UFO artefacts including crashed-UFO debris, extraterrestrial technology and cryogenically stored alien corpses.

My interest in the Home Office's involvement in the recovery of fallen space vehicles was further piqued when, in September 1997, a trusted informant gave me a copy of a still-classified eight-page Home Office circular dating from 1979.

On reading the document (which was graded at 'Restricted'

level, with a handwritten 'Confidential' note to the side), I saw that it dealt with Home Office guidelines for dealing with the possible crash of stricken space vehicles on UK soil.

Most interesting to me was the fact that the document expressed a great deal of concern about the possibility of hazardous radiation being deposited by a fallen spacecraft, and whether the general public should be informed of such an event. The document stated:

> It is for the Government to decide whether, and if so by what means, a public warning of danger from radioactivity should be given. In reaching that decision, the need to prevent unnecessary alarm would be carefully considered. Chief Officers should therefore ensure that nothing is done locally to anticipate a Government statement.

One segment of the paper, I noted, echoed the 1974 event witnessed by Roger Chambers at Cannock Chase, Staffordshire:

> When reports of suspected or actual locations have been received, the police should take such steps as may be needed locally to prevent people entering areas which may be dangerous because of radioactive material . . . some large pieces of debris might have radiation fields of significance over distances of the order of 100 metres.

The document then went on to illustrate the many and varied divisions within the British Government that had jurisdiction in the area of fallen spacecraft. As well as the Home Office, this included: the Atomic Weapons Research Establishment (AWRE) at Aldermaston; the National Radiological Protection Board (NRPB); the Ministry of Defence; Chief Officers of Police and Chief Fire Officers in the UK; and representatives from something called the 'NAIR scheme' – National Arrangements for Incidents involving Radioactivity.

Clearly, any crashed space vehicles on UK soil would be dealt with at high level and with the utmost haste. I was not surprised that such momentous events seldom reached the eyes and ears of the media – let alone those of us in UFO research.

Interestingly, towards the end of the document there was a small section headed 'Non-nuclear debris from space', which commented that:

Many non-nuclear satellites and other space debris are in orbit and there is continuing likelihood of such objects falling from space and parts of them surviving re-entry to the atmosphere and landing on the earth's surface. In that event it would be appreciated if chief officers would inform the Ministry of Defence so that the object may be examined and if possible identified.

Most pertinently, the person at Whitehall charged with the investigation of such debris was one J. Peduzie, who, at the time, was the head of a Ministry of Defence Secretariat called S4f(AIR).

In *A Covert Agenda* I had been able to show that between 1964 and 1984, S4f(AIR) was the division within the MOD that was responsible for examining UFO reports submitted to Whitehall by members of the public. And while it was clearly the case that the staff within the department responsible for looking at such reports were largely junior civil servants with limited 'need to know', the head of the division was a very different kettle of fish who liaised at a high level with other, far more covertly operated, departments within the Ministry of Defence.

Indeed, the Home Office circular made it clear that Peduzie was simply the initial 'point of contact' within the MOD when it came to the analysis of recovered space debris. Far more likely, I considered, was the probability that such material would be handed over to the elite Defence Intelligence Staff (DIS), whose involvement in UFO activity was far more significant than that of S4f(AIR).

Nevertheless, with this still-classified paper in my possession, I had been able to make a conclusive and direct link between (a) the Home Office, (b) debris from crashed space vehicles and (c) at least one division within the Ministry of Defence tasked with studying UFO data. But where was this debris stored? Was it at Rudloe Manor? The possibility could not be overlooked, and I began to take a closer look at what was taking place deep beneath RAF Rudloe Manor.

My first step was to obtain some background history on the tunnelling system itself. It transpired that the tunnels under Rudloe had originally been excavated many years previously when the surrounding area was quarried for what became known as 'Bath stone'. One of the locals told me that this was the preferred stone for building throughout the area. This accounted for the huge maze of tunnels, caves and caverns – practically the entire neighbourhood was mined for this commodity.

During World War Two, it was explained to me, circumstances naturally changed and the whole underground system was placed under the jurisdiction of the military, whereupon it served as a storage facility for weapons, TNT and so on.

In the postwar era, however, the military re-evaluated its options. While I was able to determine that certain parts of the system had been sold off, the overwhelming majority remained firmly in the hands of the authorities. That much was known publicly. But what was really going on deep under Rudloe? Matthew Williams had some ideas:

The information I obtained – most of which came from official sources – suggested we're talking about hundreds of square miles of tunnels.

These apparently link up Rudloe Manor with Colerne Airbase; the weapons storage facility at Copenacre; Monkspark, which is a weapons storage facility for the Navy; the Defence Communications Network; and the Corsham Computer Centre.

There are two points of access to the publicly accessible tunnels very near Rudloe Manor. One's at the underground quarry centre at Corsham. You can put on a hard hat and a lamp and go for a walk, and have a look at the areas where they took the Bath stone out. There are other tunnels, less sophisticated, but which are longer and more intricate. These are the ones which the professional cavers seem to like. It's some of these tunnels which seem to have a connection point with the military ones. As it's been described to me, [over] long distances in the tunnels, there are infrared security cameras which are positioned just to monitor anyone getting too close.

'Exactly how active are these tunnels?' I asked Matthew.

It's been intimated to me that there's an area for emergency housing down there and that's one of the locations where the Royal family would go in a national emergency. But I've been told that the tunnels which have been made good, which Rudloe themselves are using, are fifteen miles in length. And in the central hub, there's a labyrinth of tunnels to allow people to have offices, buildings, storage areas, et cetera.

Now, I've taken photographs while flying over Rudloe Manor in a light aircraft, and the pictures clearly show many structures in the facility which have lift shafts; and the size of the lifts . . . You can easily drive vehicles into them.[8]

Whatever was occurring at Rudloe Manor was like something out of science fiction.

Again, Matthew Williams had come through with some remarkable information; however, I needed more and so made still further enquiries.

Although Matthew's assertions of what was taking place deep below Rudloe Manor had been viewed in some quarters with scepticism, my own studies proved that Matthew was bang on target as usual.

Not long after I spoke with Matthew on this matter, for example, Flight Lieutenant Jeremy Wright of RAF Rudloe Manor made public some extraordinary facts surrounding the various caverns and tunnels in and around the vicinity of the base.

'The underground complex has forty miles of tunnel at various depths, of differing widths and heights, from tiny pot-holes to enormous caverns with floor spaces equivalent to twelve full-size football pitches.'

Twelve full-size football pitches! This was extraordinary. But there were other sources, too, who had crucial data.

Reg Bond had served with the military at the rank of corporal and in the period 1945–47 worked within one of the underground chambers below Wiltshire. 'It was a complete unit with guardroom, cookhouse and sleeping quarters,' he said, adding that, even fifty years ago, the complex was an impressive 200 feet below ground.

Even the *Independent* got in on the act when rumours about the Rudloe facility began to surface. Its reporters learned that the headquarters of the Defence Communications Network (which was housed at Rudloe Manor) was '100 acres in size and extends around 120 feet below ground. It is designed to be the seat of central government and can house 55,000 people.'

In addition, Flight Lieutenant Jeremy Wright was able to confirm that (as was the case with Dr Steve Neads of the Shepton Mallet Caving Club) tours were conducted in certain parts of the underground system. Wright noted, however, that 'The area has now been sealed off for safety reasons.'

No longer could claims be made that nothing of significance was taking place deep below RAF Rudloe Manor. Indeed, the Home Office–Rudloe Manor–UFO connections were so intriguing that I could have kicked myself for not having made the links earlier. Nevertheless, I had more than made up for lost time.

If the British Government did have its very own 'Hangar 18', then I felt that I had just come extremely close to identifying its position. But there were other possible locations, too . . .

CHAPTER THIRTEEN

OURS OR THEIRS?

'DEAR MR REDFERN,' THE LETTER BEGAN, 'I HAVE READ several of your articles in *UFO* magazine and thought you would be interested to know that my father was in the RAF in the 1950s and 1960s and I always remember him telling me that at RAF Farnborough there was supposed to be a top-secret office where the RAF carried out all its flying saucer investigations . . .'

Rumours that the sprawling one thousand-acre-plus Royal Aircraft Establishment (RAE) at RAF Farnborough, Hampshire, housed a covertly operated unit that investigated UFO encounters (and specifically UFO landings within the UK) had reached me on a number of occasions, and the above letter was one of many that convinced me that something strange was indeed afoot at Farnborough and possibly had been for decades.

While writing *A Covert Agenda*, I had unearthed a number of significant accounts implicating RAF Farnborough in the UFO subject, including that of Cyril Townsend-Withers, a senior scientific officer with the Ministry of Defence who specialised in radar development and deployment, and who ultimately rose to the rank of wing commander.

As Townsend-Withers recalled, during the 1960s he had a

number of discussions with relevant personnel in Whitehall, and was informed of the existence of a specialist UFO investigation team that operated out of Farnborough. According to Townsend-Withers, the project comprised largely RAF Intelligence people who viewed the UFO subject 'very seriously'.

There was also the woman whose husband was stationed at Farnborough for a twelve-month period in the mid-1960s, and who was directly implicated in a most strange event involving the monitoring of an unidentified radio 'signal' or 'language' that had been picked up at the base.

'They could not decode or decipher [the signal],' the woman said. '[My husband] told me that it definitely was not of human origin, and he could say no more. I think he keeps a lot to himself about his true feelings. I know he has been sworn to secrecy by the RAE – the Official Secrets Act, no doubt – but something of great importance happened that day they snatched those special signals from space, I feel sure!'

And then there was Hannah Green whom I first spoke to in 1996. She lived just about on the doorstep of RAF Farnborough, and was acutely aware that the RAE had long-standing involvement in the UFO mystery. Hannah told me, 'I've got one hell of a view: I live in a very high spot and can see the roofs of the hangars at the base.' In speaking with her, however, I learned that she had seen far more than mere aircraft hangars . . .

On a clear, bright evening in July 1977, Hannah and her family were driving through the nearby Minley Manor Woods when their attention was drawn to two 'coachloads of troops' who entered the woods by what was known as the 'Fleet Exit'.

'We had to reverse and go back,' Hannah said, 'and as we did so, I noticed just to the left what looked like a small, man-made valley with steep sides about fifteen feet deep. But inside this little valley, there were two clear burn marks, which looked like something had either landed or crashed.'

Hannah added that the presence of so many soldiers milling

about the area concerned the family so they swung the car around and drove back in the direction from which they had come. All was normal until they approached a bend in the road . . .

Standing on a gentle slope around the corner were two of the strangest-looking 'men' Hannah had ever seen. Both were of an impressive height, but were exceedingly thin and dressed in 'all-in-one white, tight-fitting suits with headgear like the astronauts in the Apollo missions wore'.

For a moment the two 'men' remained stationary; however, as Hannah and her family watched transfixed, both suddenly broke into a run and headed for a clearing. Most bizarrely of all, as Hannah continued to follow the path of the two men, they disappeared before her very eyes!

'They vanished; they simply vanished,' Hannah told me. 'I never forgot that. I came home, drew a picture of the two men, and wrote an account of it because it really shook me up. And I've never been in the woods since. It's nearly all cordoned off by the Army now.'

Hannah then explained that a number of unusual events occurred shortly afterwards which she felt were possibly related. First, she learned that, under cover of darkness, an inordinate amount of digging took place within the woods.

And who was doing the digging? None other than the Army. And what were they looking for? Hannah never found out, but the mere fact that the Army's activities were undertaken late at night certainly aroused her suspicions that it was somehow connected with the curious 'burn marks' seen in the woods, not to mention the two strange-looking 'men' who fled the area.

Hannah then recalled a second curious UFO event that occurred several months later:

It was 18 October 1977, in the mid-evening. There was what I call a 'large black cigar' over the corn fields to the back of our houses. It travelled up on to Fernhill and then headed down towards the woods.

By this time I was hanging out of the window, binoculars at the ready. I waited for around five minutes and could then see it above the trees: a white light on the back and a green light on the front.

It then headed in my direction, and I could see that it was about sixty feet long, very black, but there was no sound whatsoever. It came right over me, and within a few minutes I was feeling very sick and dizzy. I couldn't stand up, and it was all I could do to get into bed fully dressed – I couldn't even undress myself. I slept all night, and the next day I went to the bathroom and got a real shock: as I looked in the mirror, I saw that the left side of my face and forehead were burned red.

In those days we had many sightings, all of which happened as the work was going on in the woods.

I wondered if it was possible that the unusual scorch marks seen within Minley Manor Woods were the result of some form of UFO either landing or crash-landing? And what of the sudden Army presence? What was going on in the woods that required the attendance of two coachloads of troops? And who were the two tall 'beings' dressed 'like astronauts' who seemed unnaturally keen on exiting the area with the utmost haste? Given their odd garb and somewhat unusual physical appearance, I could not discount the possibility that, if a UFO had indeed become disabled in the vicinity and had come down within the woods themselves, Hannah and her family may have stumbled across the crew of the UFO as they made good their escape from the approaching military! And what of the odd digging that went on after dark? Had the military discovered 'something' within the woods that they were attempting to retrieve?

Almost twenty years later, there was an intriguing sequel to this odd affair. In early April 1996, around noon, Hannah was at home with a friend, Leahanne, when suddenly the air was filled with a tremendous roar. Hannah described what happened next:

We ran to the window and could see two black, unmarked Wessex helicopters. They were travelling from north to south and headed for the Army ground on the nearby Sandy Hills. This is above the Defence Research Agency. Well, we watched them go up there, and then, within a few minutes, two smaller helicopters – black and shiny – followed them. But one suddenly veered off to the right and headed towards one of the big hangars at Farnborough. This one helicopter took an extreme interest in that area.

Leahanne, who had seen all this, picked up my binoculars and focused them in the direction of where this one helicopter was hovering near the hangar. It's slightly surrounded by trees, but Leahanne suddenly said, 'Oh my God! It's a saucer!'

It looked like it was coming out on runners. It was being brought out of the hangar and it was definitely saucer-shaped, black or gunmetal in colour, with a hatch or triangular-shaped segment on the top.

'How big did you estimate the object to be?' I asked.

'Well . . .' Hannah thought for a moment. 'It must have been a reasonable size for us to see it from here. Probably no less than twenty feet across. There was a revolving yellow light on the saucer which would go from left to right as we watched it. But whatever the object was, it didn't stay out of the hangar for long.'[1]

Was there a connection between the strange object seen at Farnborough in April 1996 and that mysterious event that occurred within Minley Manor Woods two decades previously? Is it feasible, I asked myself, that the object brought briefly out of the hangar at Farnborough in 1996 had been retrieved from deep within the nearby Minley Manor Woods in 1977?

I prefer not to deal in speculation, but it was a possibility that I could not afford to ignore. And Hannah's was not the only account I had come across that suggested that alien technology was being stored, perhaps even duplicated and tested, at a variety of military facilities throughout the United Kingdom.

From the former civil servant Matthew Williams there came a most interesting and provocative account that had been related to him by a respected investigator: Roy Wilkinson. Matthew told me:

> The precise location was never really established, but it was a military base somewhere in the Suffolk/Norfolk area. It may in fact have been one of the US airbases, maybe Lakenheath. This happened a maximum of eight years ago.
>
> Apparently, in the vicinity of the base, there was a forest which was MOD property, and which was being used for military manoeuvres, operations and so on. A report came through that on one particular night those on manoeuvres should expect to see something being tested in the area; and when the testing was taking place, they were to ignore it: pretend it's not there and carry on as normal.
>
> They found this a bit hard to do, because when this thing came along, it was actually a ball of light and was too small to be manned – so it had to have been a remote drone of some kind. But it was pure light, no mechanics, no rockets, no noise. And this thing moved silently above the area where they were on manoeuvres – off the base, in the forest.
>
> Then the light increased in intensity and illuminated the whole area like a flare would. Everyone stopped what they were doing, and just broke their orders. They watched this thing for a minute or so, and then it diminished in size and went off at extremely high speed into the distance.

Everyone was talking about this and, really, it unnerved them to a certain degree. The whole evening's events were then called off, because everything was in such a state of disarray.

If the military experimented with things which could be perceived to be UFOs, i.e. balls of light, then – because of their knowledge that the event was going to happen – they would have to have those UFOs stored somewhere near.[2]

There was additional evidence that suggested that the British Government was working to perfect radical and highly advanced aircraft. Were these unique vehicles the result of our attempts to replicate extraterrestrial ingenuity? I surveyed the evidence.

Periodically, throughout the late 1980s and early 1990s, the skies of the UK were inundated with waves of triangular-shaped UFOs. While I was (and still am) convinced that the sheer scale of reports was evidence that some form of extraterrestrial reconnaissance operation was under way there could be another explanation. In the mid-1990s huge numbers of reports of vehicles of a triangular configuration, and usually black in colour, began to emanate from the North of England; specifically, in the vicinity of the British Aerospace facility at Warton . . .

In examining the data surrounding the Warton allegations, I was always in two minds as to who exactly was responsible for the 'triangles'. Was it Warton, or was it the 'others'? Certainly, there were grounds for believing that some form of highly advanced triangular-shaped aircraft (albeit of a small size and certainly not on the scale of some of the huge triangular-shaped objects that had been seen around the world in the 1980s and 1990s) was undergoing covert test flights from Warton; however, there was one significant problem: the claims surrounding Warton were all relatively recent. And yet craft of a triangular configuration had been seen in the area for more than forty years.

While everyone else was looking at Warton's current activities, I had gone off at a tangent and set about researching a variety of files at the Public Record Office that I felt might be useful in determining how long the British Government had been working to perfect highly advanced aircraft of an unusual design. Perusing one such file, I came across a most interesting entry: it was a two-page letter to the Air Ministry, dated 1962, from one W. Arnold of Swinton, Greater Manchester. Arnold wrote:

> The recent Flying Saucers sighted over Manchester are not a new phenomenon, and one was sighted by myself in 1956 in the early hours of the morning.
>
> It was always my belief that this aircraft was a British experimental plane. It carried no markings whatever and was of highly polished metal.
>
> If I am mistaken that this plane is British, then alternatively it could be a photo reconnaissance plane from source unknown and of an interesting design!

Most remarkably of all, Arnold had included with his letter a hand-drawn picture of the object he had viewed which, to all intents and purposes, looked almost exactly like the US military's 'Stealth Bomber': the B-2! But the Stealth Bomber was a product of the 1980s, not the mid-1950s. So what did the Air Ministry have to say about Arnold's report? In an internal memorandum generated only days later, it was reported that Arnold had probably viewed an aircraft flown from the AVRO works at Woodford. The Air Ministry Secretariat that dealt with Arnold's report was unable to give a conclusive explanation, but suggested he had seen a 'prototype Vulcan' aircraft undergoing trials.

The most important factor for me, however, was that Arnold's sighting of a delta-shaped craft in Britain's airspace had occurred in precisely the same location that advanced aircraft of an identical configuration were being seen today![3]

There were two scenarios: either AVRO and British Aerospace had been flying highly advanced aircraft throughout northern England for at least four decades or these were non-terrestrial craft. If the former, from where did British authorities acquire the technology to build a Stealth-like aircraft more than forty years ago? Was it possible that our attempts to 'back-engineer' alien spacecraft began following the UFO crash on UK soil during World War Two? I had not previously given much consideration to this theory, but I could not now afford to dismiss it.

I pondered on the evidence and built up in my mind a working scenario: on a variety of occasions dating back to the mid-1940s, British authorities had come into possession of alien technology, largely acquired from crash-retrieval operations. That same technology was then being transferred to high-security facilities (Porton Down; that mysterious Home Office-controlled chamber buried deep below RAF Rudloe Manor; RAF Farnborough; and British Aerospace at Warton were four possible locations) for storage. However, it appeared that the complexities of that same technology were now slowly being understood. The conclusion was inescapable: the British Government was building and deploying its very own prototype UFOs! Yet another facet of the crashed-UFO controversy had been exposed to me.

With such an abundance of quality material in hand, I now felt that my best recourse was to try to compare that material with the many and varied UFO-crash reports that had been made in other parts of the world. By and large this was a two-pronged attack.

First, I wanted to see if the descriptions of the UFOs retrieved elsewhere on the planet matched those found within the United Kingdom; and second, I could not rule out the possibility that British authorities might have taken an interest (or perhaps even an active role) in such retrievals.

Accounts of UFOs recovered in the USA had largely been covered in books such as those by Tim Good, Stan Friedman,

Kevin Randle and Don Schmitt, and Bill Moore. Moreover, there were the various Majestic 12 papers that gave a detailed description of the US Government's knowledge of recovered UFOs and alien remains.

Largely for that reason, I opted to concentrate on those crash reports that emanated from less explored areas of the planet: the Congo, Scandinavia, Bolivia, Australia and New Zealand, even Khartoum! Of those cases that I felt warranted extensive investigation, some were previously unheard of, while others had remained at the fringes of UFO research for decades. Once again, I was to make eye-opening discoveries, several of which had direct implications on the advances I had already made in the UK.

CHAPTER FOURTEEN

THE WORLDWIDE REPORTS

WHILE UNCOVERING CREDIBLE DATA PERTAINING TO UFO crashes within the UK was a somewhat arduous task, I had more immediate success on a worldwide basis when I was given the opportunity to access the files of a little-known US military operation known as Project Moon Dust.

Ostensibly, Moon Dust (and a related project, Blue Fly) was designed to secure for US exploitation purposes foreign space debris such as crashed satellites, rocket boosters, and so on. However, there was ample data at my disposal to show that Moon Dust had been involved in the recovery of much more than mere Earth-made technology . . .

Aside from the fact that I had come across a reference to Moon Dust in a CIA document leaked to the investigator Milo Speriglio (which made mention of a top-secret Anglo-American investigation of crashed UFOs and alien bodies in the 1940s and 1950s) there was other evidence that conclusively linked Moon Dust and the UFO issue.

A 1961 US Air Force paper, for example, a copy of which I had obtained direct from the USAF, stated:

In addition to their staff duty assignments, intelligence team personnel have peacetime duty functions in support of such Air Force projects as Moondust, Blue Fly, and UFO, and other AFCIN directed quick reaction projects which require intelligence team operational capabilities.

The author of the paper elaborated:

Unidentified Flying Objects (UFO): Headquarters USAF has established a program for investigation of reliably reported unidentified flying objects within the United States.

Blue Fly: Operation Blue Fly has been established to facilitate expeditious delivery to Foreign Technology Division of Moon Dust or other items of great technological intelligence interest.

Moon Dust: As a specialized aspect of its overall material exploitation program Headquarters USAF has established Project Moon Dust to locate, recover, and deliver descended foreign space vehicles.

Here, then, was a link between unidentified flying objects, 'items of great technological interest', and a classified project designed to 'locate, recover and deliver' non-US spacecraft to American authorities. But what could the files of Moon Dust tell me about the project's involvement in the retrieval of alien vehicles?

It was clear to me on examining the files that the vast majority dealt with crashed and recovered Earth-originated spacecraft (usually Soviet in origin). For example, when in July 1960 a 'whitish luminous cloud, about 35 feet in diameter' was seen by a number of US military personnel stationed on Pacific islands Moon Dust was quick to react:

Captain George L. Griffith, project officer for Project Moon Dust, arranged to interrogate the witnesses later in the day. He interrogated six air policemen and one civilian guard to confirm the original report, then he reported his findings in accordance with Moon Dust directives. The whole operation was nicknamed 'The Case of the Flying Doughnut.'

A TWX from Fifth Air Force to Pacific Air Forces headquarters on 6 July 1960 made it all seem worthwhile. The object sighted was evaluated as a phenomenon which accompanied one or two Soviet missile shots from the Tura Tam test area to the mid-Pacific test range, six thousand miles away. Our sighting was backed up by a civilian airline pilot who had made an almost simultaneous sighting of the doughnut cloud.

Not every report that Moon Dust came across could be explained so easily, however, including one I found within a batch of Moon Dust and Blue Fly reports forwarded to me by the US Air Force.

On 30 September 1960, a TWX report was sent to the Pacific Air Forces on a sighting of an unidentified object that entered the water near the village of Ctaru. The report originated with the Japanese Ground Self Defence Force (GSDF) headquarters and was relayed to us by the Japanese Air Self Defense Force (JASDF). According to the report, a fiery object fell from the sky and into the sea, making a fountain of water which was described as looking like a 'geyser'. Technical Intelligence personnel from Tokyo took over the case, but were not able to locate or reclaim the object.

Perhaps, I mused, almost forty years on, it was still lying dormant deep below the Pacific, its secrets waiting to be plundered . . .

As I ploughed through the Air Force files, three further unexplained Moon Dust reports captured my attention.

The White Saucer.

On 18 October 1960, a pilot of the 4th Fighter Interceptor Squadron reported that he had seen an object as large as a saucer about eight inches in diameter. The object was white, and it had a white tail about 16 to 20 times as long as the diameter of the object. It appeared from about 30 degrees above and 20 degrees to the right of the aircraft and passed by the aircraft's right side, disappearing towards the rear of the aircraft in a downward arc.

The Bubble.

On 11 October 1960, a pilot over the beach east of Kisawa observed an orange flash on the horizon. He described the phenomenon as being distinct and looking like a great bubble. The area in which the phenomenon could be observed was along the southern coast of the Soviet Kuril Islands.

The Green Pea.

On 14 September 1960, a pilot was flying an F-86D between an overcast above and below him when a greenish-white object appeared from the overcast above him. The object fell straight down, and disappeared in the overcast below. The object was described as looking like a green pea. Preliminary investigation could not identify any balloons or other known objects in the area which could have accounted for the sighting.

Come the mid-1960s, I was able to state with confidence, Moon Dust was still receiving credible data on downed and crashed UFOs. Most interesting to me was a Moon Dust record supplied by the CIA that was titled: 'FRAGMENT, METAL, RECOVERED IN THE REPUBLIC OF THE CONGO, ORIGIN BELIEVED TO BE AN UNIDENTIFIED FLYING OBJECT'. The released portions of the report read:

The purpose of this report is to present the results of the exploitation of a metallic fragment recovered near the town of [illegible] in the Republic of the Congo. Fragment recovery was the result of a ground-level search which was coordinated after an unidentified flying object exploded and fell to earth in the area. The sighting and recovery took place sometime between 10 and 15 October 1965. Other than a reported east-to-west direction of flight for the UFO specific observation and recovery details are lacking.

Also 'lacking', I noted, were any further discernible parts of the report! Was this intentional? Certainly, the opening paragraph promised revelations of extreme significance. I had to assume that this event was one that was still considered 'sensitive' by the US authorities.

Nevertheless, two years later, UFO encounters were still occupying much of Moon Dust's time and resources. In particular, two Defense Intelligence Agency reports on Moon Dust caught my eye. The first, titled 'UFO SIGHTING AT KASBA TADLA, MOROCCO', and referenced 'Project Moon Dust', stated, 'This report forwards a translation of an article which appeared in the *Potit Morocain*, 2 April 1967. This item was not carried in the other daily newspapers, but is significant as it indicates continued local interest in the subject of UFOs.'

The second report, also from Morocco, and also dated 1967, stated with regard to a UFO encounter over Agadir:

This report forwards translations of two articles which appeared in the *Potit Morocain*. Each article is separately identified as to source. Although the two articles are very contradictory, the page one coverage afforded this sighting demonstrates a high level of interest in the subject of UFOs, and presages future reporting which could be valuable in pursuit of Project Moon Dust.

But it was not just the CIA and the Air Force who were entrusted with Moon Dust data: a huge batch of material was made available to me by the US Department of State, which demonstrated a high degree of activity on the part of Moon Dust in the late 1960s and 1970s. A Department of State telegram of August 1967 from the American Embassy at Khartoum to Washington, for example, read:

> Local press 17 Aug 67 reported that a satellite, cube shaped, weighing approximately three tons discovered 3 August 50 miles from Kutum. Satellite described as made of soft metal presumably light aluminum in oblong cubes measuring two inches by one inch tightly fastened together and covered by a silky material. Nationality not identified as no inscriptions evident on outer surface. Local authorities in El Fasher have photographs and with difficulty cut samples.

In this case, I reasoned, it was difficult to ascertain whether the object was terrestrial in origin, or far more exotic in nature. The key point, however, was that Moon Dust personnel were quickly on the scene to deal with both the containment of the object and its removal back to the United States for analysis. And given the object's reported weight – 'approximately three tons' – it appeared that, however big or small an object, Moon Dust operatives were more than equipped to deal with any and all eventualities.

The one case involving Moon Dust that convinced me more than any other that crashed-UFO incidents were not exclusive to the UK and the USA occurred in Bolivia in 1978 and was of extreme interest since the event was supported by an impressive body of official documentation that I had succeeded in obtaining via the Freedom of Information Act.

The genesis of the affair appeared to lie in a US Department of State telegram transmitted from the American Embassy in La Paz, Bolivia, to the US Secretary of State, Washington, DC, on 15 May 1978. Captioned 'REPORT OF FALLEN SPACE OBJECT', the telegram read:

1. The Bolivian newspapers carried this morning an article concerning an unidentified object that apparently recently fell from the sky. The papers quoted a 'Latin' correspondent's story from the Argentine city of Salta. The object was discovered near the Bolivian city of Bermejo and was described as egg-shaped, metal and about four metres in diameter.

2. The Bolivian Air Force plans to investigate to determine what the object might be and from where it came. I have expressed our interest and willingness to help. They will advise.

3. Request the department check with appropriate agencies to see if they can shed some light on what this object might be. The general region has had more than its share of reports of UFOs the past week. Request a reply ASAP.

The Department of State, I learned, was not the only branch of the US Government that took an interest in the case, as a CIA report, also of 15 May 1978, made abundantly clear:

Many people in this part of the country claim they saw an object which resembled a soccer ball falling behind the mountains on the Argentine–Bolivian border, causing an explosion that shook the earth. This took place on May 6. Around that time some people in San Luis and Mendoza provinces reported seeing a flying saucer squadron flying in formation.

The news from Salta confirms that the artificial satellite fell on Taire Mountain in Bolivia, where it has already been located by authorities. The same sources said that the area where the artificial satellite fell has been declared an emergency zone by the Bolivian Government.

Scanning the CIA's declassified UFO files, I was able to locate a second report that referenced the crash, and that added important data to what was already in hand. Dated 16 May and titled 'REPORTS CONFLICT ON DETAILS OF FALLEN OBJECT', the document read thus:

We have received another phone call from our audience requesting confirmation of reports that an unidentified object fell on Bolivian territory near the Argentine border. We can only say that the Argentine and Uruguayan radio stations are reporting on this even more frequently, saying that Bolivian authorities have urgently requested assistance from the US National Aeronautics and Space Administration in order to determine the nature of that which crashed on a hill in Bolivian territory. Just a few minutes ago Radio El Espectador of Montevideo announced that there was uncertainty as to the truth of these reports. Argentine sources indicated that the border with Bolivia had been closed but that it might soon be reopened. They also reported that an unidentified object had fallen on Bolivian soil near the Argentine border and that local Bolivian authorities had requested aid from the central government, which, in turn, had sought assistance from the US National Aeronautics and Space Administration to investigate the case.

A La Paz newspaper said today that there is great interest in learning about the nature of the fallen object, adding that local authorities for security reasons had cordoned off 200 km around the spot where the object fell. The object is said to be a mechanical device with a diameter of almost 4 metres which has already been brought to Tarija. There is interest in determining the accuracy of these reports which have spread quickly throughout the continent, particularly in Bolivia and its neighboring countries. Is it a satellite, a meteorite or a false alarm?

I continued to peruse the files of both the CIA and the Department of State, and discovered that on 18 May 1978 the US Embassy in La Paz again forwarded a telegram to the Secretary of State, Washington, DC. Classified 'Secret', the telegram disclosed that:

Preliminary information provided has been checked with appropriate government agencies. No direct correlation with known space objects that may have re-entered the Earth's atmosphere near May 6 can be made; however, we are continuing to examine any possibilities.

Your attention is invited to State Airgram A-6343, July 26, 1973 which provides background information and guidance for dealing with space objects that have been found. In particular any information pertaining to the pre-impact observations, direction of trajectory, number of objects observed, time of impact and a detailed description including any markings would be helpful.

Six days later a communication was transmitted from the US Defense Attaché Office in La Paz to a variety of US military and government agencies, including NORAD, the US Air Force and the Department of State. Its contents made for interesting reading:

This office has tried to verify the stories put forth in the local press. The Chief of Staff of the Bolivian Air Force told DATT/AIRA this date that planes from the BAF have flown over the area where the object was supposed to have landed and in their search they drew a blank. Additionally, DATT/AIRA talked this date with the Commander of the Bolivian army and he informed DATT that the army's search party directed to go into the area to find the object had found nothing. The army has concluded that there may or [may] not be an object, but to date nothing has been found.

So what exactly did occur on that fateful day back in May 1978? While the available US Government records certainly pointed towards the probability that something out of the ordinary occurred, they also left me with a major problem.

The CIA's report of 15 May 1978 clearly stated that the object had fallen to earth on Taire Mountain, Bolivia, and had 'already been located by authorities'. Furthermore, on the following day, the CIA learned that the object had 'been brought to Tarija'. In contrast, the Bolivian Army and Air Force advised the US Defense Attaché Office that their search for the mystery object had drawn a blank and nothing was found. I reasoned that both 'explanations' could not be correct. I wondered if the CIA was misinformed? Or were the Bolivians keeping the Department of State in the dark? At that stage I could not be sure.

However, the matter did not end there. Tantalising information reached me that suggested that the object was in fact recovered by US authorities, and that both the CIA and NASA played a key role in the recovery operation. From Leonard Stringfield, I learned that in June 1979 he had been contacted by the Argentinian investigator Nicholas Ojeda, who had some interesting data to impart with regard to the crash:

> There is a report of a group of investigators who vanished mysteriously in the area. I really think something big happened in Salta. NASA investigated, but there was no news of it. I have to tell you that in La Paz, Bolivia, a huge Hercules C-130 carried 'something' from the area where the UFO crashed.

In addition, Stringfield's research led to a disclosure that a CIA source known to the researcher Bob Barry confirmed that the C-130 flight took place and that he was aboard the aircraft. 'No comment' was the reply that Barry received when the issue of the aircraft's cargo was raised . . .

So, unfortunately, the available evidence still did not answer that crucial question: what was it that crashed at Bermejo, Bolivia, in May 1978?

I discounted the possibility that the object was a meteorite, primarily because of the description given in the Department of State's telegram of 15 May: 'The object was . . . egg-shaped, metal and about four metres in diameter'.

What of the possibility that the object had been a manmade satellite? Again, that theory was thrown into doubt by the Department of State's 'Secret' telegram of 18 May, which clearly stated that 'No direct correlation with known space objects that may have entered the Earth's atmosphere near May 6 can be made.' Moreover, what of the statement of the CIA that 'people in San Luis and Mendoza provinces reported seeing a flying saucer squadron flying in formation'; and the Department of State's revelation that 'the general region has had more than its share of reports of UFOs the past week'?

Faced with this overwhelming body of official evidence, I concluded that there was a strong argument for believing that the object that plummeted to the ground on Bolivian soil was indeed extraterrestrial in origin. It was by no means a unique event in Bolivia . . .

While filing routine Freedom of Information Act requests with a variety of agencies to determine if additional data on the Bolivian crash of 1978 existed, I came across a batch of reports from the Defense Intelligence Agency that showed that in the following year (specifically in August) a number of strange objects had been found on farmland in the Santa Cruz area of Bolivia.

As I scrutinised the reports, there did not seem to be a direct link between the later events and the initial incident of the previous year, but the evidence was nevertheless compelling. For example, a series of Department of Defense papers forwarded to me by the DIA (and referencing Moon Dust), revealed that:

On late afternoon [8 August 1979] the Embassy here received information that a strange object had been found on a farm near Santa Cruz, Bolivia. Source stated that the object was about 70 centimetres in diameter and two metres in circumference with a hole in one side and a metal skin covering of approx one-half inch thickness. Later the object was described as 'about three times the size of a basketball'.

A second report, filed shortly afterwards, showed that the US authorities were taking a considerable interest in the affair:

A second fire ball fell from the sky early in the morning of the same day that the first one was found near Cotoca. This second one was found 200 kilometres north of the city of Santa Cruz on the farm of Juan Saavedra by the Campesiono Gonzalo Menacho Viveras. The place is in the area of Buen Retiro near the Yapacane River. According to the information given by the Campesino, around 12.30 a.m. on Friday last week he heard a loud whistling sound and saw a fire ball followed by an explosion. He said that the next evening a silent aircraft that had three lights was flying over the explosion area.

After dawn on Friday morning the Campesino started looking around the area of the impact and found a sphere. As it was not heavy, he took it home where he kept it until his friend, Nataniel Mendez Hurtado, learned of the other sphere in Cotoca and passed on information concerning this second sphere.

The mystery of finding these two spheres, exactly alike, is that according to the witnesses they were fire balls. That is to say that these spheres became real balls of fire when they entered the atmosphere because of the friction and after a high speed fall they hit the ground. However, in the area where they've been found, there were no signs of the impact and [it] looks as though the spheres landed smoothly.

As I continued to peruse the various reports at my disposal, I noted with interest that the US authorities had received '[A] roll of 35 mm film for color prints and a roll of Kodachrome 40 movie film. The 35 mm film will be developed and printed here in La Paz. The movie film will be forwarded to DIA.'

Questions abounded. From where did the spheres originate? What was the 'silent aircraft' that flew over the crash site displaying three lights? And how had the spheres apparently negotiated a smooth landing? Perhaps the still photographs and movie footage in the possession of the Defense Intelligence Agency would supply the answers.

Naturally, I was keen to get my hands on this invaluable photographic evidence, and duly fired off a further FOIA request in an attempt to obtain copies. Regrettably, the material appeared to have vanished from the archives of the Defense Intelligence Agency and my quest turned up no additional data . . . with one exception.

Having filed numerous FOIA requests with a host of US governmental and military agencies over the years, I was used to receiving through the mail all manner of envelopes and packages adorned with official emblems and stamps; however, on filing requests for data pertaining to the Bolivian crashes, I noted that on each envelope I received there was a small emblem with which I was not familiar.

Closer scrutiny revealed that the emblem was in fact that of a little-known body called DIALL – the Defense Intelligence Agency Liaison Office, which had its headquarters at the British Ministry of Defence's main building at Whitehall!

What was so important about UFO crashes in Bolivia that it required such high-level Anglo-American liaison? Was it possible that both parties were implicated in the crash-retrieval operations? Given that the event occurred well away from UK territory, no other explanation seemed reasonable. Yet again, I had uncovered evidence to show that British Government interest in UFO crash-retrieval operations was not limited to incidents that had occurred within the confines of the UK.

I considered the evidence I had succeeded in putting together on Moon Dust: here was a US military operation, the goal of which was to recover as expeditiously as possible (a) 'descended foreign space vehicles' and (b) 'items of great technological interest'. Moreover, Moon Dust had an undeniable link with the UFO phenomenon. More significantly, from my point of view, I had uncovered two pieces of evidence linking Moon Dust with the British authorities: the 1962 CIA report secured by the investigator Milo Speriglio; and the involvement of DIALL in the 1978 UFO crash at Bermejo, Bolivia. Were the British somehow tied in with Moon Dust? Such a possibility could no longer be ruled out.[1]

Moon Dust aside, there were numerous other ways and means at my disposal as I sought to determine the true extent to which UFO-crash retrievals had occurred in overseas countries. From the CIA, I was able to obtain several pieces of intriguing data relating to a UFO-crash incident that allegedly occurred off the northern coast of Norway on the island of Spitsbergen in mid-1952. I reviewed the CIA's papers for August of that year:

Writing in the German magazine 'Der Fliger', Dr Waldemar Beck says that a flying saucer which recently fell at Spitsbergen has been studied by eminent Norwegian and German rocket experts. He writes that Dr Norsal, a Norwegian expert in rocket construction, went to the place where the flying saucer had fallen a few hours after it had been discovered in the mountains of Spitsbergen by Norwegian jet planes. In the wreck of the apparatus the expert is said to have discovered a radio piloting transmitter with a nucleus of plutonium transmitting on all wavelengths with 934 hertz, a measure that has been unknown so far. The investigation has also shown that the flying saucer crashed because of a defect in its radio piloting system. The saucer which carried no crew has a diameter of 47 metres. The steel used in the construction is an unknown alloy. It consists of an exterior disc provided at its peripheral with 46 automatic jets. This disc pivots around the central sphere which contains the measurement and remote control equipment. The measurement instructions have an inscription in Russian.

Was there some substance to the affair? And if so, was the object Soviet in origin, as the news report picked up by the CIA maintained? I dug further, and came across several pages of US Air Force material that showed that shortly after the incident was reported by the media, the intelligence arm of the USAF made enquiries with the Norwegian military who asserted that they had no knowledge of the crash. But still the story refused to die.

Three years later, I discovered, a seldom-seen account of the crash was printed in a Stuttgart newspaper, the *Stuttgarter Tageblatt*. A translation of the account read:

Oslo, Norway, Sept. 4, 1955 – Only now a board of inquiry of the Norwegian General Staff is preparing publication of a report on the examination of remains of a UFO crashed near Spitsbergen, presumably in early 1952. Chairman of the board, Colonel Gernod Darnbyl, during an instruction for Air Force officers stated: 'The crashing of the Spitsbergen disc was highly important. Although our present scientific knowledge does not permit us to solve all the riddles, I am confident that these remains from Spitsbergen will be of utmost importance in this respect.'

I continued to review the article, and was intrigued to see that Colonel Darnbyl was now specifically denying that the disc was Russian in origin: 'Some time ago,' he began, 'a misunderstanding was caused by saying that this disc was of Soviet origin. It has – this we wish to state emphatically – not been built on earth. The materials used in its construction are completely unknown to all experts who participated in the investigation.'

The *Stuttgarter Tageblatt* had still more data to impart: 'According to Colonel Darnbyl, the Board of Inquiry is not going to publish an extensive report until some sensational facts have been discussed with US and British experts. We should reveal what we found out, as misplaced secrecy might lead to panic.'

Looking at what the newspaper had to say on the case, I noted with mounting interest that Colonel Darnbyl's decision to bring 'British experts' into the investigation was made only four months after the US columnist Dorothy Kilgallen reported that an elite team of 'British scientists and airmen' was involved in the study of yet another crashed UFO. Was the same team investigating both crashes? I read on:

Contrary to information from American and other sources, Second Lieutenants Brobs and Tyllenson, who have been assigned as special observers of the Arctic regions since the event at Spitsbergen, report the flying discs have landed in the polar regions several times. Said Lieutenant Tyllenson: 'I think that the Arctic is serving as a kind of air base for the unknowns, especially during snow storms when we are forced back to our bases. I have seen them land and take off on three separate occasions. I notice that, after having landed, they execute a speedy rotation around their discs. A brilliant glow of light, the intensity of which is variable with regard to speed at landing and at take off, prevents any view of the things happening behind this curtain of light and/or inside the disc itself.'

These were certainly fantastic revelations, but how much could be authenticated? As had been the case on so many occasions, I pursued every possible lead. Philip Mantle, I learned, had looked into the case in 1985 and had received an outright denial that anything remotely resembling the Spitsbergen crash had ever occurred on Norwegian soil. 'The whole story seems utterly unfounded,' Philip was told by Arild Isegg, the head of the Information Division, Norwegian Royal Ministry of Defence.

Again, however, Spitsbergen refused to roll over and die: Bill Moore (who had worked hard to determine the truth behind the Roswell UFO crash) spoke with the French investigator Jean Sider, who had uncovered a clipping from a Nancy-based newspaper that referred to a Nazi-developed craft built in the closing stages of World War Two, the description of which sounded remarkably like the craft recovered at Spitsbergen.

By far the most baffling addition to the whole saga, however, came from the US National Security Agency (NSA) – an agency with extremely close links to Britain's Government Communications Headquarters (GCHQ) at Cheltenham.

From the NSA I had obtained via the Freedom of Information Act a translation of a 1960s Russian media article on the UFO subject. Contained within the article, I was interested to see, was a passing reference to the Spitsbergen incident:

An abandoned silvery disc was found in the deep rock-coal seams in Norwegian coal mines on Spitsbergen. It was pierced and marked by micrometeor impacts and bore all traces of having performed a long space voyage. It was sent for analysis to the Pentagon and disappeared there.

This was certainly a new slant on the case, but what really caught my eye was the National Security Agency's reaction to the mention of Spitsbergen. Instead of dismissing the matter as a hoax, a still-unidentified NSA agent circled the paragraph of the article referencing Spitsbergen, and wrote in the margin the word 'PLANT' in bold capitals.

I spent several hours reviewing my files on Spitsbergen, and was able to state firmly that those who had investigated the case fell broadly into two camps: there were the 'believers' and there were those who felt the case was nothing more than a lingering hoax that refused to give up the ghost.

The National Security Agency's belief that the matter was some form of 'plant', however, was a new one on me. Had the NSA been exposed to data that could conclusively lay the legend of Spitsbergen to rest, once and for all? If that was the case, the NSA weren't saying, and no further evidence pertaining to National Security Agency involvement in the Spitsbergen incident came to light.

And yet, that curious one-word note, scrawled many years previously by an anonymous NSA employee, continued to niggle at me. Rather than indicating an outright hoax, the 'plant' reference suggested that the Spitsbergen story (even if bogus) had been disseminated officially, possibly to cloud the rumours surrounding crashed-UFO incidents in the late 1940s and early 1950s. And make no mistake, such rumours were ten a penny in the early years of UFO research.[2]

In *The FBI Files*, for example, I had devoted two chapters to the Bureau's (and specifically J. Edgar Hoover's) attempts to ascertain the truth surrounding the UFO crashes in New Mexico in 1947 and 1948. As I was able to demonstrate, the Bureau was almost certainly misled by the military over what was recovered at Roswell in July 1947, and was without doubt thwarted in its attempts to resolve the issue of Majestic 12.

Nevertheless, as documents secured under the Freedom of Information Act made clear, the FBI had succeeded in putting together a large dossier on a variety of UFO crashes that had occurred within the United States. The complete facts may have eluded J. Edgar Hoover, but he was certainly aware of bizarre things afoot in late-1940s New Mexico.[3]

Of the many accounts relating to retrieved UFOs throughout the world that caught my attention, I considered one of the most credible to be that of Wilbert Brockhouse Smith, who in the 1950s worked – in a top-secret capacity – with the Canadian Government's Department of Transport.

Although it was clear to me that Smith was very careful about what he said and to whom he spoke, he had made a number of positive statements on the issue of recovered UFOs. In response to questioning from the investigators C.W. Fitch and George Popovitch in November 1961, Smith said:

Our Canadian Research Group has recovered one mass of very strange metal . . . it was found within a few days of July 1, 1960. There is about three thousand pounds of it. We have done a tremendous amount of detective work on this metal. We have found out the things that aren't so. We have something that was not brought to this Earth by plane nor by boat nor by helicopter. We are speculating that what we have is a portion of a very large device which came into this solar system . . . we don't know when . . . but it had been in space a long time before it came to Earth; we can tell that by the micrometeorites embedded in the surface. But we don't know whether it was a few years ago – or a few hundred years ago.

In addition to this important statement, Smith had made a significant announcement to an audience of the Illuminating Engineering Society in Ottawa on 11 June 1959:

We have in addition to visual evidence a variety of confirmation in other forms. Many sightings have been confirmed by radar with identical positions being established. Physical evidence of witnessed landings, such as imprints in soft ground, broken bushes, withered vegetation, etc., is plentiful and well confirmed. Various items of 'hardware' are known to exist, but are usually promptly clapped into security and therefore are not available to the general public.

But from where did Smith obtain such important evidence? Declassified Canadian Department of Transport documentation in my possession showed that in 1950 Smith spoke extensively with Dr Robert Irving Sarbacher, a consultant scientist to the American Research and Development Board.

Smith came away from his meeting with Sarbacher armed with some crucial data. 'Flying saucers exist,' Smith wrote in a top-secret DOT memorandum shortly after his meeting with Sarbacher. 'The matter is the most highly classified subject in the United States Government, rating higher even than the H-bomb.'

Despite Dr Sarbacher's relative anonymity, more than three decades after his meeting with Wilbert Smith, he made an extraordinary admission to the investigator William Steinman. Commenting on the accounts of crashed UFOs that had been retrieved by the US authorities, Sarbacher revealed:

About the only thing I remember at this time is that certain materials reported to have come from flying saucer crashes were extremely light and very tough . . .

There were reports that instruments or people operating these machines were also of very light weight, sufficient to withstand the tremendous deceleration and acceleration associated with their machinery.[4]

From the former Soviet Union, there were equally astonishing disclosures. Bryan Gresh, Senior Vice-President of Altamira Communications Group, and the investigator George Knapp conducted an interview with Valeriy Burdakov. In the 1950s Burdakov worked in a scientific capacity with the Moscow Aviation Institute and he revealed that the Russian premier Joseph Stalin had taken a keen interest in the UFO crash at Roswell. Soviet agents operating in New Mexico at the time were even directed to look into the matter and report back their findings. Stalin was informed, 'The phenomenon was real . . . UFOs were not dangerous to our country, but they were not manufactured in the United States, or any other country.'

Interestingly, Gresh and Knapp, commenting on a number of classified Russian papers on UFOs to which they had gained access, noted, 'The documents make it clear the Russian military maintains an ongoing, high level interest in the UFO subject . . . The documents also show the Russians are monitoring ufology on a worldwide basis. We have found references to MJ-12.'[5]

The comments of Knapp and Gresh were of no surprise to me: periodically my research into what the US Government knew about the UFO mystery had thrown up data pertaining to UFO encounters in the former Soviet Union; and in February 1997, an extraordinary report reached me via the Defense Intelligence Agency. Titled 'SOVIET AIRCREW SIGHTINGS OF UNEXPLAINED PHENOMENA', the three-page document read thus:

> Unidentified Object. In the spring of 1984, a friend [censored] was sent by the Regimental Commander to intercept an object which had been observed flying near Mikha Tskhakaya Airfield at a supersonic speed. However, the object did not make a sonic boom as it flew north to south over the base. The pilot, flying a MIG-23/Flogger in full afterburner at Mach 1.2 was unable to close on the object. By the time both MIG-23 and unidentified object approached Mach 1.6 the pilot activated his infrared search and track system (IRSTS) approximately 12 km from the target and observed the largest bloom he had ever seen on his indicator. The pilot immediately reported this information to the controller. By the time they reached a speed of nearly Mach 2, the pilot had to break off the intercept due to low fuel.

A further (undated) report forwarded to me by the DIA, also commenting on UFO encounters in Russia, revealed:

During night flights in the Azerbaijan area, several air-
crews reported an ellipse shaped object flying more than
20 km from them which emitted a light in one direction.
The aircrew were unable to acquire a radar contact on the
object. All of the pilots which observed the unidentified
object were instructed to land immediately. The crews
were ordered to never discuss the object they had
observed.

There was no doubt in my mind that sightings of unidentified flying objects in Russia were just as extraordinary as in
other areas of the world – including Australia . . .

In his 1991 book, *Alien Liaison*, Tim Good had related the
fascinating account of a man who, from 1956 to 1960, was
employed as a radio technician at the Weapons Research
Establishment, Salisbury, South Australia.

As the man recalled, in either 1958 or 1959, a strange,
spherical object was recovered at the Woomera Test Range. 'It
was a sphere about 2 feet 9 inches in diameter. Its colour was a
mid-grey metallic, somewhat darkened by extreme heat . . . We
tried to cut it, and could not even mark it with hand tools –
saws, drills, hammers, chisels – nothing.'

Shortly afterwards, Tim was informed, US authorities
claimed the material was American space debris, whereupon it
was transferred to Wright-Patterson Air Force Base – which for
many years was the rumoured resting place for a host of
crashed UFOs and deceased alien beings.

'Perhaps this is foolish,' Tim's source advised him, 'but for
many years now I have believed that what we held in those
several days was not merely space debris, was perhaps not even
some material left by a UFO, but that it was perhaps some
form of UFO itself.'[6]

I was intrigued by this account, and vowed to look into it
deeper: I made some significant discoveries.

From the Joint Intelligence Bureau of New Zealand's
Ministry of Defence (a division with close ties to the British

MOD's Defence Intelligence Staff), I learned that numerous such 'spheres' had been recovered throughout Australia in the period 1963 to 1972, and, curiously enough, all had been claimed by US authorities as having originated with their space programme.

All of the spheres were approximately two feet in diameter, and had been recovered in areas including New South Wales, Western Australia and Queensland. Whether the Australian authorities were satisfied with the explanations put forth by the Americans as they sought to explain the discovery of the spheres was not made clear from a reading of the files; however, it was evident that the governments of New Zealand and Australia were involved in the recovery of at least twelve such spheres in less than ten years. The New Zealand Joint Intelligence Bureau went as far as to classify its findings at 'Restricted' level.

By far the most interesting piece of evidence made available to me by Australian and New Zealand authorities was a 1972 newspaper clipping that referenced one of the 'sphere crashes' on Australian territory in 1963. According to the report, two spheres had been recovered approximately one hundred and fifty miles north of Broken Hill, and the Broken Hill Police had arranged to have the objects flown to the National Weapons Research Establishment (NWRE) at Adelaide for examination. Unfortunately for the police, the pilot of the aircraft refused to allow the mystery spheres on board lest they explode!

Ultimately, the police were forced to transfer the spheres by road. However, after examination by specialist staff at the NWRE, it was determined that the spheres were neither Soviet nor American in origin. From where, then, did they originate? The newspaper apparently did not know, and those in authority were saying nothing. It was yet another bizarre episode in my attempt to chronicle the many and varied UFO crashes that had occurred throughout the world since at least the late 1940s.[7]

I closed my four-inch-thick file titled 'UFO Crashes – Worldwide'. The evidence was incontrovertible: the recovery of alien spacecraft was a global phenomenon.

CHAPTER FIFTEEN

REFLECTIONS

IN AUGUST 1998 I LOOKED BACK ON MY JOURNEY TO ascertain what British authorities knew about the crashed-UFO issue with a mixture of satisfaction, triumph, wonder and bafflement.

I smiled when I recalled the words of my agent, Andrew Lownie, after I told him of my proposal for *Cosmic Crashes*: 'I've spoken with Nick Pope and I asked him if there had ever been a British equivalent of the Roswell crash. Nick said there hadn't.'

I have a lot of respect for Nick, but based on everything I had gone through, in no way could I agree with his assertion.

I examined all of the evidence I had obtained. There was absolutely no doubt in my mind: somewhere within the United Kingdom there existed an immensely powerful, and incredibly well hidden, body of individuals (almost certainly with close ties to the defence and intelligence services) who were sitting on the story of the millennium: Plant Earth was not alone in harbouring intelligent life.

I thought of the witnesses, of those with whom I had liaised, and of those whose accounts I had been fortunate enough to come across: Roger Chambers, Harold South, Hannah Green, Jenny Randles, Bob Fall, Jonathon Turner, Leonard

Stringfield, Dorothy Kilgallen, Ray Wardle, Margaret Fry, and perhaps even Marilyn Monroe and John F. Kennedy.

These were not anonymous sources hiding behind some impenetrable screen. They were, I concluded, as genuine as you or I.

Then there was that small (but certainly significant) body of official documentation surrounding the various crashed-UFO incidents that had occurred since the mid-1940s. I was always striving to locate official backup for the many accounts I had come across, and felt that the varied government and military files – on for example, Dorothy Kilgallen and the World War Two crash, the Charlton Crater and the Cosford affairs of 1963, the 1964 incident at Walthamstow, the series of events at Rendlesham Forest in December 1980, and RAF Rudloe Manor and the Provost and Security Services – were all prime examples of what could be uncovered if one pushed hard enough.

But even when coupled with witness testimonies, the official documents did not tell the whole story. There were cloak-and-dagger episodes; for example, my dealings with the elusive Francis Kent, the Central Intelligence Agency files pertaining to Marilyn Monroe's knowledge of an Anglo-American project concerned with crashed UFOs and alien bodies, Jenny Randles's exposure to British military knowledge of Majestic 12 and the UFO crash at Roswell, and even that stealthy removal by sources unknown of Provost and Security Services files on UFOs from the Public Record Office. And just what was going on deep beneath RAF Rudloe Manor amid that dark and forbidding mass of sealed-off caverns and tunnels?

Undoubtedly, Jenny Randles's experience with a faction of the British Army, which had at its disposal information on Majestic 12, was officially sanctioned. I was as certain as I could be that that episode could have been nipped in the bud immediately if those in authority had so desired. Instead, the operation was allowed to run, and was only concluded precisely when Jenny was due to receive the crucial evidence on

Majestic 12. In other words, it appeared that someone was 'toying' with the UFO research community, and was trying to gauge the effect that exposure to information on recovered UFOs and alien bodies would have on the populace at large.

Similarly, my experience with Francis Kent was illuminating. The idea that an intelligence source would simply telephone out of the blue a member of the public and relate top-secret facts pertaining to classified Air Ministry investigations of UFO incidents was absurd. I was positive that Kent was only the front man for a hidden organisation that enjoyed playing a very manipulative game.

There was also Irene Bott's and my dealings with Harold South, who was witness to the UFO recovery at Penkridge in 1964. As you will recall, shortly before our visit to him, Harold had received a most strange telephone call from the Ministry of Defence Police. If there was a desire to prevent Harold from talking, why was it made so incredibly easy for Irene and me to trace the MOD's telephone call back to Whittington Barracks? All that this achieved was to convince both of us of the veracity of the accounts of the crash. There were, I concluded, experienced and subtle manipulators at work.

But to what end was this manipulation being played out? As exploitative and as hidden as my quarry certainly was, I never gained the impression that my investigations were frowned upon: I was never threatened; nor was I ever told to back off from an investigation. Indeed, it appeared that the opposite was the case: it was almost as if I was being spurred on to blow the lid on the UFO controversy!

Perhaps, I mused, that was the intent, after all. More than half a century had gone by since the first reported UFO crash within the United Kingdom. Maybe those in officialdom had determined that the time had arrived to entrust to the general public the true facts, and a suitable outlet for information was being sought. Was I that outlet?

Frankly, I did not envy those officials who had to make the

decision back in the 1940s to deny the populace and the media access to the guarded secrets of the UFO issue. With the world having only just recovered from World War Two, it could not have been easy for those in positions of authority to learn that our planet was receiving regular visitations from alien cultures infinitely more advanced than our own.

Was the cover-up now so huge that it was becoming unwieldy? I could see nothing more catastrophic than to have the awesome (and possibly terrifying) truth come tumbling out, mixed as it surely would be with a wealth of scaremongering, exaggerated rumours and God knows what else.

In view of this, perhaps those of us in UFO research had a purpose to serve beyond simply informing the public of the facts: we were also preparing them for the day when all would be revealed.

Twenty years had gone by since I had first become interested in the subject of unidentified flying objects. It had been an extraordinary two decades. As far as the British Government's involvement in the UFO subject was concerned, however, I felt that my work was now over.

The facts, as I had been able to ascertain them, were in print for all to see. *A Covert Agenda* had documented what I had been able to learn about the UFO problem within the United Kingdom at an official level. And, now, *Cosmic Crashes* was taking the issue a stage further and revealing those long-denied – and utterly astounding – truths surrounding the actual recovery of alien spacecraft and bodies. It was now down to those in power to capitalise on the increased public awareness of the UFO mystery. The truth, I was certain, was destined to surface.

When? It was surely only a matter of time . . .

ACKNOWLEDGEMENTS

I WOULD LIKE TO THANK THE FOLLOWING FOR THEIR welcome contributions to this book:

Graham Birdsall, who, back in 1979, learned that RAF Rudloe Manor, Wiltshire, was no ordinary Royal Air Force base; Mark Birdsall, for his help over the last decade; my research assistant and President of the Staffordshire UFO Group (SUFOG), Irene Bott, for data relating to the UFO crash near Penkridge in 1964, and the startling incident over the Wash in 1996; the Central Intelligence Agency; Roger Chambers, for having the courage to speak out on the Cannock Chase UFO incident of 1974; Robin Cole, for a wealth of fascinating material on the Government Communications Headquarters (GCHQ) at Cheltenham; Richard Conway, for his sterling research; the Defense Intelligence Agency; Jonathon Dillon of the National Union of Journalists, for numerous leads; the Federal Bureau of Investigation, for releasing to me its files on Marilyn Monroe and Dorothy Kilgallen; Chris Fowler, for the use of extracts from his fine paper on the Public Record Office's UFO files; Stanton Friedman, who in the 1970s was responsible for uncovering the truth behind the UFO crash at Roswell, New Mexico, in 1947; Margaret Fry, for her diligent investigation of the UFO crash on the Berwyn Mountains in 1974; Paul Fuller, for the use of material from *Crop Watcher* and *New Ufologist* magazines; Timothy Good, for reviewing the initial manuscript of *Cosmic Crashes*, and for his comments and advice; Barry Green, for helpful insights into the UFO event at RAF Cosford in 1963; Hannah Green, for her recollections of UFO-related activity at the Royal Aircraft Establishment (RAE) at Farnborough; the Home Office, for their helpful responses to my questions; John Lear, for his comments on the crash of a UFO on British soil during World War Two; my agent, Andrew Lownie, to whom I am once again eternally grateful for all of his hard work in selling the book; Philip Mantle, for his comments on the 'alien autopsy' film footage; the Ministry of Defence; the National Security Agency; Richard Newman, for interesting data on the Roswell incident; the New Zealand Ministry of Defence; the BBC *Out of this World* team, particularly Adelene Alani and Chris Choi; Sarah Pepin of the House of Commons Public Information Office, for supplying me with copies of parliamentary questions and answers on the UFO problem; Nick Pope, for kindly answering my questions on his UFO investigations undertaken on behalf of the Ministry of Defence, and for his personal comments on the subject in general; the Public Record Office, for the use of previously classified UFO data; Jenny Randles, for her comments on the UFO crash on the Berwyn Mountains in 1974, and her 1986 dealings with a former British Army source; my father, Frank Redfern, who set the ball rolling for me back in the late 1970s; the Royal Air Force; Neil Rusling, of the Royal Air Force Police Association, for much appreciated information on the workings of the RAF Police and Provost and Security Services; Colin Ridyard, for trying to break down the barriers of secrecy constructed by the British Government back in the late 1940s; Ray Santilli, for helpful answers to my questions on the 'alien autopsy' film footage; everyone at Simon & Schuster for their fantastic work and support, but particularly Martin Fletcher, Lisa Shakespeare,

Jacquie Clare, Gillian Holmes, Glen Saville, Anna Kiernan, Salma Blackburn, Robert Rimmer and Katharine Young; Harold South, who pushed the UFO crash at Penkridge, Staffordshire, in 1964 to a whole new level; Jonathon Turner, for information on RAF Rudloe Manor; the US Department of State; Ray Wardle, for his memories of the UFO incident at RAF Cosford; and Matthew Williams, for allowing me to conduct an extensive series of interviews with him, and for the use of a number of his excellent photographs.

REFERENCES

INTRODUCTION

1. *The Roswell Incident*, Charles Berlitz and William Moore, Granada, 1980.
2. *The UFO Crash/Retrieval Syndrome*, Leonard Stringfield, The Mutual UFO Network, 1980.
3. *Above Top Secret*, Timothy Good, Sidgwick & Jackson, 1987.
4. *The UFO Report, 1992*, Timothy Good, Sidgwick & Jackson, 1991.
5. *A Covert Agenda*, Nicholas Redfern, Simon & Schuster, 1997. *The FBI Files*, Nicholas Redfern, Simon & Schuster, 1998.

CHAPTER 1: THE ALIENS, THE ACTRESS AND THE ASSASSINATION

1. *Sightings*, Vol. 1, No. 8, 1996.
2. Project Sign Report No. F-TR-2274-1A, 1949.
3. *UFO*, Vol. 12, No. 1, 1997.
4. *Los Angeles Examiner*, 23 May 1955.

5. *Flying Saucer Review*, Vol. 25, No. 4, 1979 and Vol. 31, No. 1, 1985.

6. Letter to the author from John Lear, 6 May 1991.

7. *The UFO Crash/Retrieval Syndrome*, Leonard Stringfield, The Mutual UFO Network, 1980.

8. Letter from Olavo Fontes to Coral Lorenzen, 27 February 1958.

9. *Alien Liaison*, Timothy Good, Century, 1991. *Alien Contact*, Timothy Good, Morrow, 1993.

10. *Exploiting The High Ground*, Naval Space Command Headquarters, 1989.

11. Documentation released to the author by the Defense Intelligence Agency in 1996.

12. Letter to the author from Bruno Pappalardo, Search Department, Public Record Office, 21 September 1990.

13. *The Marilyn Conspiracy*, Milo Speriglio with Steven Chain, Corgi, 1986. *UFO*, Vol. 10, No. 2, 1995.

14. Federal Bureau of Investigation files on Marilyn Monroe.

15. *Bill Cooper and the Need For More Research*, William Jones and Rebecca Minshall, 1991.

16. Central Intelligence Agency files on Dorothy Kilgallen.

17. *UFOs, Aliens and 'Ex'-Intelligence Agents: Who's Fooling Whom?*, Lars C. Hansson, Paragon Research & Publications, 1991.

18. Statement released by John Lear, 1987.

CHAPTER 2: CRASHES AND CRATERS

1. *Flying Saucer Review*, Vol. 39, No. 3, 1994. Interview with Stephen Meeson, 28 April 1998.

2. Letter to the author from Nick Pope, Ministry of Defence, 5 July 1993.

3. Public Record Office file: AIR 2/17318. Crown copyright exists.

4. *Daily Sketch*, 17 and 30 July 1963. *Daily Express*, 23 July

    1963. *Sunday Express*, 21 July 1963. *Daily Telegraph*, 27
    July 1963. *Daily Mirror*, 27 July 1963. *Daily Herald*, 27
    and 30 July 1963. *Daily Mail*, 30 July 1963. *Guardian*, 29
    July 1963.
5. *Crop Watcher*, September 1992.
6. *Flying Saucer Review*, Vol. 10, Nos 2 and 4, 1964.
7. Public Record Office file: AIR 2/17318. Crown copyright
    exists.

CHAPTER 3: INCIDENT AT COSFORD

1. *Above Top Secret*, Timothy Good, Sidgwick & Jackson,
    1987.
2. *Flying Saucer Review*, Vol. 10, Nos 2, 3 and 4, 1964.
3. Letter to the author from Squadron Leader C.J.
    Browning, RAF Cosford, 1988.
4. Various letters from Waveney Girvan to the Air Ministry,
    1964. Various letters from Wilfred Daniels to the Air
    Ministry, 1964. Public Record Office file: AIR 2/17526.
    Crown copyright exists. *Tyneside UFO Society Journal*,
    January 1964. *Express & Star*, 7 January 1964. *Kensington
    News*, 22 May 1964.
5. Interview with Barry Green, 20 December 1996.
6. *UFO Retrievals*, Jenny Randles, Blandford, 1995.
7. Interview with Alistair Blake, 6 January 1996.
8. *UFO*, January/February 1996.
9. Interview with Ray Wardle, 20 January 1996.
10. Conversation with Francis Kent, 22 January 1996.

CHAPTER 4: UFO DOWN!

1. *UFO Crash/Retrievals: The Inner Sanctum*, Leonard
    Stringfield, 1991.
2. Ibid.

3. Public Record Office file: AIR 2/17526. Crown copyright exists.
4. *New Ufologist,* No. 5, 1996.
5. Interview with Harold South, 11 December 1996.
6. Interview with Mr Law, Ministry of Defence Guards Service, Whittington Army Barracks, 11 December 1996.
7. Interception of Communications Act, 1985.
8. *Alien Encounters,* January 1997.

CHAPTER 5: ACCESSING THE ARCHIVES

1. *Walthamstow Guardian,* 17 April 1964. Letter from Ronald Caswell to the Air Ministry, 29 April 1964. Public Record Office files: AIR 2/17982 and AIR 2/17983. Crown copyright exists.
2. Public Record Office files: AIR 2/17526 and AIR 2/17527. Crown copyright exists.
3. *Grimsby Evening Telegraph,* 8, 9, 10, 11 and 13 October 1992.
4. Interviews with Nick Pope, 29 March 1994 and 22 January 1997.
5. *UFO,* Vol. 11, No. 5, 1992.
6. *The Flying Saucerers,* Arthur Shuttlewood, Sphere Books, 1976.
7. Interview with Rita Hill, 5 June 1998.

CHAPTER 6: OFFICIAL CENSORSHIP

1. Letter to the author from Roger Chambers, 6 August 1996.
2. Interviews with Roger Chambers, 28 November and 9 December 1996.

CHAPTER 7: THE MOUNTAIN OF MYSTERY

1. *A Covert Agenda*, Nicholas Redfern, Simon & Schuster, 1997.
2. Interview with Margaret Fry, 3 December 1996.
3. *UFO*, September/October 1996.
4. Interview with Matthew Williams, 17 January 1997.
5. Interview with Margaret Fry, 3 December 1996.
6. Interview with Matthew Williams, 17 January 1996.
7. Interview with Jenny Randles, 28 March 1997.

CHAPTER 8: STUMPED!

1. Letter to the author from Captain John E. Boyle, USAF, chief of the Public Affairs Office, RAF Bentwaters, 30 September 1980.
2. Lecture given by Charles Halt, 31 July 1994.
3. *Northern UFO News*, No. 152, December 1991.
4. *The Cerealogist*, No. 13, Winter 1994/5. *Salisbury Times*, 23 August 1994. *Sunday Telegraph*, 18 December 1994. *Air Forces Monthly*, November 1994 and June 1997. *New Ufologist*, No. 3, 1995.
5. *Worcester Evening News*, 2 November 1994. *Eversham Journal*, 3 November 1994.
6. *Alien Encounters*, January 1997. *Eastern Daily Press*, 8 and 11 October 1996. *Eastern Evening News*, 30 October 1996. *Scotsman*, 4 November 1996. *Sightings*, Vol. 1, Nos 7 and 8, 1996 and Vol. 1, No. 9, 1997.

CHAPTER 9: THE KEEPERS OF THE SECRET

1. Project Blue Book Fact Sheet, USAF, 1988.
2. *Top Secret/Majic*, Stanton T. Friedman, Marlowe & Company, 1996. *The MJ-12 Documents: An Analytical*

Report, William Moore and Jaime Shandera, The Fair Witness Project, 1990.

3. *The FBI Files*, Nicholas Redfern, Simon & Schuster, 1998.

4. Interview with Nick Pope, 22 January 1997. *Open Skies, Closed Minds*, Nick Pope, Simon & Schuster, 1996.

5. Interview with Matthew Williams, 25 October 1997.

6. Interview with Robin Cole, 20 November 1997. *GCHQ and the UFO Cover Up*, Robin Cole, 1997.

7. *Encounters*, No. 3, 1996.

CHAPTER 10: THE SOLDIER'S STORY

1. Interview with Jenny Randles, 28 March 1997.

2. *Alien Autopsy: Frequently Asked Questions*, James Easton, 1996.

3. Interview with Nick Pope, 22 January 1997.

4. *Beyond Roswell*, Michael Hesemann and Philip Mantle, Marlowe & Company, 1997.

5. Interview with Ray Santilli, 3 December 1996. Interview with Philip Mantle, 7 December 1996. *Beyond Roswell*, Michael Hesemann and Philip Mantle, Marlowe & Company, 1997.

6. Letter to the author from Stanton T. Friedman, 30 November 1995.

7. *Northern UFO News*, No. 171, 1995.

8. Statement of Dr Christopher Milroy, 2 June 1995.

9. *Alien Contact*, Timothy Good, Morrow, 1993.

10. Interview with Jenny Randles, 28 March 1997.

11. *UFOs, MJ-12 and the Government: A Report on Government Involvement in UFO Crash Retrievals*, Mutual UFO Network.

CHAPTER 11: RUDLOE MANOR: UFO HQ?

1. *Quest International* (now *UFO* magazine), Vol. 8, No. 3, 1988.
2. *Above Top Secret*, Timothy Good, Sidgwick & Jackson, 1987. *Alien Liaison*, Timothy Good, Century, 1991.
3. Letter to the author from Flight Lieutenant A.F. Woodruff, RAF Rudloe Manor, June 1994.
4. *Alien Liaison*, Timothy Good, Century, 1991.
5. Interview with Nick Pope, 29 March 1994.
6. Public Record Office file: AIR 2/16918. Crown copyright exists.
7. Interview with Neil Rusling, Royal Air Force Police Association, 7 December 1996.
8. *Top Secret/Majic*, Stanton T. Friedman, Marlowe & Company, 1996.
9. Letter to the author from Air Commodore J.L. Uprichard, RAF, Director of Security and Provost Marshal, 4 May 1994.
10. Letters to the author from Jonathon Turner, 17 and 21 September 1994 and 10 May 1995.
11. Interviews with Chris Fowler, 10 January and 18 January 1997. *Truthseekers' Review*, Vol. 2, No. 13, 1997. *Out of this World*, BBC Television, 1996.
12. Interview with Anne Leamon (née Henson), 2 February 1998. *Western Daily Press*, 25 November 1996. *Woman's Own*, February 1997.
13. *Truthseekers' Review*, Vol. 2, Nos 14 and 15, 1997. *Truthseekers' Review, Special Edition: MOD Documents on UFOs*, 1997.
14. Interview with Neil Rusling, Royal Air Force Police Association, 7 December 1996.
15. Interview with Matthew Williams, 17 January 1997.

CHAPTER 12: THE HOME OFFICE LINK

1. *Above Top Secret*, Timothy Good, Sidgwick & Jackson, 1987.
2. *Flying Saucer Review*, Vol. 28, No. 3, 1983.
3. Interview with the Press Officer, Home Office, 20 December 1996.
4. Interview with the Space Information Officer, RAF Fylingdales, 20 December 1996.
5. *The Times*, 19 January 1994.
6. Interview with Nick Pope, 22 January 1997.
7. Interview with Matthew Williams, 17 January 1997.
8. Interview with Matthew Williams, 25 February 1997.

CHAPTER 13: OURS OR THEIRS?

1. Interviews with Hannah Green, 25 February and 3 December 1996.
2. Interviews with Matthew Williams, 17 January and 14 June 1997.
3. Public Record Office files: AIR 2/16918 and AIR 2/17318. Crown copyright exists.

CHAPTER 14: THE WORLDWIDE REPORTS

1. Department of State files on Project Moon Dust. Defense Intelligence Agency files on Project Moon Dust. Central Intelligence Agency files on Project Moon Dust. Department of the Air Force files on Project Moon Dust. *A Covert Agenda*, Nicholas Redfern, Simon & Schuster, 1997. *The UFO Crash/Retrieval Syndrome*, Leonard Stringfield, The Mutual UFO Network, 1980. *UFO Crash/Retrievals: Amassing the Evidence*, Leonard Stringfield, 1982.

2. *The Spitzbergen Saucer Crash*, William Moore, William L. Moore Publications and Research, 1986. *Saarbrucker Zeitung*, 28 June 1952. *Stuttgarter Tageblatt*, 5 September 1955.

3. *The FBI Files*, Nicholas Redfern, Simon & Schuster, 1998.

4. *Flying Saucers – Serious Business*, Frank Edwards, Lyle Stuart Books, 1966. *UFO Crash At Aztec*, William Steinman, UFO Photo Archives, 1987.

5. *MUFON UFO Journal*, No. 306, 1993.

6. *Alien Liaison*, Timothy Good, Century, 1991.

7. New Zealand Ministry of Defence files, 1974–5.

INDEX